ANONYMOUS SPEECH

Anonymous Speech: Literature, Law and Politics discusses the different contexts in which people write anonymously or with the use of a pseudonym: novels and literary reviews, newspapers and political periodicals, graffiti, and now on the Internet. The book criticises the arguments made for a strong constitutional right to anonymous speech, though it agrees that there is a good case for anonymity in some circumstances, notably for whistle-blowing. One chapter examines the general treatment of anonymous speech and writing in English law, while another is devoted to the protection of journalists' sources, where the law upholds a freedom to communicate anonymously through the media. A separate chapter looks at anonymous Internet communication, particularly on social media, and analyses the difficulties faced by the victims of threats and defamatory allegations on the Net when the speaker has used a pseudonym. In its final chapter the book compares the universally accepted argument for the secret ballot with the more controversial case for anonymous speech.

Anonymous Speech

Literature, Law and Politics

Eric Barendt

·HART·
PUBLISHING
OXFORD AND PORTLAND, OREGON
2016

Hart Publishing
An imprint of Bloomsbury Publishing plc

Hart Publishing Ltd
Kemp House
Chawley Park
Cumnor Hill
Oxford OX2 9PH
UK

Bloomsbury Publishing Plc
50 Bedford Square
London
WC1B 3DP
UK

www.hartpub.co.uk
www.bloomsbury.com

Published in North America (US and Canada) by
Hart Publishing
c/o International Specialized Book Services
920 NE 58th Avenue, Suite 300
Portland, OR 97213-3786
USA

www.isbs.com

HART PUBLISHING, the Hart/Stag logo, BLOOMSBURY and the
Diana logo are trademarks of Bloomsbury Publishing Plc

First published 2016

© Eric Barendt

British Library Cataloguing-in-Publication Data

A catalogue record for this book is available from the British Library.

ISBN: HB: 978-1-84946-613-4
       ePDF: 978-1-50990-406-8
       ePub: 978-1-50990-407-5

Library of Congress Cataloging-in-Publication Data

Names: Barendt, E. M., author.

Title: Anonymous speech : literature, law and politics / Eric Barendt.

Description: Oxford ; Portland, Oregon : Hart Publishing, 2016. | Includes bibliographical
references and index.

Identifiers: LCCN 2016008648 (print) | LCCN 2016009289 (ebook) | ISBN 9781849466134
(hardback : alk. paper) | ISBN 9781509904075 (Epub)

Subjects: LCSH: Freedom of speech. | Anonymous writings. | Privacy, Right of.

Classification: LCC K3254 .B367 2016 (print) | LCC K3254 (ebook) | DDC 342.08/53—dc23

LC record available at http://lccn.loc.gov/2016008648

Typeset by Compuscript Ltd, Shannon
Printed and bound in Great Britain by
CPI Group (UK) Ltd, Croydon CR0 4YY

Preface

Anonymous speech and writing may have significant political and social repercussions. This was clearly shown in the case of the notorious 'Trojan horse' letter. At the end of 2013 an anonymous letter was passed on to Birmingham City Council, though it came to light only in the following March. The letter outlined a hard-line Islamist plot to take over schools in Birmingham and offered advice to a contact in Bradford on how to do this by, for example, orchestrating complaints by parents and installing new school governors. At first it was widely regarded as a hoax, but four subsequent inquiries concluded that it revealed a real conspiracy. But its status has not been definitively settled. The episode reveals a major problem with anonymous writing: it is impossible to question its author, so it may be difficult to discover the accuracy of its claims. Moreover, moral and legal responsibility for its contents cannot easily be determined. This may not matter very much in the case of novels and poetry, but it does matter for other types of anonymous writing, perhaps for literary reviewing and certainly for communications on the Internet: see the discussion of trolling and defamatory communications on the Net in chapter 6.

This book explores the varieties of anonymous writing: for example, of novels and in literary reviews, newspapers and periodicals, and political pamphlets. In some of these contexts, the virtues of anonymity (or more commonly the use of a pseudonym) are very clear, and there may be only a few drawbacks to it. But in other contexts its vices are more apparent. The force of the competing virtues and vices of anonymity was vigorously contested in the nineteenth century, largely in the context of literary reviewing, and to some extent the arguments are now replayed in the context of the Internet. The drawbacks of anonymity may be mitigated when an intermediary (a publisher, a newspaper or journal editor) takes responsibility for the book or article whose author has refrained from using his real name; the intermediary may put readers in touch with the author or may accept liability himself for any illegal content. That often happens in the case of novels and journal articles, but it is much less likely with Internet communications. This book considers these arguments at some length; its conclusion is that there is no overwhelming case for recognising a strong right to anonymous speech, though there are some situations, in particular that of whistle-blowing, where there are good reasons to support a qualified right or freedom.

My own interest in this subject was aroused by the decision in the *Author of a Blog* case in 2009: see chapter 1, section V and chapter 4, section III.

I was unsure then, as I still am, whether it did full justice to the arguments for a right to anonymous speech, which have rarely been canvassed in England. In contrast there is a significant corpus of legal writing on the topic in the United States, where the Supreme Court has recognised a constitutional right to anonymity under the First Amendment free speech guarantee. In contrast to the dearth of legal writing in England, the pros and cons of anonymity have been explored by literature scholars, notably by John Mullan in *Anonymity: A Secret History of English Literature*, a book to which I am much indebted. These pros and cons are now also extensively discussed by writers on the Internet.

I owe an enormous debt to a number of people who have helped me in various ways. Maya Anaokar provided valuable research assistance on the topic of Internet anonymity. Many people drew my attention to relevant arguments and literature, or put me in touch with useful contacts: Roderic Ballantine, David Bentley, Nigel Fountain, Charles George, Sheila Grandison, Bernie Hogan, Kirsty Hughes, Cathy James, Paul Laffan, Lyrissa Lidsky, Paul Mitchell, Judith Märten, John Murdoch, Richard Nelsson, Karl-Nicolaus Peifer, Jake Rowbottom, Geoffrey Rowell, Tom Stern, and some newspaper lawyers who prefer to remain anonymous. I am grateful to all of them for their time and for their interest in this project. I am indebted to David Anderson, David Bentley, Rafi Cohen-Almagor, Cathy James, Gillian Morris and Jake Rowbottom for reading and commenting on drafts of specific chapters. Ian Peel and Roma Shallow helped with essential IT support. And I could not have finished this book without the skilful work of Mr Alexander Montgomery at the Royal London Hospital, for which I remain most thankful.

In the course of doing research for this book, I worked in a number of libraries: at University College London, the London School of Economics and Senate House. I am particularly indebted to the marvellous holdings and to the most helpful staff at the London Library, whose rich resources were used to the full, particularly for work on the second chapter. I am grateful to Mel Hamill and her colleagues at Hart Publishing for the prompt production of the book and to Elizabeth Davison for her careful editing of the text. But my greatest debt as ever is to my wife, Sheila, with whom I have discussed the ideas in this book over the last three years. I could not have written it without her constant encouragement and support.

Eric Barendt
December 2015

Contents

Note on Abbreviations

Three books are cited frequently, so it is convenient to refer to them in an abbreviated way. They are:

Barendt   Eric Barendt, *Freedom of Speech*, 2nd edn (Oxford, OUP, 2005/2007)

Ciuraru   Carmela Ciuraru, *Nom de Plume: A (Secret) History of Pseudonyms* (New York, Harper Perennial, 2012)

Mullan   John Mullan, *Anonymity: A Secret History of English Literature* (London, Faber and Faber, 2007)

Table of Cases

United States

Table of Statutes and Constitutional Provisions

United States

1

Introduction

I. THE PROBLEM OF ANONYMITY

A NONYMOUS WRITING IS both an old and a new phenomenon. Before the Renaissance most writing was anonymous; many of the early poems in anthologies are ascribed to 'Anon'. The medieval *auctor* (the term from which the word 'author' derives) was generally little more than a scribe, transcribing earlier texts. The name of the writer was irrelevant to the readers of a text, so it was immaterial that generally he was anonymous.[1] The identification or naming of authors has been associated with the development of printing, and then subsequently with the role of copyright in ascribing property rights to them and the birth of the Romantic Author as a heroic figure at the end of the eighteenth century.[2] But even then a high proportion of novels were anonymous; between 1770 and 1800 over 70 per cent of novels were published without a named author, and during the 1820s the proportion rose to nearly 80 per cent.[3] There has certainly been a marked decline in anonymous writing in the late nineteenth and twentieth centuries, though some notable writers in this period have always, or sometimes, used pseudonyms (see section IV of this chapter and chapter 2, section II), among them George Orwell (the pseudonym of Eric Blair), Sylvia Plath and Doris Lessing.

The Internet is responsible for the revival of anonymous writing and indeed for many of the problems now associated with it. Many blogs are written under a pseudonym, though often the identity of the author is well known, as with Paul Staines, the author of the Guido Fawkes political blog. Comments on websites are frequently posted anonymously, as are communications on some social media (see chapter 6, sections I and II). Anonymity on the Net creates real difficulties for the victims of cyber-bullying and hate speech, or for those who wish to secure redress for a defamatory allegation; these issues are considered in chapter 6, sections II and III. Put simply, it may

---

[1] A Bennett, *The Author* (London, Routledge, 2005) 38–43.

[2] Ibid 44–54, and ch 3.

[3] The figures are taken from J Raven, 'The Anonymous Novel in Britain and Ireland 1750–1830' in RJ Griffin (ed), *The Faces of Anonymity: Anonymous and Pseudonymous Publication from the Sixteenth to the Nineteenth Century* (Basingstoke, Palgrave Macmillan, 2003) 145.

be very difficult to identify the perpetrator of a damaging communication and take legal proceedings against him.

This is the central problem of anonymity: how to reconcile the interest of a writer in protecting his identity from public disclosure with the need for responsibility and accountability to injured readers. The problem is most acute when the reader, or his family, wants legal redress, for example, through a prosecution for the dissemination of hate speech or for harassment, or by bringing a civil action for libel or infringement of privacy. But anonymous writing may give rise to more general outrage on the part of readers who feel they have been deceived by the use of a pseudonym. In 1987, an Anglican vicar, Rev. Toby Forward, wrote a book of short stories under the name, Rahila Khan. Some of them depicted the lives of young Asian women. The author identified herself as a married woman with two daughters. When the publisher, Virago, discovered the use of the Rahila Khan pseudonym, the book was withdrawn and all copies were pulped; as a publisher of books by women, it felt it had been deceived, and that a hoax had been perpetrated on the Asian community.[4] There are comparable episodes in the United States; for example, the outrage felt when novels apparently written by members of minority ethnic groups turned out to have been authored by elderly white writers, or, in one instance, by an avowed segregationist.[5]

Perhaps the best recent example of the problem occurred with the publication of *Primary Colors* 'by Anonymous' in 1996, a fictional account of a Presidential election campaign, which was widely understood to be about Clinton's successful bid for the Presidency in 1992.[6] There was general indignation when it was discovered that the book was written by Joe Klein, a columnist for *Newsweek*, perhaps because he had denied in broadcast interviews that he had written it—though it was common practice in the nineteenth century for writers to disavow authorship publicly when disclosure of the fact would be embarrassing to them.[7]

This book explores in a number of different contexts how the problem of anonymous writing might be resolved. The law may play some part in this resolution, though it is very doubtful whether it can provide a satisfactory answer in every situation. As chapter 2 shows, there is an enormous variety of anonymous writing: in novels and other literature, in literary reviews, in political writing, in the peer review of academic and scientific articles, and in graffiti. There may be a strong case for disclosure of the author's

---

[4] The episode is fully discussed by Mullan, 114–18; also see K Miller, *Authors* (Oxford, OUP, 1989) 183–85. Toby Forward has subsequently written books for children under his own name.
[5] See the instances discussed by L Heyman, 'The Birth of the Authornym: Authorship, Pseudonymity, and Trademark Law' (2005) 80 *Notre Dame Law Review* 1377, 1400–1.
[6] Mullan, 30–36.
[7] See in particular the case of Sir Walter Scott, discussed in chapter 2, section II.

identity in some contexts, because the arguments for legal accountability in these circumstances, for example, financial journalism, are very persuasive and the arguments for anonymity are relatively weak. In other contexts, for example, the writing of fiction, the case for anonymity may be much stronger, outweighing the case for the disclosure of an author's identity.

An important legal question is whether a right to anonymity should be recognised as an aspect of the right to freedom of speech (or expression). A constitutional free speech right to anonymity has been upheld by the United States Supreme Court in its landmark ruling in *McIntyre v Ohio Elections Commission*;[8] chapter 3 discusses that decision and the case for recognising a free speech right to anonymity. Sweden also upholds this right under its Freedom of the Press Act and (so far as broadcasting and film are concerned) the Fundamental Law on Freedom of Expression.[9] The South Korean Constitutional Court struck down a law in effect requiring Internet users to register under their real name as incompatible with freedom of expression.[10] In contrast, the Constitution of Brazil expressly forbids anonymous communication.[11] Insofar as the law does recognise a right to anonymity as an aspect of freedom of speech, it creates a strong presumption against disclosure of a writer's identity, perhaps at the cost of any accountability for the harm resulting from the anonymous speech.

English law does not recognise a *right* to anonymous speech, though there is no legal requirement to identify the author of printed material. Anonymous communications are, as already noted, very common on the Internet and for that matter on the broadcasting media, while a number of authors write under pseudonym. There is, therefore, a *freedom* to speak and write anonymously, but it is not a constitutional right, as it is in the United States (see chapter 4). On the other hand, English law does recognise a publisher's privilege not to reveal its sources, if they prefer to remain anonymous, so in this way it does indirectly protect anonymous communications (see chapter 5). The special problems created by anonymity on the Internet are discussed in chapter 6. Although the 'virtues' of anonymous speech are particularly attractive for Net users, the ease of anonymity in this context makes it susceptible to abuse which may cause real harm to its victims. Chapter 7 contrasts the treatment of anonymous speech with the solutions applied to voting and the financing of election campaigns. All liberal democracies

---

[8] 514 US 334 (1995).

[9] Freedom of the Press Act 1949, ch 3, and the Fundamental Law on Freedom of Expression 1991, ch 2.

[10] Decision of 23 August 2012, reported in *New York Times*, 24 August 2012, and discussed in JA Martin and AL Fargo, 'Anonymity as a Legal Right: Where and Why It Matters' (2015) 16 *North Carolina Journal of Law and Technology* 311, 359–60.

[11] Brazil Constitution 1988, art 5, IV: 'manifestation of thought is free, but anonymity is forbidden'.

provide for the secret ballot, under which votes are cast anonymously; on the other hand, they usually require the disclosure of donations to political parties and contributions to campaign funds. The reasons for these different rules are explored in this final chapter.

II. VIRTUES AND VICES OF ANONYMITY

There are a number of reasons why a writer may prefer to publish anonymously or, more usually, under a pseudonym. These reasons are discussed briefly in this section, though some particular cases of anonymous writing are considered more fully in chapter 2. He or she might consider it improper, or incompatible with their position, say, at court or in society to write under their own name. Women authors in the eighteenth and nineteenth centuries frequently published anonymously, using terms such as 'By a Lady' or 'By the Author of ...' on the title page.[12] This disguise might be assumed for reasons of modesty, or from a sense that it was inappropriate for a woman to publish her work. These reasons might be coupled with other objectives; George Eliot used that name initially to give her novels, in particular her first, *Scenes of Clerical Life,* greater authority than they would probably have enjoyed if they had appeared under her real name, Mary Anne (or Marian) Evans. Like the Brontë sisters, she wished her books to be judged on their merits, quite apart from the name of the author.[13] Later when her identity became widely known, her pseudonym seems to have been kept on as a public disguise or mask, 'a kind of proclamation' of her separate identity as a distinguished novelist.[14]

Another reason for anonymity or the use of a pseudonym is to preserve privacy for the author. A well-known case is that of Charles Dodgson, who was almost pathologically shy of publicity attaching to him from his authorship as Lewis Carroll of *Alice in Wonderland* and *Alice through the Looking Glass.*[15] (His leading biographer suggests that Dodgson was also worried that the *Alice* books would damage his standing as the author of mathematical works.)[16] Anonymity has enabled a poet to write more candidly about private feelings of grief (Tennyson's *In Memoriam*);[17] a writer to explore

---

[12] Mullan, 57–75 and ch 3.
[13] Ibid 103–5. See the letter of GH Lewes to Barbara Bodichon, quoted in K Hughes, *George Eliot* (London, Fourth Estate, 1998) 311: 'the object of anonymity was to get the book judged on its own merits, and not prejudged as the work of a woman'.
[14] Mullan, 108.
[15] Ibid 41–46; Ciuraru, ch 3; MN Cohen, *Lewis Carroll* (London, Macmillan, 1995) 295–97.
[16] Ibid 298.
[17] In fact most reviewers and many others identified Tennyson as the author, but he never allowed an edition of the poem to appear with his name on the title page during his lifetime: RB Martin, *Tennyson: The Unquiet Mind* (Oxford, OUP, 1980) 341. Also see Mullan, 274–79.

family tensions and religious doubts (Edmund Gosse's *Father and Sons*);[18] and a lesbian crime writer to reveal her sexuality (Patricia Highsmith's *The Price of Salt* written under the *nom de plume*, Claire Morgan, and later published under her own name as *Carol*).[19] As John Mullan explains in his book on anonymity, one important reason for the decline of anonymous writing in the last 100 years has been the erosion of reticence; writers have become part of celebrity culture.[20] But even today some writers adopt a pseudonym to preserve their privacy and prevent the media from inquiring into their life. For example, the author of the acclaimed Neapolitan novels writes as Elena Ferrante, a pseudonym, and declines invitations to speak at conferences or accept literary prizes.[21]

Another important reason for anonymity is a writer's desire to avoid social ostracism, detention or criminal prosecution for expressing unpopular or illegal opinions. Under the disguise of anonymity he feels freer to make trouble, to question religion, to protest against harsh treatment by the police or prison authorities, or to advocate insurrection. Much controversial writing in the seventeenth century was published anonymously, including works by Andrew Marvell and John Locke's *Two Treatises on Government*, as were Jonathan Swift's satires in the early years of the eighteenth century[22] (see chapter 2, sections V and VI). This justification for anonymity, like the privacy reasons considered in the previous paragraph, now has little force for established writers. But the fear of social and legal sanctions explains why the faces of many interviewees on television (immigrants, asylum-seekers, or the neighbours of people murdered or bullied on housing estates) are pixelated in order to hide their identity. Further, such an apprehension may provide a reason, in addition to a general sense of mischief, and the distinctive Internet culture (see chapter 6, section 1(B)), why many bloggers prefer to communicate with an alias, rather than under their own name.

Finally, writers may opt for anonymity or the use of a *nom de plume* out of a desire for their work to be assessed purely on its merits without consideration being given to the gender or established standing of the author. As mentioned already, Charlotte Brontë and George Eliot did not want their gender to be taken into account. Other writers, for example, Anthony Trollope and Doris Lessing, have written one or two novels anonymously or under another name in order to see how they were received by the public, who would then not be reading them just because they came from the pen of a well-established author (see further, chapter 2, section II). Locke justified his anonymous authorship of *Two Tracts on Government* because

---

[18] Ibid 280–85.
[19] Ciuraru, ch 15.
[20] Mullan, 286–87.
[21] J Wood, 'Women on the Verge', *New Yorker*, 21 January 2013, available at www.newyorker.com/magazine/2013/01/21/women-on-the-verge.
[22] Mullan, ch 5.

he wanted readers only to consider the arguments in the book, and not the identity of the author.[23]

It is, however, unclear whether this justification can always be claimed as a virtue of anonymity. In some circumstances, particularly in the cases of political judgements or economic forecasts, readers will usually want to know the identity of the writer in order to make an assessment of his credibility: have his predictions generally been correct and consequently would it be right to accept them in this case? Anonymity deprives readers of this information, so it could be regarded as a vice rather than a virtue. Readers might even make the argument that they have a free speech right to know the author of the views or judgments which they have been invited to consider: for further consideration of this argument, see chapter 3, section III. Much the same point may sometimes apply to works of fiction. Rev. Toby Forward justified his use of a pseudonym with the argument that it enabled him to write more creatively; as a white clergyman he could not write stories about the experiences and feelings of an Asian girl.[24] But the *nom de plume*, Rahila Khan, gave the stories a credibility they were not entitled to, and will almost certainly have deceived many readers.

The main drawback, or vice, of anonymous writing is, therefore, that it enables mendacity and deception. An anonymous writer can make false claims about his product or about a political or commercial rival with less fear of detection (and legal proceedings) than someone making the same statements under his real name. Anonymity also lends itself to cyber-smears and bullying, hate speech and defamation on the Internet (see chapter 6). As Scalia J put it in his dissenting judgment in the *McIntyre* case, anonymous speech 'facilitates wrong by eliminating accountability, which is ordinarily the very purpose of the anonymity'.[25] He added that it also coarsens public debate.

The virtues and vices of anonymity cannot easily be assessed, and weighed against each other, divorced from the context of the particular type of writing. The justifications for the practice have appeared very persuasive for some types of writing, for example, poetry and novels, at particular periods of history, but may have less force now. The argument for signed, rather than anonymous, writing is particularly strong in the case of political and economic journalism, because accountability is more important in this context than it is, say, for fiction. Signed literary reviewing is now usual; anonymous reviewing has been abandoned in the twentieth century, largely because it enabled abusive reviews and because readers are entitled to know who the author is (see chapter 2, section III), though it survives in *The Economist* (see chapter 2, section IV(B)).

---

[23] Ibid 164.
[24] *London Review of Books,* 4 February 1988.
[25] *McIntyre* (n 8) 385.

An important point to consider in evaluating the virtues and vices of anonymity is that it may be possible to remove, or at least reduce, some of the latter when an intermediary takes responsibility for the anonymous work, whether it is a book, a newspaper or journal article, a broadcast or an Internet communication.[26] Normally a book or journal publisher knows the real name of an author who uses a *nom de plume*, though occasionally the author's identity may be concealed even from the publisher and is known only to his agent and a few personal friends, as with the Toby Forward stories; see also the Doris Lessing episode discussed in chapter 2, section II. Readers of the book (or journal article) will know that the writer has an established reputation, or some credibility, with the publisher (or journal editor), although they themselves are in no position to assess it. Moreover, if a reader has been deceived or defamed, he may be able to take proceedings against the publisher to secure disclosure of the author's identity, or alternatively take proceedings, say, in defamation against the publisher. Publishers then act as what may be termed 'responsible intermediaries', as do newspaper editors. Broadcasters also act as responsible intermediaries when they interview, say, an asylum-seeker on the conditions under which he is detained. He speaks anonymously (his face is pixelated and an actor's voice is used) but the interviewer knows his identity and in effect vouches for his credibility as a genuine asylum-seeker. Newspaper and other journalists should act as responsible intermediaries when they report stories given them by anonymous sources. The journalists can check whether the source is reliable, though the public cannot: for further discussion, see chapter 5, section III.

It is much less clear how far Internet intermediaries can play the same role in reducing the risks attendant on anonymous communication. Internet Service Providers (ISPs), services providing platforms for bloggers, and social media carry far too much traffic for them to check the identity of the millions of people using their services, though some social media have required users to register with their real name (see chapter 6, sections I and II). It is much more difficult for them than it is for the traditional mass media to act as responsible intermediaries. While printers and publishers were frequently held liable for defamatory and other illegal publications from the sixteenth to the nineteenth centuries (see chapter 4, section II), ISPs and website operators enjoy considerable immunity from comparable liability, largely because their exposure to liability would inhibit freedom of communication on the Net. But much communication on the Net is anonymous and there are obvious difficulties in holding anonymous authors accountable; see chapter 6, sections III(C) and (D) for further discussion of this problem.

---

[26] See S Levmore, 'The Anonymity Tool' (1996) 144 *University of Pennsylvania Law Review* 2191, 2199–202 for the idea that responsible intermediaries make anonymity more acceptable.

These difficulties perhaps make anonymity on the Net more troubling than it is in other contexts.

III. THE DEATH OF THE AUTHOR?

In a well-known essay written in 1967, Roland Barthes announced the death of the author.[27] The importance which had been attached to the personality of the author could be attributed to a number of historical factors: the personal faith emphasised by the Reformation, rationalism and capitalist ideology. This focus detracted from the primacy of understanding language and the text. It is for readers to make sense of the text, itself a 'tissue of quotations drawn from the innumerable centres of culture',[28] without recourse to nonsensical questions about the identity or intentions of the author. It is language which speaks, not the author.[29] Elena Ferrante has expressed a similar sentiment: 'I believe that books, once they are written, have no need of their authors'.[30] On this perspective, it would be a matter of indifference whether a text—novel, poem or other work—was signed by an identified (or identifiable) author or was anonymous.

A different, and richer, perspective is offered by another French writer. Michel Foucault, echoing Samuel Beckett, asked: 'What does it matter who is speaking?'.[31] It is not enough to affirm, as Barthes had done, that the author has disappeared or is dead. Literary and other works are identified as written by an author, generally named, but sometimes anonymous. The author, whose name is part of the text, should be distinguished from the person who wrote the work. An author's name permits readers to group together various texts and differentiate them from others, so permitting literary discourse and interpretation. To take a simple example, we can consider the works of Shakespeare together and use our understanding of one play, or poem, to shed light on another, without forming a view on the separate question whether they were actually written by William Shakespeare of Stratford, or the Earl of Oxford, or another candidate for their authorship. The author's name serves what Foucault terms 'author-functions' with a number of general characteristics.[32] One of them is linked to various juridical and institutional systems which determine who owns the text, or copyright, and who is responsible for transgressions. Another characteristic is

---

[27] 'The Death of the Author' in *Image Music Text* (Essays selected and translated by S Heath, London, Fontana, 1977) 142.

[28] Ibid 146.

[29] Bennett, *The Author* (n 1) 11–13.

[30] Quoted in Wood, 'Women on the Verge' (n 21).

[31] 'What is an Author?' in JV Harari (ed), *Textual Strategies: Perspectives in Post-Structural Criticism* (London, Methuen, 1980) 141.

[32] Ibid 148–53.

that the function need not refer simply to one real individual: it may be just as wrong to equate the author and the real writer, as it would be to equate the author with the narrator of a novel.

What is the significance, if any, of this literary theory for understanding and resolving the anonymity problem? One point is that Foucault's 'author function' is perfectly compatible with anonymous writing, at least if the text is entitled, 'By the Author of ...'. Readers can then easily group the text with other works by the same writer. The author-function does not require use of the name of the actual writer, or indeed any name at all.[33] A writer chooses to write with his (or her) real name, to use a *nom de plume*, or to remain completely anonymous (as with *Primary Colors*).[34] These can all be labelled 'authornyms', the term used by Laura Heyman in a significant law review article.[35] She argues that an authornym is essentially a branding choice: a statement made to the reading public which enables it to make easy, informed choices what to read, rather than have the cost and trouble of searching for something of the same quality as the book it has enjoyed. 'An authornym ... is the statement of authorship offered to the consuming public—in other words, the author's trade mark.'[36] On this perspective, as in Foucault's essay, anonymous writing or the use of a pseudonym is essentially no different from the more conventional use of an author's real name.

Foucault's conclusion that it is a matter of indifference who is speaking has been questioned by literary theorists.[37] But the anonymity problem outlined in section I of this chapter, is not a question of literary theory. It may be right to interpret literary texts without inquiring into the author's intentions, his biography or psychology, but the anonymity problem is how to reconcile or balance the writer's freedom not to disclose his real name with his responsibility (moral and legal) to his readers. The choice of a pseudonym may be regarded as a branding exercise, as apparently it was by Samuel Clemens when he registered Mark Twain as a trade mark.[38] But when he challenged (unsuccessfully) the publication of a number of his works, then in the public domain, for infringement of copyright and for dilution of his trade mark, he brought the proceedings in his own name.[39] He was prepared to remove his disguise, such as it was. Equally, the identity of anonymous authors, or those using a *nom de plume*, should usually be disclosed, when they are involved in defamation or other legal proceedings (see chapter 6,

---

[33] Griffin, 'Introduction' in *The Faces of Anonymity* (n 3) 9–10.

[34] In *Paratexts: Thresholds of Interpretation* (JE Lewin (trans), Cambridge, CUP, 1987) 39–40, G Genette wrote: 'After all to sign a work with one's real name is a choice like any other, and nothing authorises us to regard this choice as insignificant'.

[35] 'The Birth of the Authornym' (n 5).

[36] Ibid 1381.

[37] See DW Foster, 'In the Name of the Author' (2002) 33 *New Literary History* 375.

[38] Ciuraru, 88–89.

[39] *Clemens v Belford Clark and Co*, 14 F728 (CC ND Ill, 1883), discussed by Heyman, 'The Birth of the Authornym' (n 5) 1433–34.

section III(C)). The death of the author, it is suggested, has little significance for the resolution of the problem of anonymity.

IV. PSEUDONYMS

Hitherto terms such as 'anonymous writing' and the 'use of a pseudonym' have been used interchangeably, as if there are no distinctions between them. But does the adoption of a *nom de plume* differ from pure anonymity? Pseudonymity is on one view merely a subset of anonymity. A restriction on anonymous writing would certainly cover the use of a *nom de plume*; both devices are almost always used to conceal the identity of the writer, and they make it more difficult for readers to secure redress if they consider they have been harmed by a publication.[40] Pure anonymity and the use of a pseudonym both protect the author's privacy. Both devices should be distinguished from autobiographical fiction, where writers use incidents from their own life as the basis for a novel, but transform them in order to conceal the link.[41] This distinction is not always drawn properly. Two biographies of Siegfried Sassoon suggest that *Memoirs of a Fox-Hunting Man* was published anonymously;[42] in fact it was issued under Sassoon's name, but the memoirs were narrated by 'George Sherston', to spare Sassoon's family and friends any embarrassment.[43]

There is a difference between pure anonymity and the use of a pseudonym. The latter enables an author to develop a separate writing identity, particularly when it is used over a period of time for a number of novels or other works. Such an identity might be adopted for a variety of psychological and literary reasons. Often women writers have felt more comfortable when their work is published under a masculine *nom de plume*. The adoption by men of a woman's name has been much less common, although in the eighteenth century some well known works were published anonymously, but as if written by a woman, notably Defoe's *Moll Flanders* and Richardson's *Pamela*.[44] Authors may be too inhibited to write under their

---

[40] DG Post, 'Pooling Intellectual Capital: Thoughts on Anonymity, Pseudonymity, and Limited Liability in Cyberspace' (1996) *University of Chicago Legal Forum* 138, 154.

[41] Two classic examples of this genre are Tolstoy's *Childhood, Boyhood, Youth*, and Proust's *Remembrance of Things Past*. Another more recent case is Sylvia Plath's *The Bell Jar*, exploring the central character's mental breakdown and her troubled relationship with her mother: see Ciuraru, ch 10. It was also written under a *nom de plume*, Victoria Lucas, so it is both autobiographical fiction and a pseudonymous work.

[42] JS Roberts, *Siegfried Sassoon* (London, Richard Cohen Books, 1999) 224; M Egremont, *Siegfried Sassoon* (London, Picador, 2005) 328–29.

[43] The review in the *New Statesman* of 10 November 1928 begins: 'It is a pity that Mr Sassoon has acknowledged the authorship of this book; it would have been amusing to watch the efforts to fix it on different people'.

[44] Mullan, ch 4.

own name; an extreme example is the manic depressive American writer, Alice B. Sheldon, who adopted the name, James Tiptree, Jr, for her science fiction stories, after coming across Wilkin & Son jam, made in Tiptree, a village in Essex.[45] More commonly, a *nom de plume* may be used out of playfulness, or simply because a writer takes a dislike to his name; George Orwell was used partly because the writer disliked his real name, Eric Blair (see chapter 2, section II). Similar reasons operate in the case of Internet communication (see chapter 6, section I(B)).

A pseudonym also enables established writers to use a separate author name for a different genre of their work, distinguishing, say, detective stories from more literary writing. The process can work the other way; Georges Simenon in his early years wrote about 190 pulp novels between 1924 and 1931 under a variety of pen names before publishing more serious works, including the Maigret detective novels, under his own name.[46] Academics may prefer to write thrillers under a pseudonym, perhaps in the belief that the use of their real name would weaken their standing as serious scholars.[47] JK Rowling has written a number of thrillers as 'Robert Galbraith', as she has been keen to adopt a different literary persona for this genre, even though they sold less well before her authorship was revealed.[48] On the other hand, John Banville writes mystery stories as 'John Banville writing as Benjamin Black'; there is no attempt to conceal his authorship. The use of the *nom de plume* merely distinguishes the mystery stories from the author's other more literary work. This enables what has been termed a separate 'reputational capital' to be built up as an asset associated with the particular pseudonym.[49] A very good (or bad) detective novel written under a *nom de plume* would not affect the standing of the novelist's other work, let alone the author's general reputation.

Pseudonyms may therefore perform a distinctive role in the assessment of an author's literary reputation. It is less clear that they have, or should have, any impact on the anonymity problem: how to balance an author's freedom to publish without the use of his or her real name and the readers' interest in redress when they are outraged by a publication or consider that it has defamed them. The use of a pseudonym may indeed itself deceive readers, insofar as it suggests, explicitly or implicitly, that the story was written by

---

[45] Ciuraru, 252–53.

[46] P Assouline, *Simenon* (J Rothschild (trans), London, Chatto & Windus, 1997) 64–68 states that at least 17 *noms de plume* were used: P Marnham, *The Man who Wasn't Maigret* (London, Bloomsbury, 1992) 110, puts the figure at 24.

[47] JIM Stewart, Professor of English at Oxford University wrote a number of detective novels under the name, Michael Innes. Professor C Heilbrun, Columbia University, wrote mystery stories under the name, Amanda Cross, keeping her authorship secret to protect her academic reputation.

[48] See www.theguardian.com/books/2013/jul/24/jk-rowling-robert-galbraith-harry-potter.

[49] Post, 'Pooling Intellectual Capital' (n 40) 152.

a member of a particular ethnic or religious community, when it was in fact been written by an outsider—as in the Toby Forward/Rahila Khan episode mentioned earlier in this chapter. Insofar as the law does have a role in resolving the anonymity problem, whether this arises in the context of literature, political writing or in the social media and other types of Internet communication, the fact that the writer has used a *nom de plume*, rather than writing wholly anonymously, would seem to be immaterial.

V. ANONYMITY AND PRIVACY

In *Author of a Blog v Times Newspapers*,[50] one of the few English cases to discuss a right to anonymity, an unsuccessful argument was made that an anonymous blogger's privacy would be infringed when *The Times* proposed to publish an article identifying him: the significance of this case is fully discussed in chapter 4, section III. Anonymity is indeed often considered to be an aspect of privacy. In an early book on the right to privacy, Alan Westin contended that anonymity represents the desire of individuals to be free from identification and surveillance even when they are out in public or engaged in public activity.[51] Most of us prefer not to be photographed, or reported on in the media, when we are out in the streets, sunbathing on a beach, or using a public facility such as a library or a tourist information office. We prefer to remain anonymous in these situations, and this should be regarded as one of the aspects or 'states' of individual privacy. And it can be said that anonymity supports personal privacy, in that without it effective privacy protection might be reduced: see the discussion in chapter 6, section I of the relationship between anonymity and privacy in the context of Internet communication.

A right to speak anonymously may to some extent be explained in terms of privacy. Westin argued that the right to engage in political expression anonymously, which was first protected by the US Supreme Court in a 1960 decision, is a privacy interest, although the word 'privacy' was not used in that ruling.[52] The Court did use the word in its later decision in *McIntyre*, when it recognised that the motive for anonymity may be 'merely ... a desire to preserve as much of one's privacy as possible', so it is possible to interpret the case as one involving personal privacy, as well as freedom of speech.[53] But *McIntyre* is really a free speech case. It was argued

---

[50] [2009] EMLR 22.
[51] *Privacy and Freedom* (London, Bodley Head, 1967) 31–32.
[52] *Talley v California*, 362 US 60 (1960).
[53] L Tien, 'Who's Afraid of Anonymous Speech? *McIntyre and the Internet*' (1996) 75 *Oregon Law Review* 117, 173, interpreting *McIntyre v Ohio Elections Commission*, 514 US 334, 342 (1995).

successfully that a right to speak and write anonymously was protected by the First Amendment guarantee of freedom of speech (see further chapter 3, section II). A concern for personal privacy may underlie the choice to write anonymously or under a *nom de plume*, as it did most famously for Lewis Carroll, but it is another matter to conclude that it justifies a privacy right to communicate ideas anonymously.

The difficulty with basing a right to communicate anonymously on a privacy right is that, as Eady J said in the *Author of a Blog* case,[54] blogging, and presumably any form of public communication, is essentially a *public* activity; the speaker intends to contribute to public debate and influence others, so it seems hard to conclude that he has a reasonable expectation of privacy in these circumstances. It may be that Eady J did not do justice to the privacy arguments when he dismissed the blogger's application for an injunction in this case,[55] but that is not the concern of this book. It is concerned with the free speech arguments for anonymity.

The free speech arguments for anonymous communication are quite different from those which might justify recognition of a privacy right to communicate anonymously. Moreover, a privacy right to communicate anonymously might be invoked in circumstances which have relatively little to do with freedom of speech. When people answer questions in a census, public survey or election poll, it is promised or understood that their identity will not be disclosed, so they might then have a privacy or anonymity right to stop revelation of their identity. In these circumstances, unlike that of blogging, the people questioned are not really acting as speakers who are keen to communicate their views to the general public. Of course privacy concerns do frequently underlie public anonymous communications, as the Supreme Court recognised in *McIntyre*. Nor is there any incompatibility between the free speech and privacy arguments for a freedom or right to communicate anonymously. In the absence of privacy, including a state of anonymity, some people will feel constrained to remain silent, and there will be less speech. But that is primarily a free speech argument; it will be considered at length in chapter 3 of this book.

---

[54] *Author of a Blog* (n 50) para 11.
[55] This is the argument of K Hughes, 'No Reasonable Expectation of Anonymity?' [2010] 2 *Journal of Media Law* 169.

2

The Varieties of Anonymous Writing

I. INTRODUCTION

IN SEPTEMBER 1893, Emile Zola came to London to address the annual conference of the Institute of Journalists. The title of his talk, given in French but published in *The Times* in an English translation, was 'Anonymity in Journalism'.[1] Zola argued that while the practice of anonymous writing in English newspapers on political matters could be justified[2]—for it enhanced the authority of the press—the same could not be said for literary reviews. Literary criticism had a 'creative function' which distinguished it from the mere reportage of political or social events. A critic who did not put his name to a review renounced his personality as well as responsibility for its content. The signature of a writer increased his power and contributed to the intellectual vitality of public discussion. Anthony Trollope took the same view in an article in the *Fortnightly Review*,[3] a journal which adopted an explicit policy of publishing signed reviews and essays (see section III(A) below): there were good reasons for anonymous leading and other articles in the press, but they did not apply to literary reviews. If the reading public knew the name of the author of a novel or poem, it should also be told the name of the critic.[4]

Other writers have taken a different view. In a classic article, originally written in 1925 for the *Atlantic Monthly*, the novelist EM Forster argued that awareness of the identity and name of the author of a novel or poem was wholly irrelevant to its appreciation: 'all literature tends towards a condition of anonymity, and ... so far as words are creative, a signature merely distracts us from their true significance'.[5] The personality of the writer

---

[1] *The Times*, 23 September 1893, p 6.

[2] Zola contrasted the authority of the English press with the position in France, where there was a enormous variety of newspapers with signed articles, but with low circulation and little authority.

[3] 'On Anonymous Literature' (1865) 1 *Fortnightly Review* 491.

[4] Ibid 496–97.

[5] 'Anonymity: An Enquiry' in *Two Cheers for Democracy* (London, Edward Arnold, 1972) 77, 81.

becomes important only after a book has been read, when it is *studied* (my emphasis), a qualification which perhaps weakens the force of Forster's argument. In contrast, newspaper articles in his view should be signed, in order that their writers can be held accountable for any untruths in them. It was an unfortunate paradox that unsigned press articles might have greater impact, for newspapers took advantage of the apparent authority of anonymous statements.[6] Likewise, George Henry (GH) Lewes, George Eliot's partner (see section II below) and the first editor of the *Fortnightly Review*, thought that journalists and critics should be identified, as it made a difference to the reading public if it knows who they are. But that was not the case with the author of a novel or play, or a work of philosophy, for his identification would not alter the value of what he had written.[7]

So there may be good arguments for anonymity in some contexts, which do not apply, or apply with the same force, in others, though prominent writers have disagreed in assessment of their strength. This chapter examines the various contexts in which the freedom to write anonymously has been exercised, and the coherence and strength of the arguments for anonymity in these diverse circumstances. The next section discusses anonymous novels and poetry, exploring the reasons for the marked decline in anonymity and in the use of pseudonyms (a variant of pure anonymity) in the second half of the nineteenth and in the twentieth centuries. Section III is devoted to literary journals and reviews, discussing in particular the passionate debate on anonymity versus signature in Victorian periodicals and the replay of this debate in 1974 when the *Times Literary Supplement* abandoned its long standing practice of anonymous book reviews. Anonymity in newspapers and political weeklies is covered in section IV, while section V explores its use and that of pseudonyms in political writing. Section VI is concerned with their use in philosophical and religious writing. Finally, anonymity is discussed in two contexts often left out of account in writing on the topic: anonymity in art (section VII) and in the peer reviewing of articles submitted for publication in academic and scientific literature (section VIII). But this chapter does not cover anonymity on the Internet and in social media; this topic of enormous contemporary significance is discussed in chapter 6. The chapter ends with a few general reflections on the arguments for and against anonymity in these various contexts.

II. NOVELS AND POETRY

In the eighteenth and early nineteenth centuries it was very common for literary works to be published without identification of their author. As late

---

[6] Ibid 84–86.
[7] 'Farewell Causerie' (1866) 6 *Fortnightly Review* 890. (Lewes resigned the editorship after a year and was replaced by John Morley.)

as the 1820s, it has been estimated that nearly 80 per cent of novels were published without a named author.[8] Samuel Richardson's *Pamela* (1740) and *Clarissa* (1747–48) were both published anonymously, purporting to be collections of the letters and journals of the young women who gave their name to the titles. It was widely known that Richardson was the author; he probably adopted the device to give greater credibility to the novels among women readers.[9] Other writers might refrain from providing their name, because it was thought indecorous for a gentleman to write a novel, or even poetry, particularly if its content was indecent. Byron's satirical poem, *English Bards and Scotch Reviewers*, a critique of contemporary poets and reviewers, appeared first in 1809 without his name on the title page, but he was widely known to be the author;[10] after it was well received, he was happy for the second edition to be published with his name.[11] The first two Cantos of *Don Juan* were published in 1819 without the name of the author or the publisher, John Murray, who was unhappy about the poem; there was unease over its bawdy content, particularly its depiction of women as sexual predators.[12]

Women writers almost invariably were published anonymously. Jane Austen, for example, was identified, like many women, only as 'A Lady', or subsequently for *Mansfield Park* as 'The Author of "Sense and Sensibility" and "Pride and Prejudice"'.[13] It was only after her death that she was publicly identified as the author of her books, though this was well-known to her family and some friends during her life.[14] But she may have found it hard to reconcile her character as a kindly aunt who seldom voiced serious opinions with the authority of a lady novelist with firm ideas of her own.[15] More generally, reasons of modesty and sexual decorum made it difficult for women to own up to writing fiction; this continued to apply for much of the nineteenth century.

It is harder to understand why Sir Walter Scott admitted authorship of the Waverley novels only over 12 years after the first of them had been published in 1814, and when they had long received popular acclaim. In his 'Introduction' to *Chronicles of the Canongate* (1827) Scott wrote that he had never intended to reveal his authorship during his lifetime, but he had

[8] See J Raven, 'The Anonymous Novel in Britain and Ireland 1750–1830' in RJ Griffin (ed), *The Faces of Anonymity: Anonymous and Pseudonymous Publication from the Sixteenth to the Nineteenth Century* (Basingstoke, Palgrave Macmillan, 2003) 145.

[9] See Mullan, 123–26.

[10] Leslie A Marchand, *Byron: A Portrait* (London, John Murray, 1971) 57; Fiona MacCarthy, *Byron: Life and Legend* (London, John Murray, 2002) 83–87.

[11] Mullan, 239.

[12] MacCarthy, *Byron* (n 10) 348–52, 365–66.

[13] D Nokes *Jane Austen: A Life* (London, Fourth Estate, 1997) 388, 439 (and see Mullan, 66–75).

[14] Ibid 401.

[15] Ibid 393.

felt constrained to do so at a public meeting early in 1827, when his toast had been proposed as the author of the novels; he had either to admit his authorship or take undeserved praise.[16] In both this 'Introduction' and in the 'General Preface' written for the 1829 edition of the Waverley novels, Scott explained that he had originally feared the novels might fail; that they might compromise his standing as an established poet. He gave a number of reasons for continuing with anonymity after the novels proved success-ful: he wanted to avoid personal embarrassment and invitations to discuss his work in public; he was known as a poet and did not want to impose himself on readers too often; and, most plausibly, he obtained some sat-isfaction in baffling curiosity. '[The author] had challenged the public to a game of bo-peep',[17] from which he had clearly obtained a great deal of pleasure. Another reason may have been that Scott, a strong supporter of the Hanoverian monarchy, found it easier under the guise of anonymity to show some sympathy in his novels for the Jacobite cause.[18] Whatever his primary motive, Scott showed that there are many reasons why a writer may prefer anonymity; it is not always chosen for reasons of modesty or out of fear of exposure.

It was from the traditional reason of modesty that the three Brontë sisters wrote under pseudonym; Charlotte, Emily and Anne wrote their poems and novels under the names Currer, Ellis and Acton Bell. As Charlotte Brontë explained in a 'Biographical Notice' written in 1850 as a preface to Emily's *Wuthering Heights* and Anne's *Agnes Grey*, they veiled their names as 'averse to personal publicity'. Their particular choice of pseudonym was influenced by reluctance to use clearly masculine Christian names; but 'we did not like to declare ourselves women, because … we had a vague impres-sion that authoresses are liable to be looked on with prejudice'.[19] The rather teasing choice of sexually ambivalent pseudonyms naturally led to a great deal of speculation about the gender of the authors. Many reviewers of Charlotte Brontë's *Jane Eyre* thought the novel could not have been written by a woman,[20] while one detected the hand of both a man and a woman.[21] On the other hand, GH Lewes identified the book as evidently by a woman, but professed indifference to the author's gender and identity.[22] There was

[16] W Scott, *Chronicles of the Canongate* (Claire Lamont (ed), Edinburgh, Edinburgh University Press, 2000) 3–10.
[17] 'General Preface' (1829).
[18] Mullan, 28.
[19] L Gordon, *Charlotte Brontë: A Passionate Life* (New York and London, WW Norton and Co, 1995) 139–42.
[20] See the reviews collected in M Allott (ed), *The Brontës: The Critical Heritage* (London, Routledge and Kegan Paul, 1974), in particular the reviews in *Critic* (at 73), in *Era* (at 78, 79) and the controversial review by Elizabeth Rigby in the *Quarterly Review* (at 105, 111).
[21] See the review 'Novels of the Season' in *North American Review* (1848) in *The Brontés: The Critical Heritage* (n 20) 97, 99.
[22] Review in *Fraser's Magazine* (1847) in *The Brontës: The Critical Heritage* (n 20) 83, 84.

even a view for a time that Currer, Ellis and Acton were identical, which was encouraged by the publication by Thomas Newby in 1848 of the novels by Emily and Anne Brontë as by 'Mr Bell'. It was this publication which led to the famous visit of Charlotte and Anne to London to show their separate identities to Charlotte's publisher, George Smith.[23] From that time the identity of the sisters was widely known in literary circles, though the later novels of Charlotte Brontë continued to be published under her pseudonym. It was only in 1855 after her death that Elizabeth Gaskell's biography publicly identified Charlotte as the author. She and her sisters have always been known as significant writers by their real names, not under their pseudonyms.

It is quite different with George Eliot, one of the best known literary pseudonyms. Born Mary Anne Evans, she often changed her first name and signed correspondence under a number of surnames, notably Lewes, when she was living with George Henry Lewes, a married man.[24] She had used the name, Marian Evans, for her translation of Feuerbach's *Das Wesen des Christenhums* in 1854,[25] shortly before she began living with Lewes. She submitted her first novel, *Scenes of Clerical Life*, anonymously; the publisher, John Blackwood, thought the author was a clergyman, though Lewes, who conducted the correspondence, disabused him of that idea. Marian Evans then wrote to Blackwood's brother to indicate that she wished to keep her 'incognito, having observed that a *nom de plume* secures all the advantages without the disagreeables of reputation'.[26] Her name as an author would be George Eliot, the name under which she signed the letter. She chose that name because 'George' was Lewes's first name and 'Eliot' 'was a good mouth-filling, easily pronounced word'.[27] The name was kept for all her subsequent novels, even though her identity was known to the public after the appearance of *Adam Bede*, her second book.

There were a number of understandable reasons for the initial use of a pseudonym. Eliot wanted her work to be assessed on its merits and not in the context of her relationship with George Lewes, at a time when living with a married man was widely regarded as scandalous. Moreover, she was apprehensive about the possible failure of her early novels.[28] She kept the name, George Eliot, even after she became successful, perhaps as a brand-name,[29]

---

[23] Gordon, *Charlotte Brontë* (n 19) 166–72, and GM Smith, 'Charlotte Brontë' (1900) 9 *Cornhill Magazine (NS)* 778.

[24] R Ashton, *George Eliot: A Life* (London, Hamish Hamilton, 1996) 9, 118–25.

[25] Ibid 109.

[26] Ibid 173.

[27] Ashton, ibid 166, quotes this explanation, as told by Eliot to John Cross, her husband for the last few months of her life.

[28] Ibid 164. Also see K Hughes, *George Eliot: The Last Victorian* (London: Fourth Estate, 1998) 262–63.

[29] Hughes, ibid 263.

a statement of her identity as a novelist. Her biographers use that name, partly because it would be unclear which of her other names (Mary Anne Evans, Marian Evans, Marian Evans Lewes) would best identify her.[30]

Though the best known examples of anonymous and pseudonymous writing in the mid- to late nineteenth century were novels of female novelists, some men also preferred anonymity, particularly for their early work. Robert Browning's first poem, *Pauline: A Fragment of a Confession*, was published in 1833 anonymously; Browning refused to reprint the poem under his own name for nearly 35 years, as he feared it contained too much self-revelation about the attachment of the narrator-poet to his secret mistress.[31] Samuel Butler's *Erewhon* (1872) and *The Fair Haven* (1873) (respectively a satire and a mock-defence of orthodox Christianity) were anonymous works; the former was sometimes ascribed to Bulwer Lytton, an attribution which boosted its sales. Butler chose anonymity, partly because he was worried about his parents' reaction to the book and partly out of mischief.[32] Thomas Hardy's first two novels, *Desperate Remedies* (1871) and *Under the Greenwood Tree* (1872) were both published without his name on the title page;[33] his third, *A Pair of Blue Eyes* (1873), was the first to bear his name as the author.[34] A reviewer was unsure about the gender of the author of *Desperate Remedies*,[35] while the review in the *Spectator* of the anonymous serialization of his fourth book, *Far from the Madding Crowd*, in the *Cornhill Magazine* guessed that the author was George Eliot.[36] The erroneous ascription of authorship is one of the risks of anonymous writing; it also arises in the context of literary reviews and even on one famous occasion for a philosophy book.[37]

It is unusual for an established writer to choose anonymity, or the use of a pseudonym, except in those cases where the author of one genre of novel prefers to write under another name for an entirely different genre— as in the case of JK Rowling who has used the name, Robert Galbraith, for her recent thrillers. Anthony Trollope, however, decided to experiment with anonymity after five of his Barsetshire novels and several others had been published to popular acclaim. One reason is that he wanted to avoid the charge of overproduction; some critics complained that he wrote too much too quickly.[38] Further, according to his autobiography, he felt that readers

[30] See Mullan, 101.
[31] DS Thomas, *Robert Browning: A Life Within Life* (London, Weidenfeld and Nicolson, 1982) 27–33; WH Griffin, *The Life of Robert Browning* (London, Methuen and Co, 1938) 58.
[32] See P Raby, *Samuel Butler* (London, Hogarth Press, 1991) 119–20 and Mullan, 251–53. Butler's father, Canon Thomas Butler, was Headmaster of Shrewsbury School.
[33] C Tomalin, *Thomas Hardy* (London, Penguin Books, Viking, 2006) 113, 119.
[34] Ibid 122.
[35] Mullan, 130–31.
[36] Tomalin, *Thomas Hardy* (n 33) 99 and 405.
[37] See sections III(C) and VI below.
[38] N John Hall, *Trollope* (Oxford, Clarendon Press, 1991) 168–69.

and critics sometimes overvalued the work of authors with an established name, while that of younger writers would not be properly appreciated. It was in order to test this hypothesis and to see 'whether I could obtain a second identity'[39] as a writer that Trollope had two novels, *Nina Balatka* (1867) and *Linda Tressel* (1868), published anonymously. They were quite different from his earlier work; there was a greater attempt to describe the places, Prague and Nuremberg, in which they were set, and there 'was more of romance proper than had been usual with me'.[40] In one way the experiment was not entirely successful; his authorship of *Nina Balatka* was detected by Hutton, the editor of the *Spectator*, while Henry James in a laudatory review of both books, had no difficulty in identifying them as written in Trollope's inimitable style.[41] But Trollope had been right to suspect that the reading public might not have been as attracted to novels published anonymously as it was to those by well-known writers. His anonymous novels sold poorly, so he abandoned the experiment.[42] What is surprising is that he embarked on the experiment only a few months after writing the article in the *Fortnightly Review*[43] which had claimed that anonymous literature had had its day; Trollope, however, as will be discussed in the next section of the chapter, was inconsistent in his approach to anonymity.[44]

As John Mullan has pointed out,[45] anonymity has been much less common from the twentieth century, largely because of the decline in the traditions of modesty and personal reticence. Moreover, publishers use the name and personality of their authors to market their books. A pseudonym is now rarely adopted to veil the identity of a book's author, as it was in the cases of the Brontës or of George Eliot. However, a *nom de plume* is still sometimes used for other reasons. One of the best known and most fascinating examples is that of George Orwell, the name chosen by Eric Blair for almost all his literary work from 1933. Having written some short stories for the *Adelphi* and other journals under his own name, he indicated in letters in 1932 to Leonard Moore, his literary agent, that he would prefer to have his first book, *Down and Out in Paris and London*, published under a pseudonym, as he was 'not proud of it'.[46] Having rejected his publisher's suggestion that the author might be identified simply as 'X', he put forward four alternative names: PS Burton (the name he used when tramping),

---

[39] *An Autobiography and Other Writings* (Oxford, OUP, 2014) 128. *An Autobiography* was first published in 1883 after Trollope's death.

[40] Ibid 129.

[41] Hall, *Trollope* (n 38) 288, 307–8.

[42] Ibid 289, 307–8.

[43] 'On Anonymous Literature' (n 3).

[44] See section III(A) below.

[45] Mullan, 286–88.

[46] 'Letter of 26 April 1932', *The Complete Works of George Orwell* (P Davison (ed), London, Secker & Warburg, 1998) vol X, 243.

Kenneth Miles, George Orwell, H Lewis Allways: 'I rather favour George Orwell'.[47] The choice of Orwell seems to have been left to his publisher, Victor Gollancz; it has been suggested that Blair would have accepted the use of his real name had Gollancz insisted.[48] He continued to write for the *Adelphi* as Eric Blair in 1934,[49] while the use of quotation marks in a letter to *The Times* signed 'George Orwell' suggests that he was not at that time (January 1933) completely at home with his new pseudonym.[50] However, from 1935 he always seems to have published as George Orwell, though he continued on occasion to use 'Eric Blair' or 'E.A. Blair' when writing letters, even to literary friends and contacts. Apparently he considered changing his name by deed poll, but never get round to it.[51]

A number of explanations have been given for the adoption of a *nom de plume*. One is that Orwell did not want to shock his family by using his real name for his first book,[52] an account of a seedy life working in a kitchen in a Paris hotel and as a tramp in London. A second is that he disliked his Scottish surname,[53] and hated his first name, Eric, for its prim Victorian associations.[54] 'Orwell' is the name of a village in Cambridgeshire, and a river in Suffolk, which he would have known well.[55] It has also been conjectured that an old Etonian like Blair could not plausibly have written *Down and Out* under his own name,[56] though that does not explain why he continued to write virtually all his later literary work as George Orwell. Some commentators have detected a deeper reason for the use of a pseudonym: he wanted to disown his early life, a time when he considered himself a failure, and to adopt a new personality.[57] As Blair he was a self-conscious left-wing intellectual, a type of person whom the writer, Orwell, claimed to dislike.[58]

One further example of a *nom de plume* should be given, for it brings out the variety of reasons a writer may have for adopting a pseudonym. Through her agent, Doris Lessing, by the early 1980s a well-established

[47] Ibid 274.
[48] P Stansky and W Abrahams, *Orwell: The Transformation* (London, Constable, 1979) 4.
[49] Ibid 59.
[50] Ibid 18. The copyright notices in the United States for *Down and Out* and for *Burmese Days*, published there in 1934, were in the name of Eric Blair: ibid 23 and 43.
[51] G Bowker, *George Orwell* (London, Little, Brown, 2003) 298.
[52] Stansky and Abrahams, *Orwell* (n 48) 7, reporting a conversation between Blair and his sister, Avril.
[53] He even refused to meet the poet, Edwin Muir, because he disliked anything Scottish: ibid 83.
[54] DJ Taylor, *Orwell* (London, Chatto & Windus, 2003) 126–27. Frederic Farrar's *Eric, or Little by Little* (1858) was a notorious Victorian cautionary tale written for young children.
[55] Blair's parents lived in Southwold, and he may have chosen his pen-name while walking with his father along the river Orwell: S Wadhams, *Remembering Orwell* (Harmondsworth, Penguin Books, 1984) 47–48.
[56] Mullan, 291–92.
[57] See TR Fyvel, 'George Orwell and Eric Blair: Glimpses of a Dual Life' (1959) 13 *Encounter* 60, 62; K Aldritt, *The Making of George Orwell* (London, Edward Arnold, 1969) 54–55.
[58] R Colls, *George Orwell: English Rebel* (Oxford, OUP, 2013) 41–42.

writer, sent a novel, *The Diary of a Good Neighbour*, under the name, 'Jane Somers', to her publishers, Jonathan Cape.[59] It turned the book down, as did Granada. The novel was eventually published by Michael Joseph; it reminded that firm of Doris Lessing's books, so it was told of the 'plot'. However, no reviewer guessed the authorship of *The Diary*. 'Jane Somers' wrote a sequel, *If the Old Could ...*, which again was not spotted by reviewers as the work of Doris Lessing. In 1984 she republished the books under her own name as *The Diaries of Jane Somers*. In the 'Preface' she gave four reasons for writing the novels under a *nom de plume*. She wanted them to be reviewed on their merits, and to be free of the associations and constraints which every established writer has to live under. Secondly, the gesture should cheer up young writers. (Trollope in the 1860s had given much the same reasons for his experiment.) The third reason was, as Lessing admitted, a little malicious: she wanted to see what reviewers, who had disliked her recent science fiction, would make of the novels, and she seemed rather pleased that none of them had detected that they were hers. They received a number of baffling and contradictory reviews. Finally, she wanted to explore what it felt like to write under a different name. As Jane Somers, 'I wrote in ways that Doris Lessing cannot'.[60]

Michael Joseph knew that it was publishing two novels written by Doris Lessing. (It is not clear whether she would have identified herself to the other publishers, if they had taken the books.) Publishers almost always find out whom they are dealing with, even when, as with Charlotte Brontë and George Eliot, the author has initially attempted to conceal her identity from them;[61] they may get very angry if they discover that an author has deceived them (and the public), as happened when the Anglican clergyman adopted an Asian pseudonym in the episode discussed in the first chapter.[62] Publishers take responsibility for a book, ensuring, for example, that it does not carry libel risks. They can be sued for libel and prosecuted for obscenity or other criminal offences. So it is possible to agree with EM Forster that readers should be unconcerned with the identity of the author of a work of literature; they can assume, in a case of legal difficulty, that a book publisher, like the editor of a newspaper, accepts responsibility for its contents. Publishers can, and do, act as 'responsible intermediaries', so making anonymity more acceptable than it would be if the only recourse of a defamed or deceived reader was against an anonymous author.[63]

---

[59] See Mullan, 288–90 for an account of the affair with a resumé of the plot of the first Jane Somers novel.

[60] 'Preface' to D Lessing, *The Diaries of Jane Somers* (London, Michael Joseph, 1984).

[61] But see the case of Belle de Jour, discussed in section IX below.

[62] The Rev Toby Forward case discussed in chapter I, section I.

[63] See chapter I, section II for 'responsible intermediaries'.

III. LITERARY JOURNALS AND REVIEWING

A debate on the rival merits of anonymity and signature was frequently conducted in Victorian literary reviews, and was revived more recently in the contentions made before and after the abandoning of anonymous reviewing by the *Times Literary Supplement* (*TLS*) in 1974. This section outlines the gradual shift from anonymous to signed reviewing in nineteenth century journals, the strengths of the points made on each side of the argument, and finally, the reasons which impelled the *TLS* to abandon anonymous reviewing. Anonymity in newspapers and contemporary (largely) political periodicals, such as the *Spectator* and the *New Statesman,* is covered in section IV.

A. Change to Signed Reviewing in the Nineteenth Century

At the beginning of the nineteenth century,[64] as in the eighteenth, anonymous writing was standard in literary periodicals; this applied to their book serialisations, to general articles and features, as well as to book and theatre reviews. Like newspapers at that time, periodicals reflected the views of political parties and groups,[65] while editors exercised strict control to ensure that the contributors of articles took the position of the particular journal. Individual writers would not have been permitted to make a name by adopting a distinctive or unusual line. The move towards signature began when the work of well-known novelists—notably, Dickens and Thackeray—was serialised. Identification of the author would significantly promote sales of the journal.[66] *Macmillan's Magazine*, published from 1859, is the first long-standing journal in which signed articles were predominant.[67] One early issue contained an article by the author of *Tom Brown's Schooldays,* Thomas Hughes, in which he argued for signed journalism as promoting more responsible writing and as assisting readers to judge its quality.[68]

In 1865, announcements in the *Athenaeum* proclaimed that the new *Fortnightly Review* would be free of any distinctive party line and that contributors would provide their name, giving voice to their own views free

---

[64] This and the following subsection owe much to the classic article by Oscar Maurer, Jr, 'Anonymity v Signature in Victorian Reviewing' (1948) XXVII *Studies in English* 1.

[65] WJ Graham, *English Literary Periodicals* (New York, Thomas Nelson, 1930) 229. *Blackwood's Magazine* and the *Quarterly Review* were Tory periodicals, while the *Edinburgh Review* supported the Whigs.

[66] Maurer, 'Anonymity v Signature in Victorian Reviewing' (n 64) 2–4.

[67] GJ Worth, *Macmillan's Magazine, 1859–1907* (Aldershot, Ashgate, 2003) 32. Other journals, such as the *London Review* (1809) and the *New Monthly Magazine* (1820) had also contained signed articles and reviews, but they had been discontinued during the nineteenth century: Graham, *English Literary Periodicals* (n 65) 239–40 and 285–86.

[68] 'Anonymous Journalism' (1861) 5 *Macmillan's Magazine* 157.

from the opinion of the editor or other contributors.[69] All the articles in the *Fortnightly* in its first year of publication (1865) were signed, though there were some shorter anonymous notes on 'Public Affairs'. At the outset the signature policy was vigorously defended in the journal by its first two editors, GH Lewes[70] and John Morley,[71] though Morley subsequently doubted the wisdom of abandoning anonymous writing altogether; it was unclear to him in 1882 whether signature had improved the quality of literary writing, while readers may have become more interested in the 'star' quality of a writer than in the correctness of his views.[72] Interestingly, Trollope, who had expressed in the *Fortnightly* strong criticism of unsigned reviewing,[73] also soon became more sympathetic to anonymity. For the new journal, *St Pauls Magazine*, which he established in 1867 and edited for its first three years of publication, anonymity, rather than signed writing, was the rule; it has been conjectured that he preferred to follow the practice of the successful *Cornhill* periodical where articles at that time were unsigned, rather than that of the less prosperous *Fortnightly*, and that politicians would express themselves more freely if they were unidentified.[74]

A signature policy was adopted by two leading periodicals, the *Contemporary Review* (1866) and the *Nineteenth Century* (1877). Gradually, towards the end of the nineteenth century anonymity became less common.[75] For example, the *Saturday Review*, long a bulwark of anonymous writing, began to publish signed reviews in the 1890s. In 1896, the leading scholar, George Saintsbury,[76] identified the change from almost universal anonymous reviewing at the beginning of the nineteenth century to signed criticism at the end of it as one of the most significant literary developments in that period.[77] Anonymous reviewing and other writing in literary periodicals became even less common in the twentieth century,[78] though it continued

---

[69] See the announcement in the *Athenaeum* (1865) no 1957, 602. For discussion of the policy, see S Nash, 'What's in a Name? Signature, Criticism, and Authority in The Fortnightly Review' (2010) *Victorian Periodicals Review* 57, 57–63.

[70] 'Farewell Causerie' (n 7).

[71] 'Anonymous Journalism' (1867) 8 *Fortnightly Review* 287.

[72] 'Valedictory' (1882) 38 (32 New Series) *Fortnightly Review* 511, 514–15. Also see J Morley, 'Memorials of a Man of Letters' (1878) 29 (23 New Series) *Fortnightly Review* 596, 601–5.

[73] 'On Anonymous Literature' (n 3).

[74] J Sutherland, 'Trollope and *St Paul's* 1866–70' in T Bareham (ed), *Anthony Trollope* (New Jersey, Barnes and Noble, 1980) 116, 126–28.

[75] Graham, *English Literary Periodicals* (n 65) 310.

[76] George Saintsbury, Professor of Rhetoric and English literature at Edinburgh University from 1890–1915, was a prolific writer on English and French literature, and also a distinguished wine connoisseur.

[77] *A History of Nineteenth Century Literature: 1780–1895* (London, Macmillan, 1896) 450–51.

[78] However, from a few years before the First World War and subsequently, even the *Fortnightly Review* contained some articles written under pseudonyms such as 'Diplomaticus', 'Politicus' and 'Auditor Tantum'.

in many weekly journals.[79] As noted earlier the practice was only finally abandoned by the *TLS* in 1974 (see section III(C)). It survives, however, in two English periodicals (see section IV(B) below).

B. Anonymity Arguments

The rival merits of anonymous and signed reviewing were vigorously debated in literary periodicals for much of the nineteenth century. John Galt, novelist, essayist and friend of Byron, argued against anonymity as early as 1835.[80] It enabled abuse of liberty of the press through the publication of libellous attacks in newspapers and magazines. Cowardly book reviewers could use anonymity 'to stab in the dark'.[81] Authors, as well as printers and publishers, should therefore be compelled to state their name, so they could be held legally responsible. Similar arguments were made by Trollope, and by Morley, at least in 1867 when he assumed the editorship of the *Fortnightly*.[82] Signature would induce authors to take more care in their writing and so assume responsibility for their work. Anonymity in contrast encouraged not only the writing of trivial, pot-boiler criticism, but also of 'puffing' reviews in which an anonymous author extolled the merits of a friend's or even of his own work.[83] (A modern example was a 'puffing' anonymous review on the Amazon website by an historian of his book, while trashing those of other rival historians.)[84] While defending the merits of anonymity, Saintsbury admitted that it allowed reviewers, as he had done himself, to write four or five reviews of the same book in different journals.[85] Moreover, literary criticism was essentially a personal view or impression, and that required disclosure of the reviewer's name.[86] For Trollope it was particularly important that readers should be able to know who the critic is, so they could assess the value of his comments on a book and balance them against its author's ideas.[87]

The argument for signature was particularly well made in an article by J Boyd Kinnear in the *Contemporary Review*.[88] In his view, there was no

---

[79] Graham, *English Literary Periodicals* (n 65) 343.

[80] 'Anonymous Publications' (1835) 11 *Fraser's Magazine* 549.

[81] Ibid 550.

[82] See nn 3 and 71 above.

[83] L Blake, 'Literary Criticism and the Victorian Periodicals' (1986) 16 *Yearbook of English Studies* 92, 107, and see Mullan, 198–200.

[84] 'Historian Orlando Figes admits posting Amazon reviews that trashed rivals': see *Guardian*, 23 November 2010, available at www.theguardian.com/2010/apr/23/historian-orlando-figes-amazon-review-rivals.

[85] 'Journalism Fifty Years Ago' (1930) 107 *Nineteenth Century* 426, 429.

[86] Maurer, 'Anonymity v Signature in Victorian Reviewing' (n 64) 21.

[87] 'On Anonymous Literature' (n 3) 497.

[88] J Boyd Kinnear 'Anonymous Journalism' (1867) 5 *Contemporary Review* 324.

reason why journalism should be exempt from the general principle that readers want to know who gives them information and advice, just as editors want to know the names of those who write letters to a newspaper for publication. Kinnear dismissed the argument that anonymity was necessary to allow barristers, doctors and other professionals to write for the press. Anonymity encouraged inaccurate and distorted writing, but signature promoted responsibility. Unlike Trollope in his contemporaneous article in the *Fortnightly*,[89] Kinnear thought the change to signature should be made for all types of writing—for newspaper editorials and articles as much as for book reviews. The change was resisted on grounds of custom, and because newspaper owners feared it would reduce their ability to control the contents of their papers;[90] anonymous journalists were much less likely to assert their independence.

The case for anonymity is rather less familiar now, but good arguments were made for it. Replying to Zola's call for signed reviewing,[91] one commentator suggested that anonymous criticism was more likely to be calm and dispassionate, for the critic lacked any incentive to place himself at the centre of a review. It should not matter who wrote a review; what was important was whether its assessment of the work was sound.[92] Concern at the increase in reviewing by celebrities was common; readers would be likely to accept the judgement of a 'star' reviewer, just because of his position, rather than consider it on its merits.[93] Editors would also be less likely to take on young reviewers, who found it easier to write anonymously as their judgement would then be fairly considered.[94] Some writers preferred anonymity not to avoid responsibility for their work, but from a preference for privacy; anonymity encouraged public-spirited gentlemen to write.[95]

John Morley, editor of the *Fortnightly* for 15 years, thought that signed writing had led to a decline in the position of editors, who no longer felt so responsible for ensuring that reviews were consonant with the political position or the literary standards of the journal.[96] Anonymity promoted the authority of the journal as a whole and its particular judgements on literary works.[97] This argument has prevailed for a long time with newspapers and

---

[89] 'On Anonymous Literature' (n 3) 496.

[90] Kinnear, 'Anonymous Journalism' (n 88) 337–38.

[91] 'Anonymity in Journalism' (n 1).

[92] HD Traill, 'The Anonymous Critic' (1893) 34 *Nineteenth Century* 932, 937–38.

[93] See Saintsbury, *A History of Nineteenth Century Literature* (n 77) 451; Morley, 'Memorials of a Man of Letters' (n 72) 605, and 'Valedictory' (n 72) 514–15.

[94] See [ES Dallas], 'Popular Literature: The Periodical Press' (1859) LXXXV *Blackwood's Edinburgh Magazine* 180, 183; Morley, 'Memorials of a Man of Letters' (n 72) 604.

[95] [James Fitzjames Stephen] 'Journalism' (1862) VI *Cornhill Magazine* 52, 57; D Liddle. 'Sportsmen, Mentors, Anonymity and Mid-Victorian Theories of Journalism' (1997) 41 *Victorian Studies* 31, 53.

[96] 'Memorials of a Man of Letters' (n 72) 602.

[97] [WR Greg] 'The Newspaper Press' (1855) 102 *Edinburgh Review* 470, 487–89.

was accepted by the *TLS* until 1974 when it changed to signed reviewing (see section III(C) below).

On occasion comparisons were drawn between the arguments relating to anonymous writing, on the one hand, and those concerning voting, on the other. The secret ballot, now taken to be fundamental to the conduct of fair elections, was only introduced in 1872.[98] While from that time it has been common to favour the secret ballot, but to support signed writing so the author could take moral and legal responsibility for his work, a quite different position was occasionally taken earlier in the nineteenth century. In 1859, an article in *Blackwood's Edinburgh Magazine* argued for anonymous journalism, largely on the ground that it led to the less violent and more impersonal discussion of political and literary issues.[99] But in the author's view the ballot was different, as unlike writing a journal article, voting was an act with legal effects: the choice of a Member of Parliament. The identity of individuals voting for an MP should be known; the author of the article was unpersuaded that a secret ballot was necessary to prevent intimidation in voting.[100] Morley writing in 1867 rightly thought this position very odd.[101] Trollope took a more consistent position. Generally in favour of signed reviewing on the ground that it encouraged its authors to take responsibility for their work,[102] he also opposed the secret ballot when he stood in Beverley at the 1868 General Election; voters should discharge their electoral duties openly.[103]

Reference was sometimes made in Victorian writing to the French Law of 1850 (later repealed) which had required all articles of political, philosophical or religious discussion to be signed, a measure intended to curb the influence of anonymous journalists and other writers.[104] Any move to introduce a similar requirement in England was strongly opposed by the press.[105] But it was not supported either by proponents of signature. Kinnear thought the Law had saved the quality of the French press from sinking any lower, but he did not favour its import into England.[106] The move to signature should be made because it was right, not because of any legal obligation to take this step.

The case for anonymity was certainly a strong one. It is striking that John Morley became more sympathetic to it after his long experience of

---

[98] See chapter 7, section II below.
[99] See 'Popular Literature' (n 94) above.
[100] Ibid 189.
[101] 'Anonymous Journalism' (n 71) 292.
[102] See n 3 above.
[103] See Hall, *Trollope* (n 38) 326.
[104] Maurer, 'Anonymity v Signature in Victorian Reviewing' (n 64) 7.
[105] Hughes, 'Anonymous Journalism' (n 68) 157 discussed the opposition of *The Times*.
[106] 'Anonymous Journalism' (n 88) 338. Trollope, 'On Anonymous Literature' (n 3) 492, refers to the French law, but does not call for the adoption of any comparable requirement in England.

editing a journal where the overwhelming majority of articles were signed. It is also interesting that some arguments made for it were similar to those made, albeit in rather different terms, in favour of signature: anonymity encouraged more people to write and it produced better, fairer criticism, so it was in the interests of readers. One familiar argument for anonymity was notably absent; the point that otherwise critics might feel intimidated when writing their reviews.[107] It would be difficult to make that point and at the same time argue that anonymity encouraged independently minded gentlemen to write for literary periodicals. However, whatever the merits of the objective arguments, the move to signature became irresistible towards the end of the nineteenth century, as readers became more attracted to the criticism of known, perhaps celebrity, reviewers. Periodicals with signed articles and reviews had simply become more popular.

C. *Times Literary Supplement* (*TLS*)

The *TLS* was originally (1902) issued as a supplement to *The Times* newspaper, a factor which goes some way to explaining why its reviews were anonymous at a time when many literary periodicals had moved to signature: the newspaper itself then had a strict anonymity policy.[108] The *Supplement* was only published separately in 1914. Bruce Richmond, its long standing editor until 1937, was a firm believer in anonymous reviewing, on the ground that it promoted the authority of the journal's judgements on the books reviewed. The policy was vigorously defended, notably in signed articles in 1938 (in edition no 1914) by Stephen Spender and in 1961 (no 3072) by TS Eliot. For Spender, signature deterred young writers from contributing reviews and rested on 'the modern fallacy that the expression of a writer's individuality is always and on every occasion a good in itself'.[109] Eliot emphasised the discipline of anonymity; it required individual writers to submit to the requirements of the journal and its editor, who should read its every word.[110] But there were a number of critics, for example, the historian Hugh Trevor-Roper,[111] and FW Bateson, an English scholar and founder of the leading literary journal, *Essays in Criticism*. In 1957, Bateson launched a strong attack on the *TLS* policy: anonymity obliterated the personal differences in style which should characterise literary criticism and it elevated the reviewer over the author and readers. He made the fundamental point that 'the worth of an opinion varies with the degree of respect we

---

[107] Liddle, 'Journalism' (n 95) 60.
[108] See section IV(A) below.
[109] 'A Plea for More Anonymity: The Future of Reviewing', *TLS*, 8 October 1938.
[110] 'Bruce Lyttleton Richmond: Essay on his 90th Birthday', *TLS*, 13 January 1961.
[111] Letters in *TLS* (no 2906), 8 November 1957 and (no 2914), 3 January 1958.

have for the holder of the opinion', a respect which itself depended on the value of the views he or she had previously expressed. More controversially he added that an anonymous review could not be as trusted as signed criticism, because it suppressed an important element of its meaning.[112]

The editor of the *TLS*, Alan Pryce-Jones, replied to Bateson and other critics in two leading articles, 'The Disembodied Voice' (no 2908) and 'Anonymity Again' (no 2915).[113] The policy was defended to some extent as carrying on the tradition of the nineteenth century, and also because there was value in the expression of a corporate literary personality.[114] TS Eliot supported the policy as enhancing the responsibility and authority of the editor.[115] Bateson returned to the attack in 1971, adding further points to those he had made 14 years earlier.[116] Authors on occasion attributed hostile reviews to the wrong person; in one case the *TLS* had refused to publish a letter (by Professor Barbara Hardy of Birkbeck College) protesting against such an inaccurate attribution and calling on this ground for signed reviewing. Bateson also thought that anonymous reviewers could be unduly harsh on American academic writing, so souring relations between scholars on the two sides of the Atlantic. An academic reputation could be seriously damaged by a severe review of a book, to which its author could not fully respond without knowing the reviewer's identity.

The anonymity policy was maintained by Arthur Crook, the *TLS* editor from 1959 to 1974; one interesting reason he gave for it was that it enabled reviews by civil servants and Members of Parliament to be much more open than they would be if their authors had been required to sign them.[117] Conor Cruise O'Brien, for example, had been able to write an article on French literary criticism, while he was an Irish government diplomat.[118] But John Gross, the editor from April 1974, decided the time had come to alter *TLS* policy. The change was announced in a signed leader, 'Naming Names' in the edition (no 3770) of 7 June 1974. While admitting that there were sound arguments on both sides of the controversy, Gross concluded that the case against anonymity was in the end relatively simple: readers were entitled to ask on whose authority a literary judgement was made, and critics should be responsible for their views. He admitted that signature had its

---

[112] 'Organs of Critical Opinion IV: *The Times Literary Supplement*' (1957) VII *Essays in Literary Criticism* 349, 358–59.

[113] Apparently, Bateson thought the leaders had been written by Arthur Cook, at that time deputy editor of the *TLS*: J Treglown, 'Bateson and the *TLS*' (2001) 51 *Essays in Criticism* 148, 155. This article gives an excellent summary of Bateson's successful campaign to persuade the *TLS* to change its policy.

[114] 'Anonymity Again', *TLS*, 10 January 1958.

[115] Letter in *TLS* (no 2916), 17 January 1958.

[116] Editorial Commentary, (1971) XXI *Essays in Literary Criticism* 117.

[117] See Derwent May, *Critical Times: The History of The Times Literary Supplement* (London, Harper Collins, 2001) 417–18.

[118] Ibid 323.

dangers, but editors could control its abuse by celebrity writers, if they were too anxious to promote their own views at the cost of an honest assessment of the work under review.

However, the change was to be made gradually. For example, in the edition in which the change was made, there was a review on the cover page by Denis Donoghue of a collection of essays devoted to the work of the literary scholar, William Empson, and inside a signed review by Roy Pascal of books on Kafka, while two weeks later (no 3772) there was a cover review of Philip Larkin's *High Window* by John Bayley. For the first few weeks there were only three or four signed reviews. It was only by the end of the year that virtually all reviews were signed. A number of correspondents wrote letters to the *TLS*, criticising the change of policy. Jonathan Culler, a prominent literary theorist, argued (no 3773) that anonymous judgements focussed attention on their truth rather than on the personality of the writer; the new policy also destroyed academics' Common Room pleasure of guessing reviewers' identity![119] (His view did not deter Culler from writing a signed review in no 3782.)[120] An American professor of philosophy (no 3777) drew an analogy between literary reviews, on the one hand, and on the other the secret ballot, academic peer review and personal references, though it was not quite clear what implications he would draw from it;[121] in any case, the analogy is unconvincing, as literary reviews, unlike the other communications, are published to the world at large and cannot be regarded as in any way confidential. Other correspondents welcomed the change. Bateson (nos 3775 and 3783) repeated his point that the case for signature was ultimately a moral one, for it removed the spectre of cowardly, malicious attacks; moreover, anonymity did not, as its defenders contend, encourage objectivity, but only the appearance of objectivity.[122]

Although, as John Gross had admitted, the case for anonymity was still a respectable one, there is surely no doubt that the change was long overdue. A hostile review in a respected literary journal, enjoying a world-wide circulation, can seriously damage an author's standing, and there can be little doubt that malicious and bitter reviews are more likely to be penned anonymously than by writers who are required to identify themselves. With respect to Eliot, it is now beyond the capacity of any editor (or even the team of editors) to scrutinise carefully reviews of books on the wide variety of subjects covered in the *Supplement* (literature in many languages, history, theology, philosophy, politics and the sciences) and weed out those which go beyond the limits of fair criticism. Finally, readers are surely entitled to know who the writer of a review is. Some of them (though, of course, not

---

[119] *TLS*, 28 June 1974, and also see another letter by him, TLS (no 3777), 26 July 1974.
[120] Review of books by Stephen Heath and Julia Kristeva, *TLS*, 30 August 1974.
[121] Letter by Professor DF Henze to *TLS* (no 3777), 26 July 1974.
[122] Letters to *TLS* (no 3775), 12 July 1974 and to *TLS* (no 3783), 6 September 1974.

all) are capable of assessing the coherence of his views, which is easier if they are aware of his credentials and what he has written himself on the topic.

IV. NEWSPAPERS AND PERIODICALS

A. Newspapers

In the nineteenth century (and earlier) newspaper journalism was almost invariably anonymous.[123] The reasons for this practice in literary periodicals applied even more strongly in the case of newspapers; for the most part they represented the views of the political parties, while editorial control to ensure a consistent line was particularly strict.[124] The case for signature was much weaker in the newspaper context than it was for literary reviews; newspapers at that time contained lots of news, but relatively few feature articles,[125] so writers could rarely contend that it was important to attach their name to their own distinctive contributions. Further, it would probably not have mattered much to readers which individual journalist provided them with information, whether it concerned political events at home or foreign affairs. The ethos of anonymity was strongly held at *The Times* and defended by its long serving editors, Thomas Barnes (1817–41)[126] and John Delane (1841–77).[127] It was equally firmly held at the *Daily Telegraph*, a more popular paper established in 1855. When towards the end of the century, Clement Scott, the theatre critic of the newspaper for over 25 years, asked its owner for permission to sign his reviews, this was summarily refused and he left.[128] Book reviews in the *Manchester Guardian* remained anonymous during the 1890s,[129] decades after some literary periodicals had adopted a signature policy.

During the course of the twentieth century the anonymity practice was gradually relaxed, so distinguished contributors from outside a newspaper and even some correspondents could use their own name. A women's page was introduced in the *Manchester Guardian* in 1922, with signed articles by well-known writers,[130] while Neville Cardus (on music and cricket),

---

[123] L Brown, *Victorian News and Newspapers* (Oxford, OUP, 1985) 3–4.

[124] Ibid 61, 88–90.

[125] Ibid 107–8.

[126] *History of the Times*, vol 1, *1785–1841: The Thunderer in the Making* (London, 1935–38) 205, 390–91.

[127] A Smith, *The Newspaper: An International History* (London, Thames and Hudson, 1979) 120–21.

[128] Lord Burnham, *Peterborough Court: The Story of the Daily Telegraph* (London, Cassell and Co, 1955) 40.

[129] D Ayerst, *Guardian: Biography of a Newspaper* (London, Collins, 1971) 293.

[130] Ayerst, *Guardian* (n 129) 447, and ibid 448, for the film column with initials 'CAL', identifying Caroline LeJeune.

the historian, AJP Taylor, and Alastair Cooke contributed under their own name. But home and foreign correspondents were not regularly identified with their own by-line until 1960, after the paper had changed its name to the *Guardian*.[131] Practice at the *Daily Telegraph* also changed, but was inconsistent. Sports correspondents were generally identified, but the racing column was written by 'Hotspur'.[132] Some journalists signed their columns, others wrote anonymously; the 'Way of the World' column, for example, was written by Colin Welch and Michael Wharton under the pen name 'Peter Simple'.[133] The general change to signature only occurred in the 1960s, though even then it was not uniform; for example, the front page of the edition reporting the assassination of President Kennedy in 1963 carried a mixture of signed and unsigned reports.[134] Similarly, reports in the early numbers of the *Sunday Telegraph* (1961) were usually anonymous, but it moved rapidly to signature, with Peregrine Worsthorne signing his column on the leader page.[135] The *Sunday Times* had moved to signed articles in the late 1940s, largely on the insistence of Ian Fleming, then the foreign affairs manager; he was keen that foreign correspondents had their own by-lines, and this policy spread to the whole of the paper.[136]

The *Times* held out for anonymity until 1967. William Haley, its editor from 1952 to 1966, was a strong believer in it as giving the newspaper greater authority than any individual writer could command.[137] The rule was confirmed by the Board in June 1966. But the new editor, William Rees-Mogg, decided to introduce signed articles from 12 January 1967, and after that anonymous pieces became very rare;[138] obituaries, however, remain anonymous. The change was made along with others (news rather than classified advertisements on the front page) to brighten up the presentation of *The Times* and to encourage journalists to stay with the paper, rather than move to another where they were allowed their own by-line. The same reasons impelled the *Financial Times* to make this change in March 1967. Its editor, Gordon Newton, also argued that specialist readers needed to know the identity of writers, previously known as, for example, 'Industry editor' or 'Energy editor', in order to assess the authority of their views.[139]

---

[131] The change of name was made on 24 August 1959: A Hetherington, *Guardian Years* (London, Chatto & Windus, 1981) 146.

[132] Burnham, *Peterborough Court* (n 128) 119.

[133] D Hart-Davis, *The House the Berrys Built* (London, Hodder & Stoughton, 1990) 166–69.

[134] Ibid 210 reproducing the front page of 23 November 1963. The unsigned reports were headed 'From Our Own Correspondent'.

[135] Ibid 180 (displaying the front page of 5 February 1961) and 190–91.

[136] H Hobson, P Knightley and L Russell, *The Pearl of Days: An Intimate Memoir of the Sunday Times: 1822–1972* (London, Hamish Hamilton, 1972) 259–60.

[137] 'T.L.S.' (1979–80) 49 *American Scholar* 227, 229.

[138] I McDonald, *History of the Times* (London, Times Books, 1984) vol V, 453–54.

[139] D Kynaston, *The Financial Times: A Centenary History* (London, Viking, 1988) 348.

Whatever the merits of the argument for anonymity in newspapers, commercial imperatives meant that it was difficult for one or two papers to maintain the practice when their competitors had abandoned it.

B. Periodicals

The *Spectator* is the most long-established of British political weekly journals, providing features and commentary on politics and social affairs, as well as book and arts reviews. Anonymity was one of its characteristics from the start (1828), although by 1870–80 there were occasional signed reviews and initials were sometimes used.[140] An unsigned review of the work of the theologian and Christian Socialist, FD Maurice, who opposed anonymous journalism, argued that signature tended to promote the petty vanities of writers.[141] The move to signed articles occurred only shortly before its fourth proprietor-editor, St Loe Strachey, gave up control of the journal at the end of 1925. Strachey himself then signed his weekly contributions to the journal.[142]

It might be thought that the *New Statesman*, a left-wing political weekly, established as recently as 1913, would have adopted signature from the start. But that was not the case. The unsigned 'Comments' piece by the editor, Clifford Sharp, in the first number,[143] explained that anonymity was crucial to establish the common style and tone of the new journal; it was also indicated, rather coyly, that Sidney Webb and GB Shaw would as a rule write editorials and that this first issue contained more than one contribution from each of them. In fact it also carried one signed article by Sidney and Beatrice Webb and signed book reviews by Desmond McCarthy. Contributors generally wrote under a pseudonym. For instance, Robert Lynd, a freelance writer on Ireland, was identified variously as 'X', 'XX' and 'YY', while the science correspondent, Caleeb Saleeby, wrote as 'Lens'.[144] The novelist, Arnold Bennett, used the pseudonym 'Sardonyx' for his column;[145] the socialist academic, GDH Cole, wrote anonymously from 1919 as a 'Labour correspondent', so ensuring that his column was taken more seriously by cautious middle-class readers.[146] Apparently GB Shaw

---

[140] RH Tener, 'Breaking the Code of Anonymity: The Case of the *Spectator*, 1861–1897' (1986) 16 *Yearbook of English Studies* 63, 67–69.

[141] *Spectator*, 15 March 1884, 342.

[142] W Beach Thomas, *The Story of the Spectator 1828–1928* (London, Methuen and Co, 1928) 241–42.

[143] 13 April 1913. For comment, see E Hyams, *The New Statesman: The History of the First Fifty Years 1913–63* (London, Longmans, 1963) 24–25, and A Smith, *The New Statesman: Portrait of a Political Weekly 1913–1931* (London, Frank Cass, 1996) 46.

[144] Smith, *The New Statesman* (n 143) 52 and 61.

[145] Ibid 99.

[146] Ibid 139–40.

rather enjoyed anonymity, with its freedom to use 'WE' for his expression of the journal's views, and refused to sign articles, even when encouraged by the editor to do so.[147] By the end of the 1920s the anonymity rule had gradually been relaxed and signed articles became more common, but anonymity had survived longer than it had done with the *Spectator*. Even the famous 'London Diary' column was signed 'Critic', though everyone knew that it was by Kingsley Martin, the journal's editor from 1931 to 1960. From the mid-1930s all contributions, apart from editorials and short book notices, to the *News Statesman* were signed, apparently on the suggestion of Raymond Mortimer, its literary editor from 1935 to 1947.[148]

Famously, anonymity has survived at *The Economist*, where it is a significant aspect of the journal's personality. It is adhered to rigidly, except for special reports and the occasional outside contribution from a distinguished economist. The prominent columns on Britain, Europe and the United States are written by senior writers under a pseudonym: respectively Bagehot, Charlemagne and Lexington. The policy has been strongly defended by the journal's editors, notably by Geoffrey Crowther at the centenary lunch in 1943, where he explained that it meant that *The Economist* had acquired a strong corporate personality which gave the journal greater authority than its individual writers could command.[149] The anonymity rule is discussed at staff meetings every few years when editorial policy is reviewed, but it is generally accepted, albeit not always with tremendous enthusiasm. On occasion, journalists may have left the journal, because without signature they feel that their talents cannot be publicly recognised.[150]

The risk of loss of talented journalists is perhaps not the only disadvantage of the strict anonymity policy. When he was a backbench Labour MP in the 1940s, Denis Healey thought it was unrewarding to write for *The Economist*, politically as well as financially, because he could get no credit for his views. William Plowden, a distinguished commentator on government and social policy, thought it should be changed for reasons of transparency and openness; readers should know who was addressing them.[151] Anonymity in practice may also be thought to lead to the homogenous style of the journal's articles, which for some make it less attractive to read than other journals where writers can develop—or some would say exploit—their distinctive styles. Against these arguments, anonymity can be defended as supporting the collegiate approach of the journal and as enhancing its overall authority. The policy certainly makes more sense for the detailed factual

---

[147] Hyams, *The New Statesman* (n 143) 25.
[148] CH Rolph, *Kingsley* (London, Victor Gollancz, 1973) 167.
[149] R Dudley Edwards, *The Pursuit of Reason: The Economist, 1843–1993* (London, Hamish Hamilton, 1993) 855–56.
[150] Telephone interview with Ann Wroe, Obituaries Editor, on 12 November 2014.
[151] Edwards, *The Pursuit of Reason* (n 149) 853–54.

reports of political and economic developments in which *The Economist* specialises than it is for book and other arts reviews, where it seems hard to justify. In practice, it is quite easy to identify its senior writers and editors on the journal's website, and they are free to write for newspapers and to broadcast under their own name. The policy is not so much designed to keep the identity of its writers confidential, as it is to preserve the authority of the journal.

Anonymity and pseudonyms also now characterise *Private Eye*. Surprisingly, early issues of the magazine, established in October 1961, named its contributors and identified the editors on the masthead.[152] For example, 'The Hounding of the Pooves' in Issue 19 was signed 'Dr J Miller', who later protested on the ground that the publication might be considered an unprofessional advertisement on his part![153] But from 1966 authorship was largely anonymous, and the masthead with its list of editors and contributors was not reproduced after February 1967.[154] Columns were simply headed 'Lord Gnome', 'In the City', 'In the Courts', 'Nooks and Corners' (which survives to this day), or 'Grovel'. The titles sometimes kept secret the identity of well-known contributors: John Betjeman and later his daughter, Candida Lycett-Green, wrote 'Nooks and Corners', while the Crossword was set by Tom Driberg, MP, under the name, 'Tiresias', the blind seer of Athens.[155] Other disguises were very thin; most readers knew that 'Footnotes' were written by Paul Foot, the leading investigative journalist at the *Eye* for a number of years.

Anonymity contributed a little to Foot's freedom to write without inhibition, though not as much, in his view, as the culture of the magazine.[156] Sometimes there are good practical reasons for anonymity; barristers, for example, could not write a gossip column about the courts without infringing professional rules. But the pseudonyms are generally used to create a sense of fun and mischief, and to promote *Private Eye*'s distinctive identity as a magazine which uniquely combines serious news, which other newspapers and magazines are too cautious to publish, with cartoons and satire. It follows in the tradition of eighteenth century political writing, much of which was anonymous: see the next section.

V. POLITICAL WRITING

Jonathan Swift, Dean of St Patrick's Cathedral, Dublin and the author of *Gulliver's Travels* (1726), almost always wrote without using his own

---

[152] P Marnham, *The Private Eye Story* (London, Andre Deutsch, 1982) 30, 33.
[153] Ibid 42–43.
[154] Ibid 112–13.
[155] Ibid 126–27.
[156] See the long quotation of Foot's views in ibid 131.

name.[157] His first major work, the satirical fable, *A Tale of a Tub* (1704) was published anonymously, though it was widely known that Swift was the author, and he later admitted his authorship, while condemning himself for writing it.[158] His weekly essays in the political magazine, *The Examiner,* written at the invitation of the leading Tory minister, Robert Harley, were anonymous.[159] *The Drapier's Letters* (1724) provide another example. Written under the pseudonym, 'MB, Draper of St Francis Street, Dublin', the letters protested against the patent granted to William Wood, an English manufacturer, to produce copper coins for Ireland, which would lead to massive inflation and damage the Irish economy; Swift was indignant, as on other occasions,[160] at what he considered the shoddy treatment of Irish traders by the government in London. The printer-publisher of the *Letters,* John Harding, refused to reveal their author, though Swift himself had admitted his authorship to friends. (Harding was convicted of seditious libel and sent to prison, where he died shortly afterwards.) Swift then conducted a vigorous public campaign under his own name against the conduct of the government, which climbed down and cancelled the patent.[161]

Swift probably had a number of reasons for preferring anonymity or the use of a pseudonym. Writing under his real name would almost certainly in some cases have led to prosecution or at least political embarrassment. He may well have thought that it would ruin his chance of promotion in the church; once he was identified as the author of *A Tale of a Tub* with its mocking treatment of religious doctrine, he lost all chance of preferment from Queen Anne.[162] Anonymity enabled him to choose the most opportune moment to admit authorship. Irvin Ehrenpreis, in the most comprehensive biography, considers that Swift was acting from self-protection. He preferred to see how a work was assessed by the public before deciding whether to take responsibility for it;[163] when it was safe to do so, he could admit authorship, or as in the case of *The Drapier's Letters* use them as a basis for a political campaign. Further, an anonymous author could obtain information from a variety of political sources.[164] Public reticence was perfectly

---

[157] D Nokes, *Jonathan Swift, A Hypocrite Reversed* (Oxford, OUP, 1985) 153 identifies 'Proposals for Correcting, Improving and Ascertaining the English Tongue' (1712) as almost uniquely written under his own signature.

[158] I Ehrenpreis, *Swift, The Man, his Works and the Age* (London, Methuen and Co, 1983) vol II, 334–35.

[159] Ibid 406–8. Also see V Glendinning, *Jonathan Swift* (London, Random House, 1998) 101–2.

[160] As in his anonymous pamphlet, *A Proposal for the Universal Use of Irish Manufacture* (1720), which, as in the case of the *Drapier's Letters,* led to the prosecution of the printer. Swift was widely believed to be the author, but nobody was willing formally to denounce him: see L Damrosch, *Jonathan Swift: His Life and his World* (Newhaven, Yale UP, 2013) 342–45.

[161] For a full discussion of the affair, see Nokes, *Jonathan Swift* (n 157) 280–96.

[162] Damrosch, *Jonathan Swift* (n 160) 146.

[163] Ehrenpreis, *Swift, The Man, his Works and the Age* (n 158) 331, 407–8.

[164] Ibid 410.

compatible with Swift's ready disclosure of his authorship to political and literary friends, which would carry little or no risk.

Fear of prosecution for the offence of seditious libel is almost certainly the explanation for the frequent use of pseudonyms by writers of political pamphlets and newspaper columns during the eighteenth century.[165] Among these writers were John Trenchard and Thomas Gordon who collaborated under the pseudonym 'Cato' to write a number of libertarian essays in newspapers from 1720 to 1723, which were later published in book form as *Cato's Letters*.[166] The best known example of pseudonymous political writing in England in this period are the *Letters of Junius,* which were published in the *Public Advertiser* from 1768–71. Written from a radical Whig perspective, they attacked the government and its principal ministers, the Duke of Grafton and Lord North. Even King George III was not spared. In Letter 35 the King was warned that his army might not all be loyal and was advised:

> The prince who imitates their [the Stuarts'] conduct, should be warned by their example; and while he plumes himself upon the security of his title to the crown, should remember that, as it was acquired by one revolution, it may be lost by another.[167]

The unidentified Junius could not be prosecuted for seditious libel.[168] But he has now been identified as almost certainly Sir Philip Francis, a young, but high ranking, civil servant at the War Office.[169] In private correspondence he mischievously suggested that Edmund Burke, then a prominent critic of the government's policy with regard to the American colonies, might have been the author of the *Letters*, but it would be impossible for Burke to admit to offending the King and Prime Minister.[170] Obviously Francis had thought rather carefully about the matter! A number of factors now point to the authorship of Sir Philip: handwriting evidence, a confidential French spy report identifying him as the writer, and recent linguistic analysis comparing the *Letters* to the published works of Sir Philip Francis.

Two well-known examples of anonymous political writing in America during this period may be given. The radical writer, Thomas Paine, was English by birth, but lived in America from 1774 to 1787. He established the *Pennsylvania Magazine,* writing several political essays under a number

---

[165] For the growth in prosecutions for seditious libel during this period, see chapter 4, section II.

[166] LW Levy, *Emergence of a Free Press* (New York, OUP, 1985) 109–18.

[167] Much of Letter 35 is quoted in S Ayling, *George The Third* (London, Collins, 1972) 165–66.

[168] Legal proceedings were taken, for the most part unsuccessfully, against printers and booksellers: see chapter 4, section II.

[169] A Frearson, 'The Identity of Junius' (1984) 7 *Journal for Eighteenth Century Studies* 211.

[170] Ibid 217.

of pseudonyms, for example, 'Atlanticus' (apparently his favourite *nom de plume*), 'Justice', 'Humanity' and 'Vox Populi'.[171] This device gave the impression that the journal had more contributors than it did, and also provided Paine with some cover for his more radical articles.[172] His pamphlet, *Common Sense* (1776), attacked the constitution and government of England, in particular the monarchy and the hereditary principle, and urged a republican government for an independent America. Its title page did not carry Paine's name, but stated that it was 'written by an Englishman'. Criticism of the pamphlet from 'Cato' was answered by Paine in a series of letters under the pseudonym, 'The Forester'.[173] But his subsequent writing appeared under his own name, notably the *Rights of Man* (1792) which was written on his return to England and for which he was prosecuted for sedition.[174]

The other example is the famous defence of the draft federal Constitution for the United States of America agreed at the Constitutional Convention held in Philadelphia in the summer of 1787. The essays, now known as *The Federalist Papers*, were written by Alexander Hamilton, later George Washington's Secretary of the Treasury, James Madison, fourth President of the United States, and John Jay, the first Chief Justice of the federal Supreme Court, under the shared pseudonym, 'Publius'. Hamilton, the moving figure in the project, chose this name after Publius Valerius who had established stable republican government consequent on the overthrow of Tarquin, the last King of ancient Rome.[175] So the name was a powerful symbol, representing the authors' aim of persuading the States to ratify the Constitution which had been drafted in Philadelphia. It was very common at this time, as it had been earlier in the eighteenth century, to use Roman (or Greek) names; Hamilton had written previous essays in defence of the draft Constitution under the name 'Caesar', while it had been attacked by the Governor of New York, George Clinton, writing as 'Cato'.[176] The common pseudonym gave the essays unity and greater force. Moreover, it disguised the authorship of Hamilton and Madison, both of whom had played prominent parts at the Convention; if they had signed their individual essays, it might have been thought they were defending their own work rather than making an objective case for a strong federal constitution.

---

[171] J Keane, *Tom Paine: A Political Life* (London, Bloomsbury, 1995) 95–96.

[172] C Nelson, *Thomas Paine* (London, Profile Books, 2007) 61.

[173] Ibid 94.

[174] Paine fled to France in September 1792, but was convicted in his absence. His publisher was sent to prison: ibid 228–33, 244–46.

[175] B Mitchell, *Alexander Hamilton, Youth to Maturity: 1755–1788* (New York, Macmillan, 1957) ch 25, esp 415–20.

[176] Ibid 415, and also see F McDonald, *Alexander Hamilton* (New York, WW Norton and Co, 1979) 85–86 for Hamilton's use of the classical names 'Phocion' and 'Tully' on other occasions.

It is more difficult to find instances of important anonymous political writing in the nineteenth century, at least in England and the United States, when there was much less fear of prosecution for seditious libel than there had been earlier. On the other hand, political as well as literary writing in periodicals was generally anonymous until the second half of the century (see section III(A) above). Henry Adams, a distinguished American historian, whose grandfather and great grandfather had been United States Presidents, wrote a political novel, *Democracy*, anonymously in 1880; he was not identified as its author until three years after his death in 1918.[177] There was, of course, one seminal piece of anonymous political writing. The *Communist Manifesto* was originally published in German anonymously by a group of political refugees in London as a 23-page pamphlet, *Manifest der Kommunistischen Partei* (1848).[178] Marx and Engels were identified as its authors only when the Leipzig edition was published with their co-authored Prefaces in 1872.

Mention should be made of one case in the twentieth century. In June 1947 the journal of the New York-based Council of Foreign Relations, *Foreign Affairs*, carried an article, 'The Sources of Soviet Conduct', written by 'X'.[179] It argued for containment of the Soviet Union through political, rather than by military means. The author was George Kennan, a State Department employee, who was at the time engaged in setting up the Policy Planning Staff for the Marshall Plan, and who was already well-known as the author of significant articles on foreign affairs. The article had been written earlier in the year as a paper for the Secretary of the Navy, James Forrestal, who had shown it to Arthur Krock, a *New York Times* journalist. In his column on 8 July, Krock hinted that the *Foreign Affairs* article had an official source, but did not name Kennan. But the United Press Agency did name him, identifying Kennan from his prose style as well as from Krock's tip.[180] Interestingly, Kennan had wanted to add a note to the article, explaining his long experience in Russian affairs and his inability to write under his own name in view of his position, but the editor declined to carry it.[181] John Lewis Gaddis, Kennan's biographer, argues that anonymity ensured a level of attention to the article which it might not have received if it had been written under his own name.[182] If so, it would not be the only occasion in which a writer's insistence on anonymity has excited media

---

[177] Four years later, he wrote another novel, *Esther*, under the pseudonym, Frances Snow Compton: see RA Hume, *Runaway Star: An Appreciation of Henry Adams* (Ithaca, NY, Cornell University Press, 1951) 131–50.

[178] The title page is displayed in N MacGregor, *Germany: Memories of a Nation* (London, Allen Lane, 2014) 275.

[179] See GF Kennan, *Memoirs 1925–1950* (Boston, Little, Brown and Co, 1967) ch 15.

[180] JL Gaddis, *George F Kennan: An American Life* (New York, Penguin Press, 2011) 271.

[181] Ibid 259.

[182] Ibid 274.

interest, on occasion with tragic consequences: see the Garry Bennett affair discussed in the next section of this chapter.

VI. RELIGIOUS AND PHILOSOPHICAL WRITING

These two types of writing are grouped together, partly because it is sometimes hard to characterise work as belonging to one category or the other; Kierkegaard, whose pseudonymous work raises particularly fascinating questions, may be regarded either as a philosopher or as a religious writer. Moreover, one important strand in the case for anonymity (or the use of a pseudonym) perhaps applies equally to both types of writing: their authors want their arguments to be considered on their merits and are, or should be, unconcerned with appealing to readers on the basis of their general authority or of their previous work. Religious and philosophical writing should be disinterested in a way which is not expected of political pamphlets or even now of much literary reviewing. In the case of religious writing, intellectual scrupulousness may be accompanied by a sense of personal humility—a concern to avoid personal self-regard—that persuades the writer to avoid the use of his own name. In his book on anonymity Mullan discusses the spiritual autobiography of John Newton, the author of 'Amazing Grace' and later an evangelical minister, which was written anonymously towards the end of the eighteenth century.[183] Newton was worried that he would commit the sin of pride if he were to 'boast' of his spiritual journey. Even today Carthusian monks typically write anonymously; the withholding of their name is an aspect of the silence in which they live in a Charterhouse.[184]

All save one of the 'Pauline' Epistles is explicitly asserted in its opening verses to be written by St Paul. The exception is the Epistle to the Hebrews; doubts were expressed about its authorship by the end of the second century, and it is now treated as an anonymous work. (However, in the Kings James Bible of 1611 it is attributed to Paul.) The Epistle has sometimes been ascribed to one of Paul's co-workers or disciples, among them Barnabas, Apollos, Silvanus and Priscilla.[185] As a woman, Priscilla would be likely to remain anonymous, but there is little positive evidence to suggest that either she or any of the other candidates wrote it. The authors of two leading modern commentaries accept that the identity of the writer of the Epistle remains unknown.[186]

---

[183]   Mullan, 254–57 on J Newton, *An Authentic Narrative of Some Remarkable and Interesting Particulars in the Life of* ******** (1764). Also see B Hindmarsh, *John Newton and the Evangelical Tradition* (Oxford, Clarendon Press, 1996) 13–48.

[184]   See, eg, A Carthusian, *They Speak by Silences* (London, Longmans, 1955).

[185]   D Guthrie, *New Testament Introduction* (Leicester, Inter-Varsity Press, 1981) 688–98.

[186]   Ibid, and CR Koester in D Aune (ed), *The Blackwell Companion to the New Testament* (Chichester, Wiley-Blackwell, 2010) ch 36.

There is also considerable uncertainty whether Paul wrote some of the Epistles to which he did assert authorship: 2 Thessalonians, Colossians, and more particularly Ephesians, and the three so-called 'Pastoral' Epistles, 1 and 2 Timothy and Titus. The grounds for scepticism are primarily linguistic (the use in these letters of language and a style not employed in the Epistles accepted to be Pauline) and doctrinal (teaching which differs from that in the Epistles which are accepted to be Paul's). Further, the Pastoral Epistles show a concern for the organisation of the Church on matters which were not clearly established at the time of Paul's death in AD 67.[187] On the sceptical view, these works are clearly pseudonymous. One explanation might be that the real authors, perhaps followers of Paul, intended to deceive their readers, ascribing the letters to him in order to boost their authority. Alternatively, there might have been no deception, because it was generally known at the time that Paul was not their author and it was accepted that the author was merely writing in the Pauline tradition. In his New Testament commentary, Donald Guthrie finds the sceptical argument unpersuasive. Although at the time the Epistles were written pseudonymous writing was common, it seems that the early Church did not approve of the practice. The Church communities to which the Epistles were addressed would not have accepted them as genuine if they had been written and sent by one of his followers after Paul's death. But unlike the Epistle to the Hebrews, the other Epistles were accepted as genuine; serious doubts about their authorship were not raised until the nineteenth century. Similar arguments apply to the authorship of 2 Peter and Jude; given the language and the awareness of Greek ethical ideas displayed in these Epistles, they may not have been written by the authors to which they are traditionally ascribed (and who explicitly claimed authorship of them).[188]

The Cloud of Unknowing is among 'the devotional classics of the English Church'.[189] But it is not known who wrote it, let alone whether the author chose anonymity or whether we simply do not know his identity. The anonymous author was probably a priest from the East Midlands,[190] though it has been ascribed to Walter Hilton, a fourteenth century mystic, and to Carthusian monks. Written in the second half of the fourteenth century, the book insists that God cannot be understood or approached through human reason, because a 'cloud of unknowing' separates man from God;

---

[187] JM Bassler in D Aune (ed), *The Blackwell Companion to the New Testament* (Chichester, Wiley-Blackwell, 2010) ch 21, 390.

[188] See the arguments of KP McCrudden in D Aune (ed), *The Blackwell Companion to the New Testament* (Chichester, Wiley-Blackwell, 2010) ch 35, but cf Guthrie, *New Testament Introduction* (n 185) who in chs 25 and 27 accepts that the Epistles were respectively written by St Peter and Jude, the brother of James and Jesus Christ.

[189] Introduction by C Wolters to *The Cloud of Unknowing and Other Works* (London, Penguin Classics, 1978) 9.

[190] Ibid 11–13.

only contemplative love can find a way through the cloud. One of the influences on the *Cloud's* teaching was the writing of the so-called Dionysius the Areopagite; he was a Syrian monk writing in the early sixth century, but his work was ascribed to the Dionysius who had been converted by St Paul on his mission to Athens: see Acts 17, 34.[191] The ideas of Pseudo-Dionysius—that the soul of man could achieve union with God only by leaving behind the perceptions of the senses and the intellect—were given greater authority by their ascription to a first century disciple. *The Cloud of Unknowing*, an anonymous work, thus builds on the teaching of earlier pseudonymous writing.[192]

Writers on religious matters may of course prefer anonymity for much the same reason that authors often choose it in a secular context: withholding the author's name enables him to be more open and candid. That is the reason why the literary critic, Edmund Gosse, chose anonymity for *Father and Son* (1907), his story of his claustrophobic upbringing by his father, a distinguished zoologist and member of the exclusive Plymouth Brethren sect. Gosse had earlier written under his own name a biography of his father, so it was impossible to maintain his anonymity for long. When the book was reissued a year later it carried his name. But the temporary anonymity had made it easier psychologically for Gosse to write an open account of his difficult relationship with his father, although he almost certainly realised that he would be identified very soon.[193]

The desire for candour also played a part in the final example of religious writing to be discussed; it had a tragic consequence, the suicide of Garry Bennett, the anonymous author of the 1987 Preface to a clerical directory.[194] *Crockford's Clerical Directory* has been published, generally every two years, since 1858; it contains short biographies of the clergy in the Anglican Churches in the United Kingdom, including those in the Church of Ireland and the Diocese of Europe. From the early twentieth century it contained an anonymous Preface summarising important developments in the Churches. From 1921 the Directory was published by Oxford University Press until Church House Publishing took it over in the early 1980s—an important development since it gave the impression that it was an official publication. It may also have led to the publication of bland Prefaces, though a few earlier ones had been critical of Church leaders.[195] In November 1986, the Secretary General of the General Synod of the Church of England, Derek Pattinson, invited Dr Gareth Bennett, Fellow in History at New College,

---

[191] Ibid 15–16.

[192] Dionysius is referred to in ch 70 of *The Cloud of Unknowing* (n 189).

[193] See Mullan, 280–85 for a full account.

[194] I knew Garry Bennett in Oxford; he once discussed with me an outline of his argument in the Preface, though of course I was not aware at the time that he was doing that.

[195] W Oddie, *The Crockford's File: Gareth Bennett and the Death of the Anglican Mind* (London, Hamish Hamitlon, 1989) 41, 215.

Oxford, and a prominent Anglo-Catholic member of the General Synod, to write the Preface to the 1987/88 edition of the *Directory*.[196] Garry Bennett accepted the invitation, asking for an assurance that no change would be made to his text; Pattinson gave that assurance.[197]

The opening paragraph of Bennett's Preface makes it plain that he was relying on his anonymity to subject Anglican affairs to independent scrutiny:

> It is not easy for an individual churchman to write ... an independent survey in his own name for inevitably it will point to matters which are not for our comfort and it must extend to deal with personalities.[198]

It must certainly have made uncomfortable reading for some: there was sustained criticism of the General Synod, and of its Standing Committee and the Crown Appointments Commission (to both of which Bennett had recently been appointed), and of diocesan governance by the bishops. Most striking, at least for the press and the public, was the treatment in the Preface of Archbishops Runcie and Habgood. Bennett, who knew Runcie very well and used to draft some of his addresses, doubted whether the Archbishop had a clear idea of what he was doing, except with regard to ecclesiastical appointments where a 'brief biographical study will reveal the remarkable manner in which the careers of so many bishops have crossed the career of Dr Runcie'.[199] Dr Habgood was dismissed as 'the leading theological relativist among the bishops'.[200]

It was almost certainly these personal criticisms which attracted the attention of the press when the *Directory* was published in December 1987.[201] Inevitably, there was great speculation on the identity of the Preface's anonymous author. Garry Bennett's name was frequently mentioned, and he was offered money over the telephone by a reporter from the *Daily Mail* if he admitted to authorship.[202] Some bishops in their turn suggested the author had abused his privilege of anonymity. Habgood issued a statement, dismissing the Preface as 'scurrilous' and as 'an outburst from a disappointed cleric'.[203] Garry Bennett clearly found the media pressure and the criticism

---

[196] He had also been Dean of Divinity and Chaplain of New College, but had given up this position in 1979; Geoffrey Rowell, 'Introduction' in G Bennett, *To the Church of England* (Worthing, Churchman Publishing, 1988) 12. Geoffrey Rowell was Assistant Chaplain at New College, and was subsequently Chaplain at Keble College, Oxford, and Bishop in Europe.

[197] H Carpenter, *Robert Runcie* (London, Hodder and Stoughton, 1996) 340.

[198] The Preface is republished in full in Bennett, *To the Church of England* (n 196) 189–228.

[199] Ibid 221. Also see ibid 209–10 for the criticism of Dr Runcie.

[200] Ibid 225.

[201] Geoffrey Rowell conjectures that a Synod debate on sexual morality at the end of November had increased media interest in church affairs at this time: telephone interview conducted on 15 September 2014.

[202] For an account of the events following publication, see Carpenter, *Robert Runcie* (n 197) 347–59.

[203] The whole statement is reproduced in J Habgood, *Confessions of a Conservative Liberal* (London, SPCK, 1988) 82–83.

of Church leaders too much to bear. He committed suicide two days after the Preface had been published.

One immediate consequence of this tragic affair was the decision not to carry on with the tradition of anonymous Prefaces. Indeed, the inclusion of any Preface at all had been abandoned by the early 1990s. The affair had 'rocked the Church'.[204] With the benefit of hindsight it seems odd that the tradition of anonymous Prefaces survived as long as it had done. It may have been 'considered good sport for the writer to be able to speak his mind at the expense of the establishment',[205] but clergymen should surely feel free to speak truth to power, even ecclesiastical authority, without a need for anonymity. Further, as Archbishop Habgood pointed out,[206] it was difficult to reply to the charges in the Preface, without knowing who had authored them: either the author was a member of the Crown Appointments Commission, in which case he was breaking its confidences and in the Archbishop's view presenting a distorted account, or he was not and was relying on gossip. (Bennett had been appointed to the Commission after he had written the Preface.) The anonymity of the author probably excited much more interest in the Preface than it would have otherwise have enjoyed; certainly the feverish speculation and the hunt for the author must have placed Garry Bennett under intolerable pressure which he was ill-equipped to deal with.[207] The episode brought out the great hidden dangers of speaking anonymously.

Few writers have been so anxious to protect their anonymity as John Locke was with regard to his works of political philosophy. He only admitted to authorship of the *Two Treatises of Government,* and the *Letter of Toleration*, as well as *The Reasonableness of Christianity* (1695), in a codicil (to his will) made shortly before his death in 1704 when leaving his papers to the Bodleian Library in Oxford.[208] Although it was widely known that he was the author of the *Two Treatises*, Locke destroyed his manuscript drafts, conducted negotiations for its publication through a third party, and catalogued it in his library as an anonymous work.[209] Further, he became very angry when close friends whom he had told of his authorship passed on the information to others.[210] The *Treatises* and the *Letter of Toleration* were published in the autumn of 1689, the same year in which appeared the *Essay concerning Human Understanding*, which did bear his name. There is

---

[204] Email from Brian Hanson of 17 September 2014. Mr Hanson was Registrar and Legal Adviser to the General Synod from 1974 to 2001.

[205] Ibid.

[206] *Confessions of a Conservative Liberal* (n 203).

[207] Ibid 84–85.

[208] See P Laslett, 'Introduction' to a Critical Edition of *Two Treatises of Government* (Cambridge, CUP, 1960) 3–4.

[209] Ibid 5–6.

[210] J Dunn, *Locke* (Oxford, OUP, 1985) 17; R Woolhouse, *Locke: A Biography* (Cambridge, CUP, 2007) 281–82.

no clear reason why he was so reluctant to admit to his authorship of works on political philosophy after the abdication of James II and the establishment of a rather more liberal monarchy. Perhaps he feared the return of the Stuarts. A more probable explanation is that he did not want it to be generally known that the author of the *Essay*, a philosophical examination of the foundations of human knowledge, had also written on the legitimacy and limits of government; the arguments in the two types of work might have been considered inconsistent.[211] This may reveal a philosopher's concern to keep separate his authorship of two distinct genres of philosophical writing in much the same way as modern novelists (for example, JK Rowling) may choose a *nom de plume* when they write thrillers or detective novels.

In 1792, Johann Gottlieb Fichte published his first book, *Versuch einer Kritik aller Offenbarung* [*Attempt at a Critique of All Revelation*]. The publisher (or printer) omitted to give Fichte's name, so it appeared to be anonymous.[212] That would give readers the impression that the publisher wanted to avoid censorship. Early reviews thought the book was by Kant; indeed, this might have been the publisher's calculation.[213] But a few weeks later Kant, with whom Fichte had previously discussed the ideas in the book, wrote a letter to the *Allgemeine Literaturzeitung* explaining that the work was Fichte's and expressing respect for its quality. Though the episode ended fortunately, it shows a danger of anonymous authorship: the work may be attributed to another writer and the real author loses, at least temporarily, the credit to which he or she is entitled.

Surely no writer has been so prolific a user of pseudonyms as the Danish philosopher and religious thinker, Søren Kierkegaard. He used a variety of distinct pseudonyms for eight books on philosophical and literary themes which he wrote between 1843 and 1846; in the same astonishingly fertile period he also published under his own name no fewer than 18 *Edifying Discourses* on religious themes.[214] *The Sickness unto Death* (1849) and a few other works were published later under pseudonym. The matter does not end there, for on occasion a pseudonymous work used other made up names in the course of its exposition: in *Either/Or*, Kierkegaard's first significant work, the pseudonymous editor, Victor Eremita, claims to have found the book's manuscript in a desk drawer. It is apparently the work (letters, a sermon and miscellaneous papers) of two people, Judge William (labelled 'B' by Victor) and his young friend (labelled 'A'), who adopt opposing positions on how to conduct life, generally identified as the 'aesthetic' taken by A and the 'ethical' taken by Judge William. There are further complications,

[211] Laslett, 'Introduction' (n 208) 65–66, and Dunn, *Locke* (n 210) 20.
[212] R Adamson, *Fichte* (Edinburgh, William Blackwood and Sons, 1881) 33–35.
[213] WG Jacobs, *Johann Gottlieb Fichte* (Berlin, Insel Verlag, 2012) 48–49.
[214] P Gardiner, *Kierkegaard* (Oxford, OUP, 1988) 9–10.

notably the 'Diary of the Seducer', for which A claims to be the editor, but not its author.[215]

What is the explanation for this puzzling, indeed bizarre, use of pseudonyms? The most probable is that Kierkegaard is distancing himself from the views taken by the pseudonymous writers or editors. He is not, for example, to be taken by readers as endorsing either of the visions put forward by 'A' or 'B' in *Either/Or,* or even the position taken by Victor Eremita in its Preface. In *The Sickness unto Death,* apparently authored by Anti-Climacus, and only 'edited' by Kierkegaard, the pseudonymous author is able to take a Christian position, which Kierkegaard could not all in all honesty hold himself.[216] In his stimulating biography, Josiah Thompson argues that Kierkegaard was constantly recreating himself in imagined personalities, and that it was natural for him to use ghostly made up names, eg Johannes de Silentio in *Fear and Trembling* or Vigilius Haufniensis in *The Concept of Anxiety,* to pose as the authors of his books and to represent those different personalities.[217] Kierkegaard is absent from his work as an ironist is absent from the words he chooses.[218]

Kierkegaard himself explained his use of pseudonyms in 'A First and Last Explanation', which was appended to *Concluding Unscientific Postscript* (1846).[219] After acknowledging that he was the author of eight pseudonymous works, he wrote that this course was not attributable to any fear of censorship or of the imposition of a penalty for writing them; rather there was an *essential* basis in the production itself (emphasis in the original). In his pseudonymous books he had not written a single word: 'I have no opinion about them except as a third party, no knowledge of their meaning except as a reader'.[220] His character was absolutely irrelevant to the writing of the book. He admitted that in a legal and in a literary sense he bore responsibility, for he had brought about the production in the actual world. But when quoting from a book, readers were encouraged to cite the pseudonymous author's name.[221] In this way Kierkegaard seems to have anticipated the literary theory, the 'death of the author', which argues that the personality of the author is immaterial to an understanding of his work (see chapter I, section III). But that is quite compatible, as Kierkegaard himself recognised, with the ascription of moral and legal responsibility to the actual author.

---

[215] See the short account in J Thompson, *Kierkegaard* (London, Victor Gollancz, 1974) 152–53.

[216] A Hannay, 'Introduction' in *The Sickness unto Death* (London, Penguin Books, 1989) 15.

[217] Thompson, *Kierkegaard* (n 215) 85–86, 143–46.

[218] Ibid 148–52.

[219] *Kierkegaard's Writings* (HV and EH Hong (ed and trans), Princeton, NJ, Princeton University Press, 1992) vol 12:1.

[220] Ibid 626.

[221] Ibid 627.

VII. ART AND GRAFFITI

Visitors to an art gallery are familiar with the wealth of anonymous art, particularly in rooms devoted to early European painting and sculpture. It is simply not known who the artist was, largely because he (it was almost always a he) worked at a time when it was relatively unusual for a painter or sculptor, or indeed an architect or mason, to be identified. The authenticity of a work (and the character of the artist) was much less important than its quality. Paintings are consequently labelled as, for example, by 'The Master of the Cappella Medici Polyptych', or as by 'The Master of the St Bartholomew Alterpiece'.[222] Some great Renaissance artists are known by nick-names rather than by their real names. Masaccio's proper name was Tommaso di Giovanni di Simone Giudi; the nickname can be loosely translated as 'clumsy Tom'.[223] Donatello is the nickname which was given to Donato di Niccolò di Betto Bardi, and Uccello that given to Paolo di Dono.[224] These types of name should, of course, be distinguished from pseudonyms which are deliberately adopted in order to mask the identity of the real artist for one of a variety of reasons: an artist might want for personal or commercial reasons to be known under an assumed name, or a female artist might adopt a male name because she considers that this makes her work more marketable.

Some notable artists in the last century have used pseudonyms from time to time. One of them was Marcel Duchamp (1887–1968), generally recognised as the founder of conceptual art. In 1917, with a number of colleagues he established the American Society of Independent Artists, which announced plans for an inaugural exhibition in April that year. Any artist who paid the appropriate fees was entitled to show two works at the exhibition. Under the made up name of 'Mr Mutt', Duchamp submitted *Fountain,* a porcelain urinal turned upside down, on which he had painted in large black letters the name 'R. MUTT' and the date, '1917'.[225] It was a 'ready-made', an object taken from ordinary life and used for art. When the urinal was rejected by a majority of the exhibition committee, there was a protest in a short anonymous editorial in *The Blind Man,* a magazine launched by Duchamp and two friends to accompany the opening of the exhibition.

[222] On this artist, see N Macgregor, *A Victim of Anonymity: The Master of the Saint Bartholomew Altarpiece* (London, Thames and Hudson, 1993). MacGregor's theme is that this great artist would be much better known, if he had a name.

[223] G Vasari, *The Lives of the Artists* (G Bull (trans), Penguin Classics, 1965) 125.

[224] To take another example, Palladio was the name given to Andrea di Pietro della Gondola, alluding to Pallas Athene, the goddess of wisdom.

[225] For a full account of the affair, see C Tomkins, *Duchamp* (London, Chatto & Windus, 1997) 180–86, and D Ades, N Cox and D Hopkins, *Marcel Duchamp* (London, Thames Hudson, 1999) 126–31.

Under the heading, 'The Richard Mutt Case', the editorial argued that the urinal was neither vulgar nor mere plagiarism:

> Whether Mr. Mutt with his own hands made the fountain or not has no importance. He CHOSE it. He took an ordinary article of life, placed it so that its useful significance disappeared under the new title and point of view—created a new thought for that object.

Although the sentiment was Duchamp's, Beatrice Wood, one of the friends with whom he had launched the magazine, later claimed authorship of the editorial.

Duchamp's involvement in the affair was not known for several months; he even kept it secret from his sister, Suzanne, to whom he was close. He later explained that the challenge to the Society's exhibition policy could not easily have been made by one of its directors, so it was right to have submitted the work with a pseudonym.[226] But Duchamp may also have been exercising his sense of fun, as he did a few years later with a second alias. In 1920, he used the name Rose Sélavy, attaching it to another readymade, *Fresh Widow.* Two years later, this alias became Rrose Sélavy, which was frequently used on further art works and for collections of literary puns in which Duchamp specialised.[227] The name was itself a pun on three French phrases: *rosser la vie* (give life a thrashing), *Eros, c'est la vie,* and *Eros, c'est l'avis.*[228] Duchamp apparently had contemplated using a Jewish name, but found it easier to adopt a female identity, which enabled him to masquerade as a woman when the mood suited.[229] The adoption of different identities was a characteristic of members of the Dada art movement, with which Duchamp was associated. For example, Max Ernst exhibited as dadamax.[230] The aim was to question the existence of a stable identity; the personality of the artist was not fixed, lacking in Duchamp's case even a determined sexual identity. The movement perhaps anticipated the idea of Roland Barthes that the author was dead, his or her personality being irrelevant to the understanding of a literary work (see chapter 1, section III).

An artist who used a pseudonym for entirely different purposes was Ernst Kirchner (1880–1938), one of the leading German Expressionist painters. In order to establish his position as the leading member of the Brücke

---

[226] Tomkins, *Duchamp* (n 225) 184.

[227] Ibid 231, 237.

[228] AG Marquis, *Marcel Duchamp: Eros, c'est la vie* (Troy, NY, Whitston Publishing Co, 1981) 189–90.

[229] Ibid 190, 200 and 206, for the view that the adoption of the alias enabled Duchamp to compensate for his relatively meagre production of work under his own name after the 1920s.

[230] See D Hopkins, *Dada and Surrealism* (Oxford, OUP, 2004) 40–44. Man Ray, an American photographer who worked with Duchamp and other contemporary artists, was the name adopted as a young man by Emmanuel Radnitsky because he and his brother had been teased at school for their foreign name: N Baldwin, *Man Ray: American Artist* (New York, Da Capo Press, 2000) 10–11.

movement and emphasise his distinctiveness from contemporary French artists, he used the name of an invented French critic, Louis de Marsalle, to pen articles in the magazine, *Genius*, in praise of his own work. Kirchner kept the disguise going from 1920 until 1933; he ended use of the pseudonym only when the Director of a gallery in Bern pressed him with questions about de Marsalle when preparing an exhibition of his work.[231]

Few people know that Charles-Édouard Jeanneret (1887–1965) was a distinguished architect, artist and urban planner, indeed one of the pioneers of modern architecture. That is because he is known by his pseudonym, Le Corbusier. With the Cubist painter, Amédée Ozenfant, he established a journal, *L'Esprit Nouveau*, to promote the ideas of Purism, which they hoped would replace Cubism as a leading artistic movement. It was in 1920 when the first issue of the journal came out that Jeanneret began to use Le Corbusier as a pseudonym for articles on architecture; it was a variant of the name of one of his mother's ancestors, Lecorbesier. Ozenfant had suggested to Jeanneret that they used some pseudonyms to conceal the fact that they were writing many of the articles in the journal; Jeanneret's mother's maiden name, Perret, could not be employed, as it was the name of another architect, so he had to go back further into the family history for a name he could use.[232] Le Corbusier had overtones of a noble institution, even echoing, it has been suggested, Le Christus![233] Gradually the pseudonym was adopted in his architectural practice, though Jeanneret continued to use his real name for painting, and for his writing on painting and aesthetics, until the late 1920s.[234]

The most famous pseudonymous artist now, at least in Britain, is the street artist known as Banksy. His work has become increasingly popular since it was first stencilled on street walls in Bristol in the early 1990s; it has been exhibited in New York and Los Angeles and is highly prized by art collectors. An exhibition of his work at the Bristol City Museum and Art Gallery attracted nearly 4,000 visitors a day, and was the second most popular exhibition in Britain that year.[235] So Banksy's insistence on keeping his name secret seems at first sight rather surprising. Initially, it was almost certainly attributable to an understandable fear of arrest by the police, for the spraying of graffiti and other street art amounts to damage to property, whether public or private. For that reason it is common for graffiti artists to identify their work with only a short tag, for example, 'Elk', 'Diet'

---

[231] C Weikop, 'Ernst Ludwig Kirchner as his Own Critic: The Artist's Statements as Stratagems of Self-Promotion' (2012) 48 *Forum for Modern Language Studies* 406.

[232] H Allen Brooks, *Le Corbusier's Formative Years* (Chicago, IL, University of Chicago Press, 1997) 8–9, n 11.

[233] NF Weber, *Le Corbusier: A Life* (New York, AA Knopf, 2008) 10–11 and 177–78.

[234] Ibid 180, and Brooks, *Le Corbusier's Formative Years* (n 232) 498, n 27.

[235] W Ellisworth-Jones, *Banksy: The Man Behind the Wall* (London, Aurum Press, 2012) 151–52.

or 'Zomby'.[236] But such fear hardly provides an explanation for Banksy's persistence with secrecy long after his work has received widespread public acclaim. His identity is rigorously guarded by a team of PR agents, while clauses in contracts with galleries exhibiting his work protect his anonymity. (However he has been named in one or two newspaper features, which interestingly attracted criticism for making the disclosure.) Banksy's anonymity is now really a marketing tool, which increases the sense of mystery attached to his work. It has probably made him much more of a celebrity than he would be if he were to abandon it.[237] But there are disadvantages to this insistence on anonymity. It probably makes it harder in practice for Banksy to enforce copyright in his work and may encourage others to produce fake 'Banksy' works. It has even enabled people to impersonate him for newspaper interviews.[238]

Unlike novels and other written work, works of art are generally anonymous on their face; painters and sculptors sign their work relatively rarely. But patrons, collectors, galleries and scholars have been concerned with the authenticity of a painting, drawing or other work, ever since the Renaissance when Vasari's great book promoted the personality and attributes of individual artists.[239] That is why there is so much anxiety about the forging of art works, even though it can be argued that forgers challenge general assumptions about what is valuable in art.[240] Perhaps we should be no more interested in the identity of the real artist than we should be (according to the 'death of the author' school, see chapter 1, section III) in that of an author: 'there's no such thing as a fake drawing, only a false attribution'.[241] But an art forger is in a sense using a pseudonym, the name of the old master to whom the work is falsely attributed with intent to deceive the public.[242] Moreover, artists themselves usually want to assert ownership of their creation; they may take steps to stop the unauthorised copying of their work.[243] Since 1734 engravings have been protected by UK copyright legislation,[244]

---

[236] Ibid 42–43.

[237] Ibid 102–5.

[238] Ibid 209–12 for accounts of impersonations of Banksy for interviews with the *Guardian* and the *Observer*.

[239] *The Lives of the Artists* (n 223) was first published in 1550 and celebrates the lives of mostly Italian artists from Cimabue to Titian.

[240] J Keats, *Forged: Why Fakes are the Great Art of Our Age* (Oxford, OUP, 2013) 24–25.

[241] Ibid 105, commenting on the fake drawings of Eric Hebborn, some of whose 'fake' masterpieces have still not been identified.

[242] As with the deceptions carried on for years by Han van Meegeren who persuaded art critics, directors of galleries and Hermann Goering, the Nazi leader, that his work was Vermeer's: J Lopez, *The Man who Made Vermeers* (Orlando, FL, Harcourt, 2008).

[243] Vasari thought that Dürer went to Venice to prevent unauthorised reproduction of his engravings there: W Gaunt (ed), *The Lives of the Painters, Sculptors and Architects* (Everyman's Library, 1963) vol 3, 71–72. But see JC Hutchinson, *Albrecht Dürer* (Princeton, NJ, Princeton University Press, 1990) 79–81 who considers this unlikely.

[244] Engraving Copyright Act 1734, also known as Hogarth's Act, as William Hogarth promoted the measure to protect earnings from the sale of his work.

and protection was extended to paintings and drawings by the Fine Arts Copyright Act 1862. Moreover, painters and cartoonists, like authors (see chapter I, section II), should be accountable, and may be legally responsible, for their work.[245] So the identity of the artist matters. And visitors to art galleries like to know the name of the painters and sculptors whose work they are looking at. As Neil MacGregor, former Director of the National Gallery and of the British Museum, has admitted: 'I suspect I am not alone in the slightly guilty knowledge that a label with a particular name tells me not just who the artist is, but what reaction I ought to have to the work'.[246] It may be harder to attribute, say, a drawing to a particular artist than it is to ascribe a literary work to a writer, but in principle the anonymity arguments apply in much the same way to both genres of work.

VIII. PEER REVIEW OF ACADEMIC ARTICLES

The peer review of academic and scientific articles conducted prior to publication by experts in the particular field of study is designed to ensure that only accurate findings and well-presented arguments see the light of day. Peer review is clearly crucial for medical and scientific literature, for public health or safety might be endangered if professionals rely on inaccurate studies, but it is also used in the social sciences and humanities. The procedure is also employed for the allocation of grants by the research councils and for determining the allocation of research money to universities through the Research Assessment Exercise.[247]

Traditionally peer review, at least when used to determine the suitability of an article for publication in a scholarly journal, has been conducted anonymously: the author does not know the identity of the reviewers (or referees, as they are sometimes known) and, under the system of 'double blind' review, the reviewers do not know who the author is or at which university he or she holds a post. Double blind review remains the standard practice in the humanities and social sciences, while 'single blind' review has been more usual for science and medical journals: the reviewers know the author's name and institution, but the reviewer's name is not disclosed to the author.[248] Naturally the editor of the journal knows who the author and reviewers are, but takes great care to ensure that when the reviewers'

---

[245] See, eg, the decision of the European Court of Human Rights on 2 October 2008 in *Leroy v France*, Application no 36109/03, upholding the conviction by French courts of a cartoonist. He had been convicted of the offence of defending an act of terrorism for a drawing with a caption appearing to approve the destruction of the Twin Towers on 9/11.

[246] *A Victim of Anonymity* (n 222) 19.

[247] Report of Science and Technology Committee, *Peer Review in Scientific Publications*, HC 856 (2010–12) paras 1–3.

[248] Ibid paras 15–16.

reports are sent to the author, their names (and other identifying features) are concealed.[249]

The justifications for anonymous peer review reflect the arguments for anonymity which are put forward in other contexts considered in this chapter. A reviewer's ignorance of the identity of an author, and his institution, enables him to consider the merits of the arguments in the article, uninfluenced by such factors as the general standing of the author and the institution where he works or the quality of his previous publications. The argument that readers generally have a real and legitimate interest in knowing who the author is in order to assess the credibility of his case (see chapter 3, section IV(A)) is much less persuasive in the context of peer review than it is in other contexts, because the referee is an expert in the field, who should be able to assess the strengths of the article without being made aware of these other facts. Conversely, anonymous peer review does not provide a good precedent for the anonymity, say, of newspaper or journal articles read by the general public, most of whom would not be in a position to assess the correctness of, say, financial information or advice provided in its pages.[250]

The argument for reviewer anonymity is that it enables referees to write candidly about the strengths and weaknesses of the article; some of them, notably junior lecturers or clinicians, would feel inhibited in writing a full report, especially if (as under the single review system) they had been invited to comment on material which they knew had been submitted by professors or consultants. Of course, there is the converse argument that, sheltering behind anonymity, some reviewers may produce hostile reports with abusive language, which editors have to 'censor' before communicating them to the author.

Despite the evidence that most reviewers prefer anonymity,[251] some medical (and other science) journals have now moved to open signed peer review, under which referees' names are disclosed to authors. The *British Medical Journal* (*BMJ*) took this step in 1999 after conducting a controlled trial of open review, which found that this system did not affect the overall quality of reports on medical papers. The change was made for ethical reasons: it was wrong in principle to assess these papers in secret, while openness led to accountability, with credit being given to reviewers who spent valuable time in producing their reports, and to a better tone in the reports.

---

[249] As an editor of the *Journal of Media Law* I have found that some reviewers are happy to waive their anonymity and to be in direct contact with the author.

[250] But see the view of RC Post in 'The Constitutional Concept of Public Discourse' (1990) 103 *Harvard Law Review* 603, 640, n 213, that a general right to anonymous speech is justified on the same principle as that supporting anonymous peer review.

[251] BMJ Group written evidence to the Science and Technology Committee, *Peer Review in Scientific Publications* (n 247), Ev 72, para 15. And see Public Research Consortium Report, *Peer Review: Benefits, Perceptions and Alternatives* (2008) 18–20, showing a strong preference for double blind review.

It was acknowledged that some referees might refuse to review papers if they would be identified, but that did not outweigh the desirability of open review.[252] Recently the *BMJ* has extended openness, so that the original drafts of an article, the referees' reports and names, etc, and their correspondence with journal editors are put on-line, so readers can follow the whole peer review process.[253] Although there is some evidence of reviewer bias against identified authors on the basis of their nationality or gender, it is inconclusive. Further, in medical fields where only a small number of people are conducting research on a particular topic, wrong guesses may be made about the identity of unidentified authors and the quality of their earlier work, so double blind review does not guarantee impartiality.[254]

Peer review in its traditional form is quite different from all the other types of writing considered in this chapter: it is not public speech. It is produced for the benefit of the journal editors (or the grant allocating body) to advise them whether to publish an article (or to make a grant for the applicant's research), and not for a general readership. Academic journal editors are more than 'responsible intermediaries'—persons such as book publishers or newspaper editors, who are almost always able to vouch for the integrity of an anonymous author before his material is published or used as the basis for a press report.[255] Editors, not the public, are the readers for whom the report is written. As has been noted, the arguments deployed in support of anonymous peer review are much the same as those used in the context of public speech. They surely have greater force in the former context, at least insofar as the editors of academic and scientific journals can be relied on to ensure that reviewers provide honest and accurate reports and do not abuse their anonymity.

IX. CONCLUDING REFLECTIONS

Some seven or eight varieties of anonymous writing have been discussed in this chapter: it is far from an exhaustive list. It does not cover the well-known (and best-selling) books of two authors in the last few years: the books by the Secret Footballer with inside stories on the hidden world of professional football,[256] and the sexually explicit memoirs of Belle de Jour,

---

[252] The change in policy was announced by the editor at the time, Richard Smith, 'Opening up *BMJ* Review' (1999) 318 *BMJ* 4.

[253] Telephone interview with Dr Fiona Godlee, Editor in Chief of the *BMJ*, conducted on 16 January 2015.

[254] Ibid. See also Science and Technology Committee, *Peer Review in Scientific Publications* (n 247) paras 18 and 40–43.

[255] See chapter 1, section II and chapter 5 passim for 'responsible intermediaries'.

[256] *I am the Secret Footballer: Lifting the Lid on the Beautiful Game; Tales from the Secret Footballer; The Secret Footballer's Guide to the Modern Game* (all books published by Guardian Faber, 2012, 2013, 2014).

the *nom de plume* adopted by the author when she revealed in blogs and several books her life as a call girl in London in 2003.[257] Another important category of anonymous speech is whistle-blowing, when employees expose wrong-doing at work without revealing their identity to the other employees or managers against whom the complaint is made: this category is discussed in the next chapter when the case for recognising a *right* to anonymous speech is examined.[258]

Authors resort to anonymity, or the use of a pseudonym, for a variety of reasons: to secure privacy; to escape the disapproval of their family or scrutiny by the media; to avoid arrest for committing a criminal offence; to test the waters for a new type of novel; to have a sense of fun; to promote their own work or savage that of their rivals; or to create for themselves an entirely different identity. Women have used pseudonyms to disguise their gender, fearful that otherwise their work will not be taken seriously. As Virginia Woolf wrote, 'I would venture to guess that Anon, who wrote so many poems without signing them, was often a woman'.[259] Some motives are more laudable than others. It is understandable for a novelist to adopt a *nom de plume* for a different genre of writing from that for which she has already acquired a reputation: she may want the new type of book assessed purely on its merits rather than by reference to her established standing, and there seems no good reason why she should not indulge this preference. But it is indefensible for a writer to shelter behind a pseudonym to puff his own work (or that of a friend) or to abuse that of a competitor. It was surely right for the *Times Literary Supplement* to abandon anonymous literary reviewing just to avoid that risk, though that was not the main reason for taking that step (see section III(C) above).[260]

The strength of the arguments for anonymity depends to some extent on the political and social culture in which they are made. In Victorian Britain, when reticence and privacy were prized more highly than they are now, anonymous writing in reviews and magazines was valued, partly in order to enable 'gentlemen' to contribute to public debate on literary and social affairs, even though they had no expertise on the matter on which they were writing. Anonymity contributed to the authority of newspapers and reviews at a time when the deference of readers to that authority was taken for granted, and was also considered desirable. Readers now feel entitled to know who is giving them information and advice, so they can assess how seriously to take it. Like politicians and public authorities, writers may be

---

[257] The first was *The Intimate Adventures of a London Call Girl* (London, Weidenfeld & Nicolson, 2005).

[258] See chapter 3, section V. See also chapter 4, section IV for the legal position of whistle-blowers in English law.

[259] *A Room of One's Own* (London, Hogarth Press, 1929) 74.

[260] It is right to point out that literary puffing (or log rolling) of colleagues' books exists even when reviews are signed: see *Private Eye* (no 1382), 20 December 2014–8 January 2015, 34.

held accountable. Responsibility requires open acknowledgement of their identity, so the case for anonymity is culturally much weaker than it used to be.

The argument for responsibility and signature is primarily a moral one. But it can also be legal, if a reader alleges that he has been defamed or that he is the victim of fraud, say, in a financial newspaper column. Defamation proceedings can be taken against the publisher, an important safeguard for libel victims when the author cannot be identified; but the safeguard is not so strong in the case of other civil wrongs where the claimant has to prove an intention to deceive. It may be important to discover the author's identity, so proceedings can be taken against him.[261] Usually publishers know who their author is, even when he prefers to write anonymously or under pseudonym; like the editors of newspapers and journals (whether academic or of general interest), publishers act as intermediaries, who can vouch for the credibility of an anonymous author and help a claimant identify him if that is necessary for legal purposes. But sometimes publishers may not know who their author is. That was the case with the Brontës and George Eliot, at least initially, and also occurred recently with Belle de Jour; the publisher of the call girl memoirs did not know that her real name is Brooke Magnanti until that was revealed in November 2009.[262] Apparently only her literary agent and accountant knew her identity at the time of publication;[263] they could not have been expected to act as 'responsible intermediaries', reducing the risks of anonymous authorship. So the defects of anonymity to which attention was drawn in chapter 1 may not always be cured.

[261] For discussion of English law in this area, see chapter 4, section III and chapter 6, section III(C).

[262] Dr Magnanti has been a research scientist, who did not want to reveal her identity as the author of sexually explicit memoirs when disclosure might have damaged her career.

[263] See an interview with her, available at http://freakonomics.com/2009/11/20/a-few-questions-for-belle-de-jour-call-girl-and-scientist/?_r=0.

3

Anonymity and Freedom of Speech

I. INTRODUCTION

IN THE UNITED States of America it is now accepted that there is a free speech right to speak and write anonymously (or with the use of a pseudonym). As the Supreme Court said in its landmark ruling, *McIntyre v Ohio Elections Commission*, 'an author's decision to remain anonymous ... is an aspect of the freedom of speech protected by the First Amendment'.[1] The decision has been followed in subsequent cases.[2] Although it has been distinguished in a number of others, notably in litigation concerning requirements to disclose election expenditure (see chapter 7), its fundamental correctness has rarely been questioned. This chapter criticises the arguments which have been used to justify the anonymity *right* as an aspect of freedom of speech (or expression), and it finds them unpersuasive.

In the first place, some of the reasoning in *McIntyre* itself (see section II below) is flawed. It is difficult to see how an anonymity right can be derived from the free speech rights of *speakers* to determine the contents of their speech or publication (see section III below). Probably the best argument for the free speech anonymity right is that otherwise speech may be lost, because some people will feel too inhibited to communicate their ideas or to disclose important information unless they are free to do this anonymously (see section IV below). But there are objections to that argument as grounding a general right to anonymous speech. It might, however, support a qualified right to anonymity, which would be protected in those circumstances where it is clear that any requirement to disclose the speaker's or writer's

---

[1] 514 US 334, 342 (1995) per Stevens J giving the judgment of the Court.

[2] See, eg, *Buckley v American Constitutional Law Foundation*, 525 US 182 (1999) (requirement of canvassers to wear name badge while soliciting signatures for an election initiative infringed First Amendment); *Watchtower Bible and Tract Society of New York v Stratton*, 536 US 150 (2002) (ordinance requiring persons engaging in door to door soliciting to register with mayor and receive a permit infringed First Amendment); *ACLU of Nevada v Heller*, 378 F3d 979 (2004) (requirement to identify names and addresses of persons paying for material or information relating to an election candidate on any published written matter infringed First Amendment).

identity will almost certainly lead to a 'chilling effect' on the communication of valuable speech, for example, whistle-blowing by employees exposing dishonesty or corrupt practices by their employer (see section V(B) below). But that right, like the freedom of expression guaranteed by Article 10 of the European Convention on Human Rights (ECHR), could be restricted whenever necessary to protect other rights or public interests.[3]

Scepticism about the development of a constitutional free speech right to anonymity does not mean that anonymity (and the use of pseudonyms) is not of great value to many writers. As we saw in the previous chapter, there are a number of good reasons why novelists, literary reviewers, political writers and others prefer to write without disclosing their identity, and why this choice should generally be respected. But if the law does require disclosure of their identity—perhaps to protect the public in a particular context against misleading communications or to enable the victim of a defamatory allegation to bring libel proceedings—we should require strong arguments to show that this infringes a strong *right* to anonymous speech which in the United States enjoys constitutional protection. This chapter shows that there are no such strong arguments.

II. *McINTYRE v OHIO ELECTIONS COMMISSION*

Margaret McIntyre handed out leaflets at public meetings held at a school in Ohio, expressing opposition to a proposed school tax levy. She had written the text on her own computer at home. Some of the leaflets identified her as the author, but others expressed the views of 'Concerned Parents and Tax Payers'. She was warned that it was contrary to State law to write, print or distribute campaigning literature without indicating the name and residence of the person responsible for it, but nevertheless continued with its distribution. Mrs McIntyre was fined for infringing the Ohio law, and the State Supreme Court upheld this decision.[4] In its view the disclosure requirements enabled voters to evaluate messages directed at them and identified those who sent fraudulent and defamatory communications. Despite the death of Mrs McIntyre during the course of the litigation the case was taken to the United States Supreme Court.

By a seven to two majority the Court allowed the appeal. The majority judgment was given by Stevens J.[5] Two strands to justify the anonymity

---

[3] D Vorhoof, 'Internet and the Right of Anonymity' in J Surculla (ed), *Proceedings of the Conference on Regulating the Internet* (Belgrade, Centre for Internet Development, 2010) argues for a qualified right to anonymous speech on the Internet under the ECHR.

[4] 618 NE 2d 152 (1993).

[5] Ginsburg J and Thomas J gave separate concurring judgments. The latter examined the history of anonymous political writing in America in the eighteenth century and inferred that the Founding Fathers of the Constitution intended the First Amendment to cover anonymous speech: *McIntyre v Ohio Elections Commission* (n 1) 359–71.

right can be identified in his reasoning, though it is difficult to disentangle them from each other.[6] The first is the instrumental argument that '[a]nonymity is a shield from the tyranny of the majority'.[7] It enables radicals and dissenters to express unpopular views free from the fear of retaliation or prosecution. In its earlier decision in *Talley v California*,[8] the Court had recognised 'a tradition of anonymity in the advocacy of political causes',[9] best exemplified, according to Stevens J, by the secret ballot. In short, in the absence of anonymity, some valuable political speech would not be published: the merits of this instrumental argument are considered in sections III and IV(B) below.

The second argument is more clearly rights-based. An author is free to determine the contents of his publication. As 'the identity of the speaker is no different from other components of the document's content that the author is free to include or exclude',[10] it follows that he is entitled to write anonymously (or with the use of a pseudonym). To require him to disclose his name (or address or other identifying details) is no different from compelling him to express a particular opinion. This argument was used by Stevens J to rebut the contention that readers (in this case the electorate) may have a real interest in knowing the identity of the author in order to assess his credibility and the strength of his case. The Court, therefore, rejected the Ohio State's argument that the disclosure requirement was justified because it gave the audience more information.

It also rejected the argument that disclosure was necessary to prevent fraud or libel. The danger of fraud was covered by other, more specific provisions in the Ohio Election Code. The disclosure requirement reinforced, or helped to enforce, these provisions, but that did not mean that it was necessary. Narrower rules confined to leafleting by candidates at elections, or to leaflets distributed on the day before an election when there was no opportunity for a reply, might have been upheld, but not this broad rule which was applied to leaflets distributed before a referendum.[11] Indeed, the Court regarded the disclosure requirements in this case as 'a regulation of pure speech',[12] which lies at the heart of the First Amendment, rather than as an election restriction.[13] It therefore found it easy to distinguish two earlier rulings where the Supreme Court had upheld the constitutionality of

---

[6] See the analysis of LB Lidsky and TF Cotter, 'Authorship, Audiences, and Anonymous Speech' (2006) 82 *Notre Dame Law Review* 1537, 1542–44.

[7] *McIntyre* (n 1) 357.

[8] 362 US 60 (1960).

[9] *McIntyre* (n 1) 343.

[10] Ibid 348.

[11] Ibid 350–52.

[12] Ibid 345.

[13] Ibid 346–47.

restrictions on corporate expenditure on referendum campaigns,[14] and of laws requiring the disclosure of election expenditure.[15]

There was a strong dissenting judgment from Scalia J, in which Rehnquist CJ joined. The Ohio provision protected the electoral process. Unlike the State ordinance invalidated by the Court in its earlier ruling in *Talley v California*,[16] it did not totally outlaw the distribution of all anonymous leaflets; the provision in this case was limited to the distribution of literature designed to influence an election or the outcome of a referendum. Virtually every State had similar provisions on its statute book.[17] Scalia J argued that a general right to anonymous speech would lead to 'silliness'; he asked whether a city would be required to issue a parade permit to an anonymous group, or to allow an anonymous sponsor to hire a municipal hall for a theatrical production.[18] Disclosure requirements reinforced the ban on disseminating false election literature, as a person providing his real name would be much less likely to lie than someone who could shelter behind a mask of anonymity or a pseudonym. Further, signature requirements promoted 'a civil and dignified level of campaign debate'.[19]

Some of the arguments to be made in the following sections of this chapter are relevant to an assessment of the *McIntyre* decision. But a few points should be made here. The first is that Stevens J was surely wrong to suggest that the secret ballot is an example of a tradition of anonymous writing and advocacy. The issues are completely different: see chapter 7, section II for further discussion. Put shortly, the electorate is entitled to vote secretly because voters should not be accountable to anyone (for example, an employer, landlord or a government official) for how they cast their vote. In contrast, a speaker or writer is, and ought to be, accountable in some circumstances for their publications, particularly when they are deceptive or defamatory. Further, speech forms part of a dialogue or exchange with its audience, while voting is a final act in an election campaign.

The second point is more complex. The Court held that an author's decision to remain anonymous can be equated with his decision to add material to the contents of his publication, or to omit material; both are aspects of freedom of speech, and so covered by the First Amendment.[20] There is, of course, a trite sense in which the author's name on the title page can be viewed as part of the title, or indeed the text, of the work, whether it is a novel or a political leaflet. But it is not part of the contents of a work in the same way as the information and ideas contained in the work.

[14] *First National Bank of Boston v Bellotti*, 435 US 765 (1978).
[15] *Buckley v Valeo*, 424 US 1 (1974), considered in chapter 7, section III.
[16] 362 US 60 (1960).
[17] *McIntyre* (n 1) 375–7.
[18] Ibid 381.
[19] Ibid 382–3.
[20] *McIntyre* (n 1) 342 and 349.

The use by an author of 'Anon' or a pseudonym does not give readers valuable information or provide them with ideas; indeed, arguably these devices often deprive them of information they value: the real name of the writer. (Of course, a pseudonym does indicate that the work is authored by the person who has used the same *nom de plume* on earlier occasions, but it does not provide readers with more information than they would have had if the author always used their real name).

Further, the reason for suspicion of restrictions on the content of speech is that they clearly run counter to the values of freedom of speech; these restrictions may prevent the discovery of new social and moral truths or impede the exchange of information and ideas relevant to the conduct of government. Moreover, content-based restrictions on speech enable government to discriminate by allowing the spread of ideas it approves, while penalising the dissemination of dissenting opinion.[21] Disclosure requirements in contrast do not *directly* restrict the circulation of information and ideas, though admittedly they were used in, for example, the seventeenth and eighteenth centuries to reinforce restrictive seditious libel and blasphemy laws in England,[22] and are still used in this way in authoritarian societies. But the real evil here is the suppression of, say, dissenting political or religious ideas, rather than the restriction on anonymity. Disclosure requirements may, of course, inhibit the circulation of lawful speech, because the speaker fears social ostracism or isolation if he communicates an unpopular view: see the discussion of whistle-blowing in section V(B) below. But it does not follow that his name is part of the contents of his speech, as the Court in *McIntyre* suggested. Further, there is perhaps something paradoxical in allowing an author to remain anonymous, as the Court did in *McIntyre*, partly to enable readers to assess the contents of his work on its merits,[23] divorced from awareness of his name, and then treating the name of the author as an aspect of those contents!

Finally, it can be argued that some of the leaflets circulated by Mrs McIntyre were in fact misleading, so it was right to take proceedings against her for distributing them. Insofar as they purported to give the views of 'Concerned Parents and Taxpayers', they might have given those attending the meeting the impression that the views expressed in them were held by a number of people, perhaps a large group of anxious parents, etc, when in fact they might have represented the opinion solely of Mrs McIntyre herself.[24] The inaccurate identification of the author might well have given

---

[21] See GR Stone, 'Content Regulation and the First Amendment' (1983) 25 *William and Mary Law Review* 189.

[22] See chapter 4, section II.

[23] See *McIntrye* (n 1) 342.

[24] It is very unlikely that the views were not shared by many others, for the proposed levy which Mrs McIntyre opposed was initially defeated twice, before passing on its third attempt: see *McIntyre* (n 1) 338. But that is not the point. The leaflets purporting to express the views of 'concerned parents' suggested that they had written them.

additional strength and credibility to her views, to which they were not entitled. It is odd in this context that the Court said that there was no suggestion that the text of the message was false or misleading.[25] If the identity of the author is, as Stevens J said elsewhere in the Court opinion (see the previous paragraphs), 'no different from other components of the document's content that the author is free to include or exclude',[26] then the inaccurate naming of some of the leaflets should have been treated as part of their text, and so regarded as misleading.

Much of the reasoning in *McIntyre*, therefore, seems flawed. Nevertheless, the right to speak (and write) anonymously has now been accepted as an integral aspect of the First Amendment.[27] We should now explore whether there are strong arguments for recognising this right as an aspect of freedom of speech. That entails some reflection on the point of freedom of speech and in particular on the different interests of the speaker (or writer) and of the readers (or audience) in the exercise of the freedom. It may be that the interests of an author and his readers will often clash in this context: an author might prefer to use a pseudonym to disguise his identity for one reason or other, while readers might want to know the name of the author either in order to assess his credibility or to know the identity of the person against whom they may want to secure some form of redress.

III. A *SPEAKER'S* RIGHT TO ANONYMITY?

Free speech theories vary considerably in the extent to which they emphasise either the speaker's or the audience's interest in freedom of speech. Mill's famous argument from truth places greater emphasis on the interests of the audience in the discovery of new moral and social truths than it does on those of the speaker; insofar as the speaker does have a right to communicate his view of the truth, it is parasitic on the interest his listeners have in hearing and considering his argument, either because it might be true and so persuade them to change their minds on some important matter, or because it compels them to defend the received wisdom more vigorously. Some versions of the argument from democracy also attach at least as much weight, if not more, to the interests of the electorate in access to information and to a variety of opinions on political and social matters than they do to the interests of speakers to participate in public discourse. As Alexander Meiklejohn, a leading exponent of free political speech, put it, in the context of the regulation of speech at public meetings, it is important 'not that every one shall get to speak, but that everything worth saying shall be said'.[28]

[25] *McIntyre* (n 1) 337.
[26] Ibid 348.
[27] See the cases cited in n 2 above.
[28] *Political Freedom* (New York, Harper Collins, 1960) 64.

Other justifications for freedom of speech, for example that articulated by Thomas Scanlon, have proceeded from the right of an autonomous individual to consider all the arguments for courses of action which are put before him.[29] Scanlon's view clearly treats the interests of readers and listeners as paramount, and indeed was criticised by Ronald Dworkin for ignoring the interests of speakers in the freedom to communicate their views.[30]

Since these arguments have been influential in shaping the development of constitutional free speech rights, some theorists have argued that recipients are the primary object of free speech concerns; speakers only enjoy derivative rights, which are protected to ensure effective respect for the interests of the former group.[31] If this is correct, it may be difficult to justify a general right of speakers to anonymous speech, because (as will be explained in section IV below) that right would run counter to some important recipient interests.

Nevertheless, the *McIntyre* decision rests largely on the speaker's right to determine the contents of his speech, a right which, in the Court's view, trumped the readers' interest in acquiring information about the identity of the speaker in order to assess the credibility of his publication. The Supreme Court itself in a later case treated *McIntyre* as an instance of a general First Amendment principle of speaker autonomy.[32] What might justify such a broad principle, and so derivatively a right to speak anonymously? One argument for freedom of speech which does emphasise the rights and interests of speakers, as distinct from those of their audience, is the argument that speech is an essential aspect of the right to self-development and fulfilment, or of individual autonomy, and so must be respected as an aspect of that autonomy. Ed Baker, a leading free speech theorist, argued that self-expression or self-disclosure reveals an individual person to others, and so enables him to be treated as autonomous.[33] That is why speech is important and the right to freedom of speech should be regarded as paramount. But there are some problems with this argument: other goods, such as housing, education or a minimum income, might be regarded as necessary as free speech to the development of an independent individual and so covered by the self-development right. If all these goods are also covered by the right, then it is hard to see how speech is special. Moreover, unlike the arguments

---

[29] T Scanlon, 'A Theory of Freedom of Expression' (1972) 1 *Philosophy and Public Affairs* 204.
[30] R Dworkin, 'Introduction' in *The Philosophy of Law* (Oxford, OUP, 1977) 15.
[31] See F Schauer, *Free Speech: A Philosophical Inquiry* (Cambridge, CUP, 1982) 105–6, 158–60; L Alexander, *Is There a Right of Freedom of Expression?* (Cambridge, CUP, 2005) 8–9.
[32] *Hurley v Irish-American Gay, Lesbian and Bisexual Group of Boston*, 515 US 557 (1995).
[33] See the arguments of CE Baker in, eg, *Human Liberty and Freedom of Speech* (New York, OUP, 1989) ch 3, and 'Autonomy and Hate Speech' in I Hare and J Weinstein (eds), *Extreme Speech and Democracy* (Oxford, OUP, 2009) 142–46.

from truth and democracy, the self-development rationale for free speech is difficult to distinguish from more general libertarian claims to individual freedom or autonomy.[34]

Quite apart from these difficulties which make the self-development argument perhaps the least plausible rationale for freedom of speech, there is a further obstacle to using it as support for an anonymity right. Put shortly, it would be odd to base such a right on the speaker's interest in self-development or fulfilment. How does the mask of anonymity claimed by someone who prefers to remain nameless or to publish under the disguise of a pseudonym advance that person's self-development as an individual? The anonymous spraying of political graffiti may make the artist feel better, but it is unclear how it helps his self-development. Baker's argument that self-expression reveals an individual to others, and so is uniquely valuable in developing his sense of autonomy, simply does not work for anonymous speech. As one literary critic has put it: 'in what respect can a poem ... be read or experienced as an act of "self-expression" when the self doing the expressing ... remains unidentified?'.[35] Of course, anonymity or the use of a pseudonym does enable a writer to experiment with the use of separate identities for different genres of fiction, and in that way promotes his literary development, but that seems different from the usual self-fulfilment or autonomy argument which rests on the close link between speech or writing and the development of an individual's personal autonomy. The anonymity argument in this context also seems to rest on the questionable assumption that we can develop in isolation from each other, irrespective whether our expressive acts are appreciated by others and are identified with our developing personality. Self-expression as part of the autonomy argument for freedom of speech cannot be purely self-regarding; it surely requires communication between individuals, and an identifiable speaker known to others who will appreciate the contribution his speech makes to his self-development.

These doubts about using the self-development free speech argument as a basis for an anonymity right are not dispelled by pointing to the strong motives writers have for choosing anonymity or the use of a pseudonym. As was explained in chapter 2, there are many good reasons for anonymity, particularly in the context of fiction and other literature. But these reasons have to be balanced against the arguments for disclosure which are to some extent based on the free speech interests of readers or the general audience in knowing the identity of the author in order to assess the credibility of the information or ideas put forward by the writer. Further, disclosure, as the dissent of Scalia J in *McIntyre* pointed out, makes it easier for readers to

---

[34] See *Human Liberty and Freedom of Speech* (n 33) 14.
[35] D Foster, 'Commentary: In the Name of the Author' (2002) 33 *New Literary History* 373, 383.

secure redress for any deception or defamation in the publication. Insofar as the reasons for and against anonymity have to be weighed against each other, it is difficult to justify a general right to anonymous speech, as formulated by the Supreme Court in *McIntyre*, though there may be a case for recognising more limited rights in specific contexts (see section V below) or for acknowledging a freedom to publish anonymously, as in English law (see chapter 4), albeit one which may be regulated or curtailed by law.

The Court in *McIntyre* treated the anonymous speech right as an aspect of a speaker's right to determine the *contents* of his communication.[36] However, as was explained in the previous section, there is a distinction between the contents of speech and the identity of the speaker; the reasons for the hostility to regulation of the former do not apply directly to disclosure requirements. Moreover, in the context of these general free speech arguments, the reader, or general audience, has as strong an interest in the contents of a communication as the speaker. There seems no good reason for giving greater weight to a speaker's choice of anonymity, if this can be regarded as an aspect of the contents of his speech, than the reader's interest in knowing the identity of the speaker, information which, from his perspective, adds, or gives greater meaning, to the other contents of the publication. Admittedly, the use of a pseudonym may be particularly valuable to some writers, enabling them to use a distinct branding name for different genres of their work; but that choice too has to be balanced against the reader's interest in awareness of the real identity of an author to secure redress for deception or defamation. It is hard to see why balancing of this kind should be avoided, simply by labelling the choice of anonymity an aspect of the author's freedom to determine the contents of his speech. This argument does not really add anything to the thin case for treating an anonymity right as an aspect of the speaker's free speech rights, at least insofar as these rights are based on the self-development justification for these rights.

A better argument for an anonymity right for speakers is that otherwise they might be deterred from participating at all in political life; the right would then be an aspect of a speaker's right to contribute to public discourse.[37] Members of vulnerable groups, for example, asylum-seekers, transsexuals and the mentally handicapped, might not exercise their freedom of speech unless they were guaranteed anonymity; the same would be true in some, particularly authoritarian, societies for women, gays, and members of minority ethnic or religious groups. So a right to speak anonymously, or with the use of a pseudonym, might be justified, as it was to

---

[36] See nn 19–22 above.

[37] See the free speech arguments of, among others, R Dworkin in 'Foreword' to I Hare and J Weinstein (eds), *Extreme Speech and Democracy* (Oxford, OUP, 2009); RC Post, 'The Constitutional Concept of Public Discourse' (1999) 103 *Harvard Law Review* 601; and MH Redish, 'The Value of Free Speech' (1982) 130 *University of Pennsylvania Law Review* 591.

some extent by the Supreme Court in *McIntyre*,[38] as a protection against the tyranny of the majority.

A few points should be made about this argument. The first is that, although it is based on the right of speakers to participate in political and public life, it can equally be framed in terms of the autonomy rights of readers and listeners in exposure to every type of argument—Scanlon's autonomy argument for freedom of speech mentioned earlier in this section.[39] Readers have a strong interest in access to minority views to which they might not be exposed if it were not for the anonymity guarantee. This version of the argument is considered in the next section, where many points that could be made here are fully examined (see section IV(B)). Secondly, if there is a right to anonymous speech—particularly, if it is protected constitutionally, as it is in the United States—then it can be claimed by anyone, whether or not they are a member of a vulnerable group in whose interest the right is framed. It could also be claimed, for example, by persons using a pseudonym to engage in cyber-bullying, hate speech or harassment on the Internet (see chapter 6, section I), or for the distribution of pornography or commercial advertising. That might, at least, lead us to hesitate before accepting the right.

The third point is more complex. There is surely a virtue in the open display of opinion, allowing a full examination of the speaker's arguments in the context of what the public knows about his character and his previous statements. The making of pronouncements in public, with disclosure of the identity of the speaker, exercises and develops the virtue of political courage.[40] It allows for a full and vigorous debate between people who are aware of the identity of their political opponents, or of the others with whom they are engaged in public discourse. On this perspective, anonymity is at best a compromise; it does allow some people to contribute to political discourse, but there are significant costs (see section IV below). Moreover, the resulting discussion is impoverished when it is compared to the vigorous public debate which should occur when complete disclosure is made of a speaker's identity in conjunction with his arguments. The argument from the right to political participation may well be the strongest that can be made for a speaker's right to anonymity, but it seems to justify the ascription of rights only to members of vulnerable groups and contemplates a relatively weak, unsatisfactory form of public discourse, where some participants choose not to disclosure their identity.

---

[38] See n 7 above.
[39] See the text at n 29 above.
[40] H Arendt, *The Human Condition* (Chicago, IL, University of Chicago Press, 1958) 36–37, 50–58, and see 179 where she writes: 'In acting and speaking, men show who they are, reveal actively their unique personal identities and thus make their appearance in the human world'.

IV. INTERESTS OF READERS AND AUDIENCES

A. Interest in Credible Speech

Readers' and audiences' interests are important under the truth and democracy arguments for freedom of speech. Exercise of the freedom enables them to discover new truths and insights, vital for social progress, and to acquire the information and range of political ideas and views which are crucial for full participation in a liberal democracy. Readers and (broadcasting) audiences have an interest in credible speech, which they can presume with confidence to be accurate and reliable. In many contexts it will be important for them to know the identity of the speaker, for that knowledge enables them more easily to evaluate the worth of his information and ideas. They can refer to the previous work of an author to see whether, say, his economic forecasts have been accurate in the past, or whether his political promises should be trusted. Identification makes an author's earlier pronouncements available to the public, and enables it to take account of his experience.[41]

Anonymity, or the use of a pseudonym, may also make it easier for the speaker to manipulate readers and listeners, and certainly harder for the latter to secure redress if they consider they have been deceived or defamed by the speech or publication. These problems, however, are not relevant to the readers' free speech interests, but to the protection of their economic interests or their reputation rights. They are not discussed further in this section, but some account must be taken of them in assessing any utilitarian argument for recognition of a right to speak anonymously (see section VI below).

The view of Robert Post that speech should be assessed entirely divorced from the context in which it is made, including any awareness of the identity of the speaker, seems unrealistic.[42] In an ideal world arguments should, and would, be assessed purely on their merits without regard to the status or position of their advocate. That may sometimes happen at university seminars; further, the system of blind peer refereeing of articles submitted for publication in academic journals requires them to be assessed without the referee's knowledge of the identity of their authors.[43] But in these contexts, the readers and listeners are an expert audience, who, it is assumed, can pass judgement on the quality of the material. That is much less likely to be the case with general political and economic discourse, where the public usually, and quite reasonably, wants to know something about the record

---

[41] SF Kreimer, 'Sunlight, Secrets, and Scarlet Letter: The Tension between Privacy and Disclosure in Constitutional Law' (1991) 140 *University of Pennsylvania Law Review* 1, 85–86.

[42] 'The Constitutional Concept of Public Discourse' (1990) 103 *Harvard Law Review* 603, 639–40.

[43] Discussed in chapter 2, section VIII.

and character of the person offering advice or making a commitment. Admittedly, the case for freedom of speech must assume that readers (or the audience) have some capacity to consider and assess the arguments put before them, but there is no ground for assuming that additionally they must be able to assess them without knowing the identity of the person putting them forward. Suppose readers come across an article claiming that smoking does not after all endanger health; they surely have a strong interest in knowing the identity of its author, and whether he is a medical researcher or a representative of the tobacco industry.

Of course, many members of the public may discount the value of speech from anonymous sources, treating it as of less worth than comparable communications from identified speakers. As a New York court said in a passage which was approved by the Supreme Court in *McIntyre*:[44]

> Don't underestimate the common man. People are intelligent enough to evaluate the source of an anonymous writing. They can see it is anonymous. They know it is anonymous. They can evaluate its anonymity along with its message, as long as they are permitted, as they must be, to read that message. And then, once they have done so, it is for them to decide what is 'responsible', what is valuable, and what is truth.

It is unclear, however, how much force this argument has in the case of pseudonymous speech, where the audience may be unaware that the author's real identity is masked in this way and so may fail to discount its value.[45] For example, online restaurant evaluations made by someone with the use of a pseudonym might be taken as seriously as those by a reputable newspaper correspondent writing under his real name, while clearly anonymous judgements almost certainly would not be. More importantly, the argument of the New York court does not meet the point that often readers simply want to know the identity of the speaker to enable them more easily to evaluate the credibility of the publication; they have a real free speech interest in this information. The New York court appears to have assumed that speakers do have a right to anonymity, so it was attempting merely to meet the point that exercise of that right would inevitably mislead readers.

It does not follow from the recognition of a reader's interests in credible speech that he has a free speech right to compel speakers to disclose their identity. Freedom of speech, or expression, would then be treated as granting a positive claim right to the acquisition of information from private persons. That would be a radical extension to the scope of the freedom, which is usually regarded as a liberty protected against government or state intervention.[46] But acknowledgement of these reader interests does weaken

---

[44] *New York v Duryea*, 351 NYS 2d 978, 995 (1974), quoted in *McIntyre* (n 1) 348, n 11.
[45] See Lidsky and Cotter, 'Authorship, Audiences, and Anonymous Speech' (n 6) 1567.
[46] Barendt, ch III, ss 6–7.

the case for recognising a speaker's right to anonymity, which, as was seen in the previous section of this chapter, is anyhow far from persuasive. The discussion now turns to a much better argument for an anonymity right, which in fact depends to some extent on another interest of readers and audiences—their interest in access to more speech.

B. Interest in More (Radical) Speech

One rationale for the decision in *McIntyre* is that without the safeguard of anonymity there would be less speech, because minorities would be deterred from communicating their views.[47] As has been explained in section III above, this argument can be used to support a *speaker's* right to anonymity; without anonymity, members of vulnerable groups would not participate in public discourse. But the argument can also be framed in terms of the interests of readers and listeners, and is considered more fully here than it was in the previous section. The case is that, in the absence of anonymous speech, society might be deprived of valuable truths or insights, and the electorate would lose access to important political information and ideas. Readers and the audience are the primary objects of these free speech concerns,[48] so this argument for anonymity should be considered in the context of their interests. Is there a good free speech case for anonymity, on the ground that it provides the public with more, perhaps radical, speech than it would otherwise have the opportunity to consider?

Many people may hesitate to speak, if they are required to disclose their identity as a condition for communicating their views. Among these people are immigrants and asylum-seekers; gays and lesbians; members of minority racial and ethnic groups; the victims of harassment or bullying on a housing estate or at their place of work; and whistle-blowers bringing to public attention dangerous or illegal practices by their employer. They may fear social ostracism from their neighbours, loss of their job or detention if their identity is revealed, particularly when their views are highly critical of established authority. There are other instances where anonymity may be valuable, even essential for the free dissemination of ideas or information. Students may be unwilling to be identified with their expression of radical political views, because they fear that disclosure will damage their long-term career prospects. On occasion this reluctance may even extend to senior employees or people with established positions, who would not want to be accused by their peers of damaging the reputation of their employer if they spoke freely about malpractice at work. Consequently, unpopular ideas may

---

[47] See text at nn 6–8 above.
[48] Text at n 28 above.

simply not be aired, or information disseminated by someone who is in the best position to provide it.

In contrast, it is unlikely that disclosure requirements would have much impact on the speech of people in positions of authority or on the expression of popular views. In these cases speakers will generally be very keen to be identified with their expression. So an anonymity right can best be defended as safeguarding the public interest in access to minority, unorthodox and challenging views, and to the provision of unwelcome (to some) information, which might otherwise never see the light of day.[49] An analogy might be drawn with broadcasting regulation, which in the United Kingdom (and other European states) protects the public interest in access to a range of views, including minority opinion, through an impartiality principle and rules precluding programme controllers from expressing their own political opinions.

Even though the primary beneficiaries of an anonymity right are the intended audience, indeed often the general public, clearly it is the speaker who is in the best position to assert it; it is he, not a potential reader, who knows whether the right may have been infringed and who is in a position to claim it. But the speaker's right is parasitic or dependent on the public interest in the dissemination of minority views or unwelcome information. That interest provides without doubt a stronger case for anonymity than any which is based on a speaker's right to choose the contents of his speech as an aspect of his freedom of self-expression and self-development. It also provides in some situations a much more convincing basis for an anonymity right than the *speaker's* right to political participation which was considered in section III above. It would be odd to say that a whistle-blower is relying on this participation right when he reveals to the press some malpractice on the part of his employer without disclosing his identity, but the public interest in the story might justify anonymity. Equally, a victim of domestic violence is hardly exercising her right to political participation when she insists on concealing her identity when giving a media interview, but there is a powerful argument for upholding an anonymity right on the ground that the public has a strong free speech interest in hearing her story.

The readers' interest in credible speech, as explained earlier,[50] favours disclosure of the speaker's identity and would appear at first glance to run counter to this argument for anonymity. But in many circumstances the name and identity of the speaker may not be of much importance to readers or the general audience. This seems particularly likely to be the case so far as the expression of minority or radical ideas are concerned. While

---

[49] Kreimer, 'Sunlight, Secrets, and Scarlet Letter' (n 41) 88, and see the anonymous note, 'The Constitutional Right to Anonymity: Free Speech, Disclosure and the Devil' (1961) 70 *Yale Law Journal* 1084.

[50] See section III(a) above.

readers reasonably want to know the name of the author, say, of City trading forecasts, a political report, or a book or theatre review, they would probably be much less concerned with the name of the person expressing a grievance about the conditions in which asylum-seekers are detained, or even of a whistle-blower. At most they have an interest in knowing that the person concerned is a genuine asylum-seeker or did work for the company whose alleged malpractice has been exposed. His real name and previous record will generally be a matter of relative indifference to the public, though not of course to the authorities who must investigate the complaint. The readers' interest in credible speech may not, therefore, significantly weaken the argument for anonymity based on their concern for access to challenging speech, which strict enforcement of disclosure laws would deny.

This point, however, does not end the arguments which should be considered before determining whether a right to anonymous speech should be recognised, and whether it is a right of such strength as to outweigh competing interests, as it did in the *McIntyre* decision. Though readers in the circumstances considered in the previous paragraphs may not be very concerned with the authority or credibility of the writer, they may want to challenge his views, while employers, public authorities and the media may want, or need, to investigate them. It is difficult to have a satisfactory dialogue or exchange of views with a writer who insists on anonymity. Further, a reader (or other individual) may want redress for any defamatory content in an anonymous publication, or protection from any threat of harassment or of bullying expressed in it.[51] The accountability argument for disclosure, emphasised by Scalia J in his dissent in *McIntyre*, applies as much to the dissemination of minority, radical views, or to whistle-blowing, as it does in other contexts. The free speech interests of readers (and speakers) in anonymity must be balanced against the interests of readers and others in redress for any deception, defamation or threats in the anonymous publication. Something more is said about balancing in the last section of this chapter, but we should first consider another free speech interest of readers, and then the question whether the strength of the free speech arguments for anonymity are dependent on the category of speech at issue.

C. Readers' Interest in their Own Anonymity

This chapter has been concerned with the anonymity of speakers and writers. But readers, or members of an audience, may also want to remain anonymous, and may on occasion even assert a right to anonymity. Freedom of

---

[51] This is particularly true for anonymous blogs and comments on the Internet: see chapter 6, sections II and III.

speech, or expression, protects the right to receive, as well as the freedom to disseminate, information and ideas.[52] So a right, say, to read books, periodicals or other material without disclosure of the reader's name or other identifying features can be claimed as an aspect of his freedom to receive information and ideas, just as a speaker may claim an anonymity right on the basis of his freedom to impart them. Indeed, Douglas J in a concurring opinion in *United States v Rumley* strongly implied that readers have a First Amendment right to anonymity, when he ruled that a committee of Congress could not require the secretary of an organisation, who had distributed controversial political material, to disclose the names of people making bulk purchases of the material for further distribution.[53] In a more recent case the Supreme Court of Colorado refused to grant a search warrant authorising the seizure of customer purchase records from a bookseller, on the ground that its enforcement would infringe the customers' right to purchase books anonymously.[54] It also implicated their privacy interest.[55]

Would the upholding of a right to *read* anonymously, whether on the basis of freedom of speech or of privacy, mean that a right to speak anonymously must also be recognised? The answer is surely, 'No'. The first point is that the identity of readers or the audience (for a film or broadcasting) is completely immaterial to the credibility of a report or to the character or quality of a work of fiction, review or other literary or cultural work which is read or viewed. The anonymity of the audience is, as it were, the default position. Speakers have no interest in disclosure of the names (as distinct from the numbers) of their readers or audience, comparable to the interest readers often have in the identity of the writer in order to establish his experience, authority and credibility (see section IV(A) above). Secondly, readers are rarely accountable to anyone for what they read, though there are some exceptional cases, for example, the consumption of child pornography which is often made a criminal offence.[56] But they are not accountable in the same way that speakers should be—for false reporting, deception or defamation.[57] So the grounds for reservation about recognising a general right to anonymous speech do not apply to anonymous reading. There is a strong case on grounds of both free speech and personal privacy

---

[52] The right to receive information and ideas is explicitly guaranteed by ECHR, Art 10. See also German Basic Law, art 5(1) which guarantees the right of everyone 'freely to inform himself from generally accessible sources'. For discussion of these provisions and case law applying them, see Barendt 108–12.

[53] 345 US 41, 57–58 (1953). The Court majority did not consider the First Amendment question, as it invalidated the Congressional order as outside its powers of investigation.

[54] *Tattered Cover v City of Thornton*, 44 P3d 1044 (Colo 2002).

[55] Ibid 1060.

[56] In the United Kingdom it is an offence to possess child pornography, even though the possession is without any view to further distribution: Criminal Justice Act 1988, s 160.

[57] JE Cohen, 'A Right to Read Anonymously: A Closer Look at "Copyright Management" in Cyberspace' (1997) 28 *Connecticut Law Review* 981.

for recognising a right to read anonymously; authorities, particularly totalitarian governments, may find it easier to prosecute the people who look at what they consider subversive material than it is to stop its sale or its import from abroad.[58] But we need other, stronger arguments for recognising a right to speak anonymously, when, as we have seen, there may be good grounds for disclosure.

V. CATEGORIES OF SPEECH

A. General Discussion

A French Law of 1850 required the signature of newspaper articles discussing political, philosophical or religious issues; anonymity for this type of writing was proscribed, but it was presumably allowed for other categories of material: general features, social gossip and cultural reviews.[59] The Law drew a distinction between categories of speech with regard to the permissibility of anonymity. How far is such a distinction justified and legitimate under freedom of speech principles? It is first relevant to consider the different approaches legal systems take to the protection of various categories or types of speech. In a leading privacy case in England, *Campbell v MGN*,[60] Baroness Hale in the House of Lords assessed the value of a disclosure concerning the treatment for drug problems of the celebrity model, Naomi Campbell, in balancing the newspaper's free press rights against her right to respect for her private life. While political speech was worthy of the strongest degree of protection, and intellectual, educational and artistic expression was also important, the exposure of the celebrity in this case was of little free speech value.[61] Similar distinctions have been drawn in later House of Lords decisions.[62]

The US Supreme Court has accorded pornography a lower level of protection than political speech and other contributions to political discourse.[63] Its treatment of commercial speech and advertising is also not quite as generous as it is for political speech, though a blanket proscription of commercial advertising is likely to be struck down for infringing the First Amendment.[64]

---

[58] See the decision in *Lamont v Postmaster General*, 381 US 301 (1965) invalidating a federal law which permitted delivery by post of 'Communist political propaganda' only if the addressee specifically requested it in writing.

[59] See the discussion in 'The Constitutional Right to Anonymity' (n 49) 1084–85.

[60] [2004] 2 AC 457.

[61] Ibid paras 148–49.

[62] *Jameel v Wall Street Journal Europe* [2007] 1 AC 359, para 147 per Baroness Hale; *Belfast City Council v Miss Behavin' Ltd* [2007] 1 WLR 1420, para 16 per Lord Hoffmann, and para 38 per Baroness Hale.

[63] See *Young v American Mini Theatres*, 427 US 50 (1976).

[64] *44 Liquormart v Rhode Island*, 517 US 484 (1996). For general discussion of the treatment of commercial speech in the United States, see Barendt, 407–9, 411–12.

However, zoning requirements limiting the siting of theatres showing sexually explicit films have been upheld.[65] The European Court of Human Rights is much more reluctant to uphold state restrictions on political expression than limits on commercial speech or on the display or distribution of pornography, allowing states a wider margin of appreciation in the latter two contexts.[66] But unlike courts in the United States,[67] the European Court (and the former European Human Rights Commission) have consistently declined to treat hate speech as a form of strongly protected political discourse, holding either that it falls outside the scope of ECHR, Article 10, or that a state has good grounds to restrict its dissemination in order to protect public order or the rights of others.[68]

It is relatively easy to justify this differential treatment of categories of speech. The strong protection afforded political speech, broadly defined to include the communication of all ideas and information on issues which intelligent people should consider, can be supported both on the argument for freedom of speech from democracy and Mill's truth argument. It is in contrast less easy to see why commercial speech and advertising, or sexually explicit expression, should receive a similar level of protection.[69] Moreover, there may be good grounds for their restriction, for example, the protection of consumers, children and other vulnerable groups, which do not apply to political speech. These points are relatively uncontroversial, though of course there are some types of expression which resist easy classification, for example, hate speech treated in the United States, but not in European jurisdictions, as political speech, or advertising for professional services, which may be regarded either as similar to valuable political discourse or in much the same way as advertising for commercial goods.[70]

---

[65] Ibid 387–89.

[66] See *Handyside v United Kingdom* (1976) 1 EHRR 737 (pornography), and *Markt Intern and Beerman v Germany* (1990) 12 EHRR 161 (commercial speech).

[67] See the decision of the Court of Appeals for the Seventh Circuit in *Collin v Smith*, 578 F2d 1197 (1978) invalidating a ban on the dissemination of material promoting racial or religious hatred, and of the Supreme Court in *RAV v St Paul*, 505 US 377 (1992) invalidating a ban on the placing of objects (including the Nazi swastika) on property which the accused knew was likely to cause anger or alarm on racial, religious grounds, etc on the ground that the ban proscribed some types of hate speech, but did not outlaw others.

[68] See the decision of the European Commission in *Glimmerveen v Netherlands*, Application no 8348/78, 18 D & R 117, holding inadmissible an application to challenge the proscription of possession of racist leaflets as infringing the freedom of expression guaranteed by ECHR, Art 10; the decision of the European Court in *Witzsch v Germany*, Application no 7485/03, 13 December 2005, holding inadmissible a challenge to application of a Holocaust denial law; and the judgments of the Court in *Jersild v Denmark* (1995) 19 EHRR 1, and in *Lehideux v France* (2000) 30 EHRR 665, indicating that the proscription of hate speech and Holocaust denial laws are compatible with the Convention, though on the facts the particular challenges under Art 10 were upheld.

[69] For discussion, see Barendt, 355–61 (pornography) and 399–406 (commercial speech).

[70] See Barendt, 395–99 and 409–11 for the difficulties in classifying commercial speech and professional advertising.

The question is how far these distinctions should be applied in the context of anonymous speech. The strength of the speaker and reader interests in anonymity, on the one hand, or that of the latter in disclosure on the other, does seem to vary according to the category of speech. Members of vulnerable groups want to speak out on political and social matters of public concern, and the rest of the community has a reciprocal interest in hearing their views, to which in the absence of anonymity they might not be exposed. On the other hand, readers may, as pointed out in section IV(A) above, have a strong interest in the credibility of news reports, or the experience and authority of commentators offering their opinion on a political situation, on the trading position of a commercial company, or on economic prospects. So the arguments in favour of anonymity apply particularly strongly to political discourse, though equally the arguments in favour of disclosure apply in this context as well.

With regard to commercial speech and advertising, on the other hand, it is hard to see how a strong case can be made for anonymity, while there are clear accountability arguments in favour of disclosure of the advertiser's identity; consumers and an appropriate regulatory authority, such as the Advertising Standards Authority in the United Kingdom, should know which organisation is answerable for a complaint of a misleading or offensive advertisement, or from whom they can seek redress in the courts. In this context the speakers' autonomy interest in anonymity is very low and 'the potential for abuse particularly high'.[71] Similar points apply to pornography, particularly hard-core and child pornography. While the authors of sexually explicit literary pornography have sometimes legitimately preferred to write under a pseudonym,[72] there seems no good reason for allowing the authors and publishers of mass hard-core pornography the same freedom. Unlike the writers of literary pornography, they have no reason to distinguish this genre of work from their other fiction. Anonymity is used primarily to enable them to shelter from application of the obscenity and child pornography laws, so the compulsory disclosure of their identity appears to be a reasonable requirement.

The differential treatment of diverse categories of anonymous speech is reflected in US case law. In *Watchtower Bible and Tract Society of New York v Village of Stratton*,[73] the Supreme Court held it incompatible with the First Amendment to apply to political and religious canvassers an ordinance requiring door-to-door canvassers to register with the local mayor and receive a permit; one reason for this decision was that the

---

[71] Lidsky and Cotter, 'Authorship, Audiences, and Anonymous Speech' (n 6) 1592.
[72] Pauline Réage, the author of *Story of O*, was a pseudonym for a woman whose real name was Dominque Aury: Ciuraru, ch 16. John Cleland's *Memoirs of a Woman of Pleasure* (or *Fanny Hill*) was written anonymously: Mullan, 126.
[73] See n 2 above.

canvassers would then surrender their anonymity. But Stevens J, in the opinion for the Court, indicated that the application of the ordinance to commercial canvassers might be legitimate, because the Village would then have a strong interest in preventing fraud.[74] In Internet defamation cases, courts are relatively willing to compel an Internet Service Provider (ISP) to identify the actual authors of a commercial advertisement,[75] so that libel proceedings can be taken against them. In contrast they are reluctant to take this step where the allegations were made in the course of political speech.[76] In a commercial speech case, the Court of Appeals for the Ninth Circuit said that 'the nature of the speech should be a driving force in choosing a standard by which to balance the rights of anonymous speakers in discovery disputes'.[77] The same approach was taken by a federal District Court when it ordered an ISP to identify the subscribers to its service who had posted scandalous slurs under pseudonym about the sexuality and sexual conduct of female law students at Yale University:[78] for further discussion of these cases, see chapter 6, section III.

Of course, it may sometimes be hard to characterise the anonymous speech at issue. In *McIntyre* itself, part of the disagreement between Stevens J for the Court majority and Scalia J concerned the classification of Mrs McIntyre's leaflets; the majority treated them as 'core political speech',[79] while Scalia J referred to 'anonymous electioneering',[80] so it was legitimate in his view to order the disclosure of her name as part of the state's regulation of the electoral process. Whistle-blowing and leaks of confidential government or private information may be particularly hard to categorise, both generally and in the context of anonymous speech; the issues are complex and merit full consideration.

B. Whistle-blowing

Many whistle-blowers report illegal or dangerous practices at their work anonymously—out of fear of reprisals from their employer or of hostility and ostracism from their work colleagues; the disclosure can then be characterised, rather opprobriously, as a 'leak'.[81] Should a blanket ban on

---

[74] 122 S Ct 2080, 2089 (2002).

[75] *In re Anonymous Online Speakers*, 611 F3d 653 (9th Cir, 2010).

[76] *Doe v Cahill*, 884 A 2d 451 (Del 2005).

[77] *Anonymous Online Speakers* (n 75) 661.

[78] *Doe I and Doe II v Individuals* ('AutoAdmit' case), 561 F Supp 2d 249 (D Conn, 2008); for commentary, see LB Lidsky, 'Anonymity in Cyberspace: What Can We Learn from John Doe?' (2009) 50 *Boston College Law Review* 1373, 1386–89.

[79] *McIntyre* (n 1) 347.

[80] Ibid 372–73.

[81] The distinction is drawn between whistle-blowing and anonymous leaks by R Sagar, *Secrets and Leaks* (Princeton, NJ, Princeton University Press, 2013) 6–7, 162.

anonymous whistle-blowing be upheld, or should the law recognise that in some circumstances at least anonymity is justified? It has been persuasively argued that a blanket ban would be wrong, for anonymity leads to more reporting of dangerous incidents at work and corrupt employment practices, and their subsequent investigation.[82] Whether anonymity is justified in the particular circumstances depends on a number of factors, among them the seriousness of the offence alleged by the whistle-blower, the probability of unfair retaliation by his colleagues, and the effectiveness of the anonymous reporting. With regard to the last factor, objectors to anonymity in this context argue that it is unfair to a criticised work colleague for him to face charges which have been made by an unidentified whistle-blower. Further, such charges are relatively unlikely to be taken seriously, particularly if there are reasons to suspect the motives of the person making the complaint.[83] However, it is far from clear that fairness to the criticised employee requires the identity of the whistle-blower to be known; generally a complaint can be investigated and found to be warranted or not without disclosing who made it.[84] Nor should suspicion of the motives of the whistle-blower matter; what is important is whether wrong-doing at work has occurred.[85]

When assessing the legitimacy of anonymous whistle-blowing, it would be wrong to assume that the identity of the complainant is wholly unknown. Complete secrecy will only be kept if he telephones a public interest organisation or the media to report his concerns and insists on keeping his anonymity. More frequently, he communicates them in person to a work colleague, who has the specific responsibility of considering whistle-blowers' complaints, or to an outside organisation or the media. The colleague or outside body should then act as a responsible intermediary, in a position to check the whistle-blower's credibility and the allegations of wrong-doing before giving them wider disclosure. English law, as will be explained in the next chapter,[86] recognises that anonymous allegations reported within the concerned organisation should be investigated seriously; it is enough if someone in the organisation knows the identity of the whistle-blower. When allegations are reported directly to the press or other media, it is perhaps less likely that they will be subject to full investigation, but the media should make some attempt to check the story before revealing it to the general public.[87]

---

[82] F Elliston, 'Anonymous Whistleblowing: An Ethical Analysis' (1982) 1 *Business and Professional Ethics Journal* 39, 49.

[83] S Bok, 'Whistleblowing and Professional Responsibilities' in JC Callahan (ed) *Ethical Issues in Professional Life* (New York, OUP, 1988) 331, 336.

[84] GG James, 'In Defence of Whistleblowing' in JC Callahan (ed) *Ethical Issues in Professional Life* (New York, OUP, 1988) 315, 318–19, and Elliston, 'Anonymous Whistleblowing' (n 82) 53.

[85] Ibid 50.

[86] See chapter 4, section IV.

[87] These arguments are considered fully in chapter 5, section III(C) in the context of journalists' privilege not to disclose their sources.

Whistle-blowing is clearly in the public interest, when, for example, it reveals that a commercial product is unreliable or dangerous to its users,[88] or that the government is, say, engaged in, or has attempted to cover up, torture or rendition of its citizens for detention overseas, or surreptitious surveillance.[89] Another example of a public interest disclosure was the whistle-blowing by a young civil servant (posthumously revealed to be Malcolm Wicks, a Labour MP from 1992 to 2012) of the Callaghan government's use of 'downright lies' to delay the introduction of child benefit.[90] It would be right to characterise whistle-blowing of this sort as political speech, even if it most immediately concerns the practices of a private business; there is a strong argument in these circumstances for recognising a right to make the allegations anonymously. Naturally it may be controversial whether a particular anonymous leak is in fact in the public interest, particularly when it seems likely that an exaggerated or distorted claim has been made for personal or malicious reasons. That possibility does not, however, remove whistle-blowing from the category of political speech, any more than the risk that an individual asylum-seeker makes bogus claims about his conditions removes the speech of all asylum-seekers or immigrants from that category.

When a whistle-blower's allegation or, if the term is preferred, a 'leak' is reported by the press, perhaps with some commentary to put it into context, free press arguments come into play, in addition to the free speech arguments which may be made by the whistle-blower himself. It is the responsibility of newspapers and the other media to report news of public importance, so it would be failing in its duties if it did not communicate the substance of a leak, unless its publication would clearly be damaging to national security, public order or some other important interest.[91] The personal ill-will or malice of the leaker against his employer should not be ascribed to the press, which may not even know the identity of the person who had supplied the information The fact that a leak had been made anonymously does not weaken the press freedom argument for publication, provided the journalist to whom the story had been disclosed has made some attempt to check its veracity. When the source is known to the press, then it can interview him

---

[88] See *Lion Laboratories v Evans* [1985] 2 QB 526, where the Court of Appeal lifted an interim injunction granted to the claimants to stop publication in the *Daily Express* of an article based on confidential documents supplied by former employees of the claimant that its breath-test machine (used by the police) was seriously defective.

[89] For example, the anonymous disclosure by an army reservist of the abusive treatment of Iraqi detainees in the Abu Ghraib prison: Sagar, *Secrets and Leaks* (n 81) 147–48.

[90] See *Guardian*, 20 January 2014. Wicks leaked the story to Frank Field, MP, who published the disclosure anonymously in a magazine article.

[91] This was the issue in the disclosures by the *Guardian* and the *New York Times* of the leak by Edward Snowden, a contractor working for the CIA, of documents showing that the US National Security Agency and GCHQ in the United Kingdom had engaged in mass interception of communications on the Internet.

and assess his reliability. In that event the journalist acts as an intermediary, vouching to some extent for the credibility of the story and taking responsibility for its accuracy. But the press cannot act as a responsible filter in the public interest when it knows nothing about the identity of the source, and little if anything about the truth of the leak or whether its publication might endanger public safety.[92] We return to this topic when anonymous speech is discussed in relation to the privilege of journalists and others responsible for publication not to disclose the identity of their sources: see chapter 5, especially section III.

VI. CONCLUSIONS

Lyrissa Lidsky and Thomas Cotter, the authors of a leading American law review article on this topic, concluded that it is difficult to calculate the social costs and benefits of anonymous speech.[93] Any rule that provides for its strong protection will lead to more harmful speech, while the absence of any protection, let alone a general disclosure requirement, would deter the communication of core speech, for example, the expression of minority or dissenting political ideas and whistle-blowing. Nevertheless Lidsky and Cotter argued that traditional free speech analysis in the United States suggests a clear preference for the protection of anonymous speech in most sets of circumstances: they point to the assumptions underlying the First Amendment guarantee of freedom of speech and of the press that first, 'audiences are capable of rationally assessing the truth, quality, and other characteristics of core speech', and secondly, 'more speech is generally preferable to less'.[94] Audiences can therefore be trusted to make an appropriate discount when speech is made anonymously; they can protect themselves against the increased risks of fraud and deception from speakers who conceal their identity. Moreover, it should be presumed that anonymous speech is valuable.[95]

  This argument is far from persuasive. The first assumption ignores the point that readers often want to know the identity of a speaker in order better to assess the credibility of his arguments; this seems be as important a free speech interest as the interest the speaker has in anonymity. Further, the ability of audiences to discount the worth of anonymous communications does not apply to the use of a pseudonym, which they may understand, perhaps wrongly, to stand for an authoritative and experienced speaker (see section IV above). It is true that much anonymous speech is valuable, but

---

[92] For a full discussion of these complex arguments, see Sagar, *Secrets and Leaks* (n 81) 162–70.
[93] Lidsky and Cotter, 'Authorship, Audiences, and Anonymous Speech' (n 6) 1578–81.
[94] Ibid 1581.
[95] Ibid 1588.

equally much of it (for instance, cyber-bullying and harassment, commercial spams, extreme and child pornography) is of little or no value. Lidsky and Cotter admit that a government may legitimately require speakers to disclose their identity when the autonomy interest is particularly low and the risk of abuse is particularly high.[96] So anonymous commercial e-mails, or spam, can be regulated or perhaps even banned.

This surely entails that it would be wrong to formulate a constitutional right to speak anonymously, as the Supreme Court did in its decision in *McIntyre* (see section II above). Claims to free speech anonymity rights could then be made in a variety of inappropriate circumstances, as Scalia J pointed out in his vigorous dissent in that case.[97] One of these circumstances might be the ban on the dissemination of anonymous Internet communications intended to be annoying to, or abuse, threaten or harass anyone, which was imposed by Congress in the Violence Against Women Act of 2005.[98] Lidsky and Cotter are confident that the ban would be held unconstitutional, for First Amendment jurisprudence has affirmed a right to communicate ideas which are annoying.[99] But this misses the point; the question is whether there is a right to disseminate *anonymously* annoying or threatening messages over the Internet, which will generally be received by isolated individuals at home, not whether there is a right to communicate annoying, etc, messages at, say, a demonstration or at a public meeting.

The category of the speech may be important in determining whether it is legitimate to require disclosure of the identity of the speaker (see section V above). There are good arguments for allowing a freedom to disseminate radical political ideas anonymously (see sections III and IV(B) above), but few for allowing a similar freedom for cyber-bullying or harassment, or for commercial speech and advertising. A major objection to the formulation of a strong constitutional right to anonymous speech is that it makes it much harder to engage in a nuanced analysis which takes full account of the type or category of anonymous speech at issue. This objection does not apply so clearly to the coverage of anonymous speech by a provision such as Article 10 of the ECHR, for then the right to freedom of anonymous expression may be restricted when necessary in order to protect other rights and public interests.

Another objection to the recognition of a strong constitutional right is that it would make it more difficult for an authority to find out the identity

---

[96] Ibid 1592.

[97] 514 US 334, 381 (1995).

[98] Violence Against Women and Department of Justice Reauthorization Act 2005, s 113, amending Communications Act 1934, s 223(a)(1). The measure has been re-enacted in the Violence Against Women Reauthorisation Act 2013, with the deletion of the word 'annoying' which arguably made the earlier law overbroad. In its present form it would almost certainly survive constitutional challenge: see chapter 6, section I(A).

[99] *Cohen v California*, 403 US 15 (1971).

of a speaker when it has a legitimate interest in determining this point. For example, under the UK Education (No 2) Act 1986, universities must take reasonably practicable steps to ensure that freedom of speech within the law is secured for members of staff, students, employees and visiting speakers.[100] The identity of the speaker is relevant in this context. It matters whether he is a member of the university or has been invited to speak at, say, a seminar or a student society meeting. The university authorities are entitled to know whether a speaker is covered by the statute, so it would be wrong to recognise a statutory free speech right to circulate anonymous leaflets on a campus or university premises, or to use university computers for anonymous or pseudonymous communication.[101] Public and private employers may have a legitimate interest in establishing whether the source of a leak of confidential information is an employee, or a member of the public who happens to have come across the information; that provides a good, though not a decisive, argument against recognition of a right to leak such information anonymously which trumps other interests irrespective of the circumstances.

These points show why it would be wrong to recognise a general free speech right to anonymity or to use a pseudonym, with the consequence that disclosure requirements should necessarily be invalidated. It does not follow, of course, that a freedom to communicate anonymously is without value. On the contrary, in many circumstances, as pointed out in both the preceding chapter and in this (see especially sections III and IV(B) above) it is important for liberal societies not to interfere with the exercise of this freedom. But this object can be achieved, as it is in English law, through a general tolerance of the liberty of anonymous speech (see chapter 4), coupled perhaps with the recognition of limited legal rights to anonymous speech in those circumstances where its value clearly outweighs the risks of deception and defamation which anonymity makes more likely. The social utility of anonymous speech should also be recognised in law, where responsible intermediaries can take steps to vouch for the reliability of the speaker and check the accuracy of his report: see the discussion of the privilege of journalists not to disclosure their sources in chapter 5. In these ways the value of anonymous speech can be accommodated without taking the unjustified step of recognising in all circumstances a strong constitutional right for speakers to communicate their ideas without revealing their identity.

---

[100] See Barendt, 501–2.
[101] See the US Federal Court of Appeals decision in *Justice for All v Faulkner*, 410 F3d 760 (5th Cir, 2005), which upheld a right of a student anti-abortion group to circulate leaflets anonymously on campus, but which recognised that a duty to notify the university authorities of the identity of persons circulating leaflets might be upheld.

4

Anonymous Speech in English Law

I. INTRODUCTION

THERE HAS BEEN a long tradition of important anonymous writing in England, including, of course, writing under a pseudonym: see chapter II, especially sections I–V. But this has not led to the recognition, as it has in the United States (see chapter III, section II) of a strong, constitutional right to anonymous speech. This is largely attributable to the general treatment in English law of freedom of speech, where it has usually been regarded as a liberty, rather than a right: it exists only where the law does not restrict its exercise. There is complete freedom of speech, including a freedom to voice controversial and unpopular views, except where that is limited by the laws of defamation, obscenity, incitement to commit a crime, contempt of court, and so on. It follows that individuals are free to write anonymously, unless the law prohibits this by requiring, for example, a book or other printed matter to bear the author's real name. English law has not imposed requirements of this kind since the seventeenth century, when they sometimes formed part of licensing schemes designed to limit the spread of politically or religiously subversive literature. This history is discussed in section II below.

During the seventeenth and eighteenth centuries it was more common for proceedings to be taken against the printers rather than the authors of material which was regarded as subversive or dangerous. It was relatively easy to identify a printer who worked from fixed premises and whose assets could be confiscated, while an author might be anonymous, or if identified could disappear and so escape the clutches of the authorities. As section II below explains, legislation frequently required the printer to disclose his name and residence. This requirement survives in the present law: see section III below. Disclosure obligations are imposed on printers (and newspaper publishers) but not on authors. Writers are free to be anonymous or use a pseudonym, but it is very unlikely that they could challenge successfully, as they could in the United States, a statutory disclosure requirement for infringing freedom of speech. Nor could they take proceedings against anyone who revealed their identity on the basis of an infringement of their privacy rights, let alone for interfering with their right to freedom of expression: see the discussion of *Author of a Blog v Times Newspapers Ltd*[1] in section III below. There are, however, some sets of circumstances where English law does recognise limited or qualified anonymity rights. First, a whistle-blower may be entitled to raise a concern anonymously, in the sense that his identity is not disclosed to the fellow employee whose conduct is the subject of the concern, though it is known to an appropriate person dealing with the matter (see section IV below). More generally, the sources of stories disclosed to the media are entitled under the Contempt of Court Act 1981 to anonymity, unless disclosure of their identity is necessary for one of a limited number of ends, notably the prevention of crime or the interests of justice.[2] The relationship of this qualified *entitlement* to speak anonymously through the media to the general legal position, under which there is a bare freedom, but no entitlement, to anonymous speech is discussed in the next chapter.

II. A LEGAL HISTORY OF ANONYMITY RESTRAINTS

The history of restraints on anonymity can be traced back to the reign of Henry VIII, when a Proclamation of 1546 issued under the Royal Prerogative required a printer to set out on each copy of a book his own name, that of the author and the date of printing. The requirement supplemented a comprehensive licensing scheme which had been introduced by an earlier Proclamation of 1538.[3] Comparable requirements were imposed in the reign of Elizabeth I by Royal Proclamations and then by a Star Chamber Decree of 1586, which continued in force until 1637.[4] The licensing scheme was in effect challenged by the famous Marprelate tracts, when a number of books and pamphlets were written in 1588–89 under the pseudonym, Martin Marprelate ('bad prelate'); they mocked from a Puritan perspective the Church of England and in particular ridiculed the High Church Archbishop of Canterbury from 1584 to 1604, John Whitgift, and various other bishops. The authorities eventually tracked down one of the printers, who had moved the press on several occasions to avoid arrest, but the author was never discovered.[5] It was, of course, relatively easy to trace the printer responsible for a particular publication; links might be made with previous subversive material which came from his press and he might find it difficult to move his press with sufficient speed to evade arrest. Authors would generally be much harder to detect; the identity of the author of the Marprelate tracts has never been conclusively established, though it was probably

---

[1] [2009] EMLR 22.
[2] Contempt of Court Act 1981, s 10.
[3] FS Siebert, *Freedom of the Press in England 1476–1776* (Urbana, IL, University of Illinois Press, 1952) 49–51.
[4] Ibid 56–63.
[5] Ibid 98–100, and for a fuller account see Mullan, 146–50.

Job Throkmorton, a prominent Puritan and Member of Parliament for Warwick, who in addition to the tracts wrote over 100 works under different pseudonyms.[6]

The 1586 Decree was replaced during the reign of Charles I by another Star Chamber Decree of 11 July 1637, which required two copies of any book or pamphlet to be submitted for approval by a person authorised to license publication. It was an offence to print any material without setting out the printer's name and that or those of the author(s), on pain of seizure of the printing press and fine or imprisonment.[7] But with the advent of the Civil War the Star Chamber was abolished in 1641 and control over the press moved from the Crown to Parliament. The House of Commons issued an Order on 29 January 1642 to the effect that printers should not print or reprint any material 'without the Name and Consent of the Author'.[8] This was a response to the flood of unregulated news-sheets and other printed material in 1640 after the Star Chamber lost effective control;[9] authors complained that their work was circulated without their consent, so the Order can be taken as a first recognition by Parliament of their interests.[10]

It was indeed only in the middle of the seventeenth century that authors emerged from the shadows to claim rights in their work. More than half the books published in 1644 and in 1688 were printed without an author's name. Collaborative works involving a number of writers and also the active participation of printers and booksellers were common.[11] Much of Milton's early work, including *Comus*, *Lycidas* and four of the five anti-episcopal pamphlets published in the 1640s, was written anonymously.[12] However, his famous attack on censorship, *Areopagitica, A Speech of Mr John Milton For the Liberty of Unlicenc'd Printing*, clearly indicated

---

[6] LH Carlson, *Martin Marprelate, Gentleman: Master Job Throckmorton Laid Open in All His Colors* (San Marino, CA, Huntington Library, 1981) argues strongly for the authorship of Throckmorton, while P Collinson in *Richard Bancroft and Elizabethan Anti-Puritanism* (Cambridge, CUP, 2013) suggests there may have been a consortium of authors, including Throckmorton and George Carleton, a Puritan lawyer and MP: ch 5, esp 63–64.

[7] Star Chamber Decree of 11 July 1637, cl VIII, available at British History Online. John Rushworth, 'The Star Chamber on Printing, 1637' in *Historical Collections of Private Passages of State*, vol 3, *1639–40* (London, 1721) 306–16, available at www.british-history. ac.uk/rushworth-papers/vol3/pp306-316. For commentary, see Siebert, *Freedom of the Press in England 1476–1776* (n 3) 142–44.

[8] Available at British History Online; 'House of Commons Journal Volume 2: 29 January 1642' in *Journal of the House of Commons*, vol 2, *1640–1643* (London, 1802) 402–4, available at www.british-history.ac.uk/commons-jrnl/vol2/pp402-404.

[9] LG Schwoerer, 'Liberty of the Press and Public Opinion' in JR Jones (ed), *Liberty Secured? Britain Before and After 1688* (Stanford, CA, Stanford University Press, 1992) 199, 202.

[10] Siebert, *Freedom of the Press in England 1476–1776* (n 3) 171, and M Rose, *Authors and Owners* (Cambridge, MA Harvard University Press, 1995) 22–23.

[11] SB Dobranski, *Milton, Authorship and the Book Trade* (Cambridge, CUP, 1999) ch 1, esp 16–20.

[12] WR Parker, *Milton: A Biography* (G Campbell (ed), Oxford, OUP, 1996) 155–56, 167, 196, 219–22, and A Beer, *Milton* (London, Bloomsbury, 2008) 82–83, 90, 129, 140.

its author, though it did not disclose the printer or publisher.[13] Moreover, Milton argued there that licensing dishonoured authors and their work, and was an affront 'to the dignity and privilege of Learning'.[14] It also, Milton argued, created problems for an author if he wanted to alter the text after the work had been approved. But interestingly Milton had no quarrel with the earlier Ordinance of 1642, which had required that no book be printed without registering the name of the printer and author.[15] These requirements were enough to ensure that seditious and libellous material could be appropriately punished.

The licensing scheme against which Milton protested was ineffective, largely because of the turmoil of the Civil War.[16] But a comparable scheme introduced by the Parliamentary government in 1649 did manage to suppress unlicensed news-sheets and weeklies, at least for the first year or so after its enactment.[17] The Act of 20 September 1649 'against Unlicensed and Scandalous Books and Pamphlets, and for better regulating of Printing' required printers to imprint on the title page the author's name, 'with his quality and place of Residence', or the licenser's name where a licence was required (as it was for books, pamphlets and news-sheets), as well as the printer's own name and place of residence.[18] This measure eventually became less effective in controlling either Royalist material or the tracts issued by the radical Levellers, but it was revived in 1653.[19]

The Regulation of Printing Act 1662, generally known rather misleadingly as the Licensing Act,[20] was enacted soon after the Restoration of Charles II. It adopted much the same licensing principles as those in the Star Chamber Decree of 1637 and in the Civil War and Protectorate measures. It also restricted printing to the master printers of the Stationers Company in London and the university presses at Oxford and Cambridge, though the press established at York during the Civil War was allowed to continue; the master printers were to be limited to 20, a significant reduction on the

---

[13] The title page is reproduced in Beer, ibid 166, and Dobranksi, *Milton, Authorship and the Book Trade* (n 11) at 110.

[14] *Areopagitica*, republished in J Milton, *Prose Writings* (London, Dent, Everyman Paperback, 1958) 145, 167.

[15] Ibid 184.

[16] See J Frank, *The Beginnings of the English Newspaper 1620–1660* (Cambridge, MA, Harvard University Press, 1961) 32, 41–43.

[17] Ibid 197–98.

[18] British History Online: 'September 1649: An Act against Unlicensed and Scandalous Books and Pamphlets, and for better regulating of Printing' in CH Firth and RS Rait (eds), *Acts and Ordinances of the Interregnum, 1642–1660* (London, 1911) 245–54, available at www.british-history.ac.uk/no-series/acts-ordinances-interregnum/pp245-254. For commentary, see Siebert, *Freedom of the Press in England 1476–1776* (n 3) 222–23.

[19] Ibid 224–32 on the attempts by the Protectorate, 1649–60, to regulate the press.

[20] J Walker, 'The Censorship of the Press During the Reign of Charles II' (1950) 35 *History* 219, 224.

number which had existed during the previous two decades.[21] Clause VI of the 1662 Act required a printer to set his own name on every piece of writing, and to 'declare the Name of the Author ... if he be thereunto required by the Licenser'.[22] The Licensing Act remained in force (except for the period, 1679–85) for over 30 years, but was not renewed in 1695, primarily because the House of Commons accepted the printing trade's argument that the legislation limited its commercial freedom by privileging those printers who were members of the Stationers Company.[23] Since then, any system of licensing for the press and other printed material has been resisted as contrary to freedom of the press, though this argument of principle had played little part in the non-renewal in 1695 of the 1662 Act.

Without a licensing system and any regulation of the printing presses, more attention had to be given to effective enforcement of the criminal laws of seditious and blasphemous libel in order to stop the spread of subversive literature.[24] Further, there was more such literature to control, for newspapers (tri-weeklies and new daily papers) expanded in both number and circulation throughout the eighteenth century.[25] The anonymity of authors could be tolerated relatively easily, if the licensing system ensured that radical political and religious publications did not see the light of day, but that position was hardly tenable after 1695. Indeed, the relationship of licensing and author/printer anonymity had been appreciated before the lapse of the Licensing Act. When the renewal of the 1662 Licensing Act was debated in 1693, an amendment was unsuccessfully moved in the House of Lords by three aristocratic authors and literature patrons, under which no licence would be required for a book to be printed, provided it carried the names of its author and printer.[26] In 1704, Daniel Defoe argued that the name of the author, printer or bookseller should be affixed to any book or other publication, in order to ensure that someone would carry responsibility for a publication infringing the criminal law; that would remove the need for a licensing system, which could only be justified if it were difficult to identify the author of a book. Anyone found selling a book without the name of

---

[21] Ibid 225–26, and see Siebert, *Freedom of the Press in England 1476–1776* (n 3) 239–41.
[22] Ibid 238–41.
[23] GC Gibbs, 'Press and Public Opinion: Prospective' in JR Jones (ed), *Liberty Secured? Britain Before and After 1688* (Stanford, CA, Stanford University Press, 1992) 231, 236–37. For a fuller account, see R Astbury, 'The Renewal of the Licensing Act in 1693 and its Lapse in 1695' (1978) 33 *The Library* 296, 314–16.
[24] P Hamburger, 'The Development of the Law of Seditious Libel and the Control of the Press' (1985) 37 *Stanford Law Review* 666, 722–24 argues that there was increased reliance on prosecutions for seditious libel to control subversive publications after the lapse of the Licensing Act.
[25] Gibbs, 'Press and Public Opinion' (n 23) 241; RB Walker, 'The Newspaper Press in the Reign of William III' (1974) 17 *Historical Journal* 691, 698–702; J Black, *The English Press in the Eighteenth Century* (Aldershot, Gregg Revivals, 1991) 12–14; H Barker, *Newspapers, Politics and English Society 1695–1855* (Harlow, Longman, 2000) ch 2.
[26] Astbury, 'The Renewal of the Licensing Act in 1693' (n 23) 302–3.

the author affixed would be deemed to be its author.[27] Authors would be encouraged to state their name on a book because they would then enjoy the property rights conferred by the recent Copyright Act 1710.[28]

Anonymous publications frequently caused concern in the early eighteenth century. John Asgil, a libertarian lawyer, opposed measures to re-introduce licensing, but argued (ironically in an anonymous pamphlet) that authors should be required to identify themselves, as anonymity was responsible for 'licentiousness'.[29] In 1712, a Bill was drafted to compel the registration of all printing presses and the disclosure of the names of authors, printers and publishers, but it lapsed when Parliament was prorogued in July that year.[30] Bills prohibiting the anonymity of authors met strong opposition.[31] Joseph Addison, writing as a 'Tory Author' opposed any restriction on anonymity; he argued that it would discourage important contributions to political debate.[32] As an alternative to the lapsed Bill, the government led by the Earl of Oxford, formerly Robert Harley, introduced a stamp duty under the Stamp Act of 1712, which required publishers of all newspapers and pamphlets to register their publications with the Stamp Office and to disclose their names and addresses in them; it also imposed a charge on newspapers depending on their size, and taxes on advertisements in the press.[33] But it did not require disclosure of authors' names. The measure was designed to raise revenue to fund a public lottery and to reduce the volume of opposition propaganda.[34]

One reason for tolerating anonymous writing (very widespread in the early eighteenth century)[35] is that prosecutions for seditious libel could easily be brought against printers, publishers and booksellers. Although identified authors were sometimes prosecuted, it was far more common to take proceedings against printers for seditious libel, as it had been in the seventeenth century for infringement of the licensing requirements.[36] Publishers

---

[27] *An Essay on the Regulation of the Press* (1704) in *Political and Economic Writings of Daniel Defoe* (WR Owens and PN Furbank (ed), London, Pickering and Chatto, 2000) vol 8, 145–59. Hamburger, 'The Development of the Law of Seditious Libel' (n 24) 744, n 256, argues that this did not represent Defoe's real view, but reflected his gratitude for a lenient sentence after he had been convicted of seditious libel in 1703.

[28] M Rose, *Authors and Owners* (Cambridge, MA, Harvard University Press, 1995) 34–36.

[29] *An Essay for the Press* (London, 1712): for discussion, see LW Levy, *Emergence of a Free Press* (New York, OUP, 1984) 104.

[30] JA Downie, *Robert Harley and the Press: Propaganda and Public Opinion in the Age of Swift and Defoe* (Cambridge, CUP, 1979) 150.

[31] Gibbs, 'Press and Public Opinion' (n 23) 239.

[32] *Thoughts of a Tory Author, Concerning the Press* (1712), discussed by Levy, *Emergence of a Free Press* (n 29) 107.

[33] Siebert, *Freedom of the Press in England 1476–1776* (n 3) 306–12; Gibbs, 'Press and Public Opinion' (n 23) 240–41.

[34] Downie, *Robert Harley and the Press* (n 30) 158–61.

[35] Ibid 13–14.

[36] Hamburger, 'The Development of the Law of Seditious Libel' (n 24) 681, 687–90, 717–19; see also Schwoerer, 'Liberty of the Press and Public Opinion' (n 9) 207–8, and Walker, 'The Censorship of the Press' (n 20) 233–35 discussing the *Twyn* case (1664) when a printer was

and booksellers could also be prosecuted, while, if necessary, measures could be taken against hawkers and the coffee houses where newspapers were read.[37] Obviously, it was much easier to identify a printer or bookseller than an author who was keen to remain anonymous, and then to search the printing premises or a publishing house and confiscate the press and offending copies.[38] There was a rebuttable presumption that a printer was aware of the contents of any seditious material he had printed, while its publication provided evidence of the required malice, so there was generally little difficulty in establishing guilt.[39] Further, a successful prosecution of a printer or bookseller would probably have a greater deterrent effect on the circulation of subversive literature than the conviction of an individual author.

The best known example of prosecutions for seditious libel of printers and a bookseller in the eighteenth century concerns the anonymous *Letters of Junius*, written in 1769.[40] Letter 35 was particularly incendiary; it called on George III to dismiss his ministers and to pardon John Wilkes, the author of radical articles in the *North Briton*, and warned the King not to follow the example of the Stuart monarchs who had lost their throne.[41] Five printers of the Letter, which first appeared in the *Public Advertiser*, and which was then reproduced in other newspapers and a monthly journal, were charged with seditious libel, but they were either acquitted or found guilty 'of printing and publishing only', though not of publishing a libel.[42] Only the bookseller, John Almon, was convicted of this offence, and then fined and bound over to be good behaviour for two years.[43]

The origins of the modern law requiring the disclosure of printers' names and addresses on printed material can be traced back to the legislation introduced during the Napoleonic wars at the end of the eighteenth century when there was great anxiety over the publication of radical literature, which was sympathetic to the Jacobins and the French Revolution.[44] The Newspaper

---

convicted of treason and hung, drawn and quartered, though he may not have known the contents of the offending publication.

[37] Schwoerer, 'Liberty of the Press and Public Opinion' (n 9) 215–16.

[38] Black, *The English Press in the Eighteenth Century* (n 25) 157–61.

[39] Hamburger, 'The Development of the Law of Seditious Libel' (n 24) 700–8 discusses the elements of the offence of seditious libel.

[40] See chapter 2, section V for discussion of the real author of the *Letters*.

[41] For extracts from the text of Letter 35, see S Ayling, *George the Third* (London, Colllins, 1972).

[42] At that time judges claimed the right to determine whether a publication was seditious or not, a matter which under Fox's Libel Act 1792 is determined by the jury.

[43] Siebert, *Freedom of the Press in England 1476–1776* (n 3) 385–89; Black, *The English Press in the Eighteenth Century* (n 25) 177–78.

[44] C Manchester, 'The Newspapers, Printers and Reading Rooms Repeal Act 1869: A Case for Repeal?' (1982) 2 *Legal Studies* 180, 181–86. Also see Barker, *Newspapers, Politics and English Society 1695–1855* (n 25) 69–70.

Publication Act 1798 was enacted 'for preventing the mischiefs arising from the printing and publishing newspapers, and papers of a like nature, by persons not known';[45] it obliged the Stamp Office to send stamped paper for the publication of newspapers only to persons known to the Commissioners, and required the 'true and real' names and addresses of its printer and publisher to be stated on each copy of the paper.[46] The Unlawful Societies Act 1799 tightened these requirements by requiring the registration of all printing presses, and the disclosure of the names and addresses of the printers and publishers on all printed material (books, pamphlets and every category of paper) as well as the newspapers and comparable papers covered by the earlier legislation.[47] Penalties were imposed on anyone publishing or dispersing any material which did not comply with the disclosure obligation. It is not clear why these provisions did not also require disclosure of the names of authors and editors, though the use of pseudonyms during the late eighteenth century was very common, particularly in letters to the editor;[48] it seems reasonable to conjecture that, as in previous periods, it was thought that imposing requirements on printers would be the most effective method of discouraging the circulation of radical and subversive material.[49]

The disclosure obligation imposed in the Act of 1799 was preserved in amending legislation, the Printers and Publishers Act 1839, though it reduced the penalty for non-compliance with the obligation to print the name and address of the printer from £20 for each offending copy to £5.[50] It also required proceedings under it to be brought in the name of the Attorney General or the Solicitor-General, so removing the opportunities for private prosecutions.[51] These requirements have been preserved in the present law. There is an obligation to disclose the name and address of printers, but not the author of any printed paper. Two witnesses to the House of Lords Committee, which was set up to review the law of defamation and criminal libel in 1843, considered authors should be encouraged to acknowledge by signature publications for which they were responsible; anonymity allowed

---

[45] This is the long title of the Act.

[46] Newspaper Publication Act 1798, s X.

[47] Unlawful Societies Act 1799, ss XXVI and XXVII. For discussion of these provisions and their implications, see A Aspinall, *Politics and the Press c 1780–1850* (London, Home and Van Thal, 1949) 38–40; C Emsley, 'Repression, "Terror" and the Rule of Law During the Decade of the French Revolution' (1985) 99 *English Historical Review* 801, 817–19.

[48] See H Barker, *Newspapers, Politics and Public Opinion in Late Eighteenth Century England* (Oxford, OUP, 1998) 38–40 and 79–80, where it is pointed out that letter writers often used classical Roman pseudonyms (eg Cato, Gracchus, Brutus) to remind readers of the ideas of republicanism and democracy.

[49] Manchester, 'The Newspapers, Printers and Reading Rooms Repeal Act 1869' (n 44) 181–82.

[50] Printers and Publishers Act 1839, s 2.

[51] Ibid s 4. See Manchester, 'The Newspapers, Printers and Reading Rooms Repeal Act 1869' (n 44) 182.

them to commit libel with impunity.[52] But the Committee did not adopt any recommendation to discourage anonymity, and no obligation to disclose authors' names was imposed by the Libel Act 1843. Indeed, no attempt has been made to require by legislation the automatic disclosure of the name of an author since the early eighteenth century, although steps can be taken in litigation to compel the revelation of his identity.[53]

III. LEGAL POSITION TODAY

The obligation to disclose the name and address of the printer of any paper or book has been kept in force by Schedule 2 to the Newspapers, Printers and Reading Rooms Repeal Act 1869. Any publisher or person responsible for dispersing copies of material not complying with that obligation is liable to a fine of £5 for each offending copy.[54] Newspapers must register their titles, and the names, occupations, places of business and residences of their proprietors.[55] These requirements ensure that libel and other claimants can identify someone on whom writs may be served. But there is no comparable obligation to disclose the name and address of authors, who are therefore free to write anonymously or under a pseudonym.

But what is the legal weight of this freedom? English law has traditionally treated freedom of speech, or expression, as a bare or residual liberty, existing only insofar as the laws of, say, obscenity, libel and contempt of court have not restricted its exercise. The freedom lives, as it were, in the gaps of the criminal and civil law. Sometimes, however, the courts have invoked a stronger, active principle of freedom of speech to place a narrow interpretation on legislation, so that it interferes as little as possible with exercise of the freedom.[56] The courts have also articulated a common law right to freedom of speech, when they formulated and developed the defences of fair comment and public interest privilege to libel actions,[57]

---

[52] Report of the Committee with Minutes of Evidence, 31 July 1843, para 5 (Lord Brougham and Vaux, Lord Chancellor 1830–34), and paras 787–97 (John Robertson, former editor of the *Westminster Review*).

[53] See chapter 5, section III, and chapter 6, section III.

[54] *Attorney-General v Beauchamp* [1920] 1 KB 650 held that publishers, as well as printers, were liable for the offence, although on a literal interpretation of the complex provision in the 1839 Act, preserved under the Schedule to the 1869 legislation, the penalty might appear only to apply to printers: Manchester, 'The Newspapers, Printers and Reading Rooms Repeal Act 1869' (n 44) 185–86.

[55] Newspaper Libel and Registration Act 1881, s 9.

[56] *Brutus v Cozens* [1973] AC 854, where the House of Lords held that the word 'insulting' in the public order legislation should not be interpreted to penalise the use of offensive language during an anti-apartheid demonstration at Wimbledon.

[57] See *Silkin v Beaverbrook Newspapers Ltd* [1958] 1 WLR 743, per Diplock J; *Spiller v Joseph* [2011] 1 AC 852, paras 107–8 (fair comment defence); *Reynolds v Times Newspapers Ltd* [2001] 2 AC 127, HL; and *Jameel v Wall Street Journal Europe* [2007] 1 AC 359, HL (qualified privilege).

and when they declined to grant an injunction to stop the showing of a distressing television programme in circumstances when there was no clear legal basis for the grant of such an order.[58] The Human Rights Act (HRA) 1998 incorporated the rights guaranteed by the European Convention on Human Rights (ECHR) into English law, including the right to freedom of expression protected by Article 10 of the Convention. Under the HRA 1998, courts must take account of the right when developing the common law,[59] and must interpret legislation in conformity with the right.[60] This has further strengthened the protection afforded freedom of expression, so it is no longer possible to regard it as a mere residual liberty. The courts must now consider its scope and meaning in a variety of circumstances, balancing its weight, for example, against the right to respect for private life which is also guaranteed by the ECHR.[61]

What is the significance of these developments in English law for the freedom to write anonymously? Does that freedom carry weight, so that any legislation which might be introduced to restrict its exercise, either generally or in particular circumstances, should be narrowly construed, although it could not be invalidated as it could be in the United States? As will be discussed at length later in this book, the recent Defamation Act 2013 provides website operators with a defence to libel actions where the operator did not itself post the allegedly defamatory statement on the website, as long as the claimant can identify the person who did post the statement or the operator takes steps to provide the claimant with the poster's full name and address or, if the poster prefers, to remove the statement from the website.[62] It will no longer be possible for anonymous posters to keep their defamatory statements up on websites without the co-operation of the website operator, which would then itself be exposed to liability; anonymous communication on the Internet is therefore to some extent discouraged. It is conceivable that these complex provisions could be challenged for limiting the freedom of anonymous speech, but an English court is unlikely to uphold an argument that they should not be applied when they are invoked to protect the victims of defamatory attacks.

There might be stronger protection for anonymous speech in English law if there was any indication that a free speech anonymity right had been upheld by the European Court of Human Rights in Strasbourg. An English court must take account of such a decision, though it would not be bound by the ruling of the European Court.[63] But the Strasbourg Court has so far

---

[58] See *R v Central Television plc* [1994] Fam 192, CA.
[59] HRA 1998, s 6(1), discussed in Barendt, 43.
[60] HRA 1998, s 3, discussed in Barendt, 44.
[61] As in the leading privacy decision of the House of Lords, *Campbell v MGN* [2004] 2 AC 457.
[62] Defamation Act 2013, s 5, and SI 2013/3028, discussed in chapter 6, section III.
[63] HRA 1998, s 2(1).

not been invited to hold a limit on anonymous speech incompatible with ECHR, Article 10, and it is unlikely that it would accept the invitation if it were presented. In these circumstances, a state would probably make a persuasive argument for restricting an anonymity freedom, for example, on the basis of its need to protect the effective exercise of the right to privacy (including the right to reputation) which requires in some circumstances, as under the UK Defamation Act 2013 explained in the previous paragraph, disclosure of the speaker's identity.

However, the Court has recently expressed some support for freedom of anonymous speech in its decisions in *Delfi AS v Estonia*.[64] The issue in that case was whether there had been an infringement of the freedom of expression of the owner of Delfi, an Internet news portal service, when it was required by the courts in Estonia to compensate the victim of threatening and defamatory comments which had been posted on its service, even though it operated a notice-and-take down procedure when readers complained of these messages. In upholding the compatibility of the Estonian Supreme Court's ruling with the ECHR, the Grand Chamber of the Court said '[it] is mindful … of the interest of Internet users in not disclosing their identity.'[65] Anonymity promoted the free flow of ideas and information, particularly on the Internet. So it rejected Delfi's argument that defamation victims must bring libel proceedings against the authors of the comments after the identity of the latter had been established.[66] The importance of anonymity on the Net has also been emphasised by other Council of Europe institutions. A Declaration of the Council of Ministers on freedom of communication on the Internet, considered by the Court in the *Delfi* case,[67] states that the desire of users of the Net not to disclose their identity should be respected to ensure protection against online surveillance and 'to enhance the free expression of information and ideas'.[68] An earlier Recommendation had called for recognition of anonymity in the context of Internet communications as an aspect of personal privacy protection.[69] But these provisions stop well short of recognition of a *right* to anonymity on the Net, let alone the constitutional right to anonymous speech which has been upheld in the United States; they would not appreciably strengthen an argument for recognition of such a right in English law.

---

[64] Application no 64569/09, Decision of First Section Chamber of the Court, 10 October 2013, (2014) 58 EHRR 29, upheld by the Grand Chamber of the Court in a Decision of 16 June 2015, [2015] EMLR 26; for further discussion of this case, see chapter 6, section III(D).

[65] [2015] EMLR 26, para 147.

[66] Ibid para 151.

[67] Ibid para 44.

[68] Declaration of Council of Ministers adopted on 28 May 2003, Principle 7 (Anonymity).

[69] Recommendation (99) 5 of the Committee of Ministers, For the Protection of Privacy on the Internet, 23 February 1999, Guidelines 3 and 4.

A right to anonymity as an aspect of personal privacy has been considered in one recent English case. In *Author of a Blog v Times Newspapers Ltd*,[70] Eady J rejected the claim of a blogger, known as 'Night Jack', for an interim injunction to stop *The Times* from revealing his identity; the blog, which had been awarded the Orwell Prize for citizen journalism in 2009, discussed the claimant's work as a serving police officer and was severely critical of both government ministers and of police operations. The judge rejected the claim on the ground that 'blogging is essentially a public rather than a private activity',[71] so the claimant had no reasonable expectation of privacy, a threshold requirement for a successful action for misuse of private information. But even if that requirement had been satisfied, Eady J ruled that the privacy right would be outweighed by the public interest in the revelation that a particular police officer was expressing strong criticism of political figures and of the police itself.[72]

The claim was argued in terms of the blogger's right to privacy, but that case was supported by freedom of expression arguments; it was said by his counsel, Hugh Tomlinson, QC, that the claimant and other bloggers would be 'horrified' if their anonymity could not be protected against unmasking,[73] and that revelation of their identity would inhibit their rights to impart information and ideas guaranteed by ECHR, Article 10.[74] Eady J did not explicitly accept or reject these free expression points, though he did uphold the defendant newspaper's argument that the public was entitled to know who the author of the blog was in order to assess the strength of his criticisms of the police force in which he was serving.[75] That interpretation of freedom of expression would run counter to the case for a speaker's right to anonymity; as explained in the previous chapter, readers and audiences have an interest in credible speech and therefore in knowing the identity of the speaker.[76] The decision in the *Author of a Blog* case is far from a definitive ruling, but it certainly suggests that the freedom of anonymous speech has little more weight today than it has traditionally enjoyed in English law. Further, it should be noted that even if there is a Convention right to freedom of anonymous speech, it is unclear that it would be protected against interference from a private person or organisation, as distinct from the state or public authority.[77] This is particularly doubtful when the private

---

[70] [2009] EMLR 22.
[71] Ibid paras 11 and 33.
[72] Ibid paras 21–23 and 33.
[73] Ibid para 4.
[74] Ibid para 18.
[75] Ibid para 21.
[76] See chapter 3, section IV.
[77] Under the HRA 1998, s 6(1), it is unlawful for public authorities to act incompatibly with Convention rights, but private individuals and organisations are not directly bound in the same way.

organisation is a newspaper, which itself can claim the protection of the freedom of expression guarantee.

However, it can be argued that the decision in *Author of a Blog* makes nonsense of the journalists' privilege not to disclose their sources of information, under which the anonymity of sources is strongly, though not absolutely, protected.[78] The point is that if the blogger had gone to *The Times* with his criticisms of government ministers and the police force, it might have published them and then refused to disclose the identity of its source. It would have argued that the importance of the story outweighed any interest the police force had in unmasking its employee. Eady J's decision appears on one view to have the effect of unduly privileging the institutional media; it is entitled to claim immunity from disclosing its sources, while it is also free to identify a citizen journalist who independently publishes a story for which it could claim journalists' privilege. The relationship of the journalists' privilege to keep their sources confidential to the freedom of anonymous speech is considered in the next chapter; if journalists act as responsible intermediaries, checking the reliability of their sources, then the privilege can be justified, even if we remain sceptical of the case for a right to anonymous speech.[79]

IV. ANONYMOUS WHISTLE-BLOWING IN ENGLISH LAW

Whistle-blowing has been protected in the United Kingdom since the passage of the Public Interest Disclosure Act 1998. The law was introduced after it became clear from a number of public inquiries into disasters during the 1980s and 1990s that often staff had known of the risks which had led to the tragedy, but had hesitated to speak out because they feared that this would put their job in jeopardy.[80] Under the provisions of the 1998 legislation, which have subsequently been incorporated in the Employment Rights Act (ERA) 1996,[81] employees are protected against dismissal for making a 'qualifying disclosure', provided that certain specified conditions are satisfied.[82] A 'qualifying disclosure' means the disclosure of information which the employee reasonably believes to be in the public interest,[83] and

---

[78] For this argument, see E Barendt, 'Bad News for Bloggers' (2009) 2 *Journal of Media Law* 141, 146–47.

[79] See chapter 5, in particular section III.

[80] A Myers, 'Whistleblowing: The UK Experience' in R Calland and G Dehn (eds), *Whistleblowing Around the World* (Open Democracy Advice Centre and Public Concern at Work in partnership with British Council, South Africa, 2004) 101–5.

[81] ERA 1996, ss 43A–43H. For a full account of the legal provisions, see J Bowers, *Whistleblowing Law and Practice*, 2nd edn (J Bowers, M Fodder, J Lewis and J Mitchell (eds), Oxford, OUP, 2012).

[82] ERA 1996, s 103A.

[83] The 'public interest' requirement was inserted into the ERA 1996 by the Enterprise and Regulatory Reform Act 2013, s 17.

which tends to show one of a number of facts, for example, that a crime has been or is likely to be committed; that the health or safety of anyone has been or is likely to be put in danger; that the environment is being or is likely to be damaged; or that any of these (and other specified) matters has been, or is likely to be, covered up.[84] The conditions for protection are more onerous for a disclosure to a regulator or for a public disclosure than they are for disclosure to the employer itself. They are most strict for public disclosure, for example, to the media, requiring, among other things, the employee to show that it was not made for personal gain, that it was reasonable to make the wider disclosure, and that one of three further conditions is satisfied—one of them being that the worker reasonably feared victimisation if disclosure was made to the employer.[85]

Some employees will only be prepared to blow the whistle if their identity is not disclosed to their managers or to other members of staff; they may fear reprisals from colleagues, even if their allegations are substantially true and they themselves are in no danger of dismissal from their work.[86] It is clear from a number of decisions of the Employment Appeal Tribunal (EAT), which hears appeals from employment tribunal decisions on whether an employee has been dismissed unfairly, that anonymous allegations must be investigated seriously and may lead to the proper dismissal of the employee against whom they were made. Guidelines for dealing with them were given by the EAT in *Linford Cash and Carry Ltd v Thomson and Bell*,[87] where the informant insisted that his identity should not disclosed because he feared reprisals. He was interviewed by the security officer, but declined to appear at the hearing before the regional officer where his allegations against two colleagues were considered. Wood J, the President of the EAT, emphasised that a careful balance must be struck between the protection of an inform-ant who was genuinely afraid of reprisals and the provision of a fair hearing for the employees accused of dishonesty. An anonymous informant should provide a detailed statement in writing, though some parts of it might be omitted or erased when it was shown to the accused employees to prevent his identification. Enquiries should be made into the character and back-ground of the informant, and it should be noted whether he had any reason to fabricate his allegations, whether out of a personal grudge or from mis-guided principle. The person in management responsible for conducting the hearing should usually himself interview the informant.

In a later decision, the EAT emphasised that, when investigating alle-gations that a manager had used hard drugs, it was appropriate for an employer to give a promise of confidentiality to an informant who did not

---

[84] ERA 1996, s 43B.
[85] Ibid s 43G.
[86] For the arguments of principle for protecting a right to anonymity in these circumstances, see chapter 3, section V(B).
[87] [1989] IRLR 235.

want his identity to be revealed. Moreover, knowledge of his identity was not necessary for a fair hearing of the allegations made against other employees. Their representative could cross-examine the investigating officer who had looked into the whistle-blower's allegations.[88] The guidelines in *Linford* should be treated flexibly, so that in the *Ramsey* case[89] it was held that the employment tribunal could properly hold it was enough for the informant to be interviewed by a human resources manager; it was not necessary for the other managers involved in the disciplinary process to see him. Moreover, in a departure from the *Linford* guidelines, the informant's statement need not provide details about the nature and location of his job, or of the date and time of the incident leading to his allegations, where these details would enable discovery of his identity. But the EAT appreciated that allowing anonymity limited the ability of employees accused (as in the *Ramsey* case itself) of criminal conduct to meet the allegations.[90]

In all these cases it was perhaps misleading for the allegation to have been characterised as 'anonymous'. At least, they were not absolutely anonymous, for someone in the organisation (in *Ramsey* the human resources manager) knew the informant's identity. A distinction should be drawn between a *confidential* disclosure, as in the cases discussed in the two previous paragraphs, and a wholly *anonymous* allegation. This distinction is made in the Code of Practice recommended by the Whistleblowing Commission set up by Public Concern at Work (PCaW)[91] to review whistle-blowing arrangements and to make proposals for good employer practice in this area. Written procedures for raising and handling concerns should require an assurance to be given to workers that their identity will be kept confidential if requested;[92] confidentiality should be 'a clear option for anyone to use when raising a concern'.[93] An organisation should also assess a completely anonymous statement of concern, where no name is given at all, as best it can to see whether it has any merit, but the Commission clearly thought it was better to encourage a culture at work where concerns could be raised openly to reduce the risk of anonymous, or malicious, leaks.[94]

It may, of course, be much more difficult for an employer to investigate an anonymous statement of concern, although that is not always the case. Nor is it really material whether it was made out of spite; the real question is whether the allegation was true or not.[95] The Chief Executive of PCaW

---

[88] *Asda Stores v Thompson* [2012] IRLR 245, paras 15–16.
[89] *Ramsey v Walker Snack Foods* [2004] IRLR 754.
[90] Ibid para 55 per Judge Ansell, President of the EAT.
[91] PCaW is a charity set up in 1993 to support and advise whistle-blowers and to encourage employers to establish effective whistle-blowing procedures at their place of work.
[92] Draft Code of Practice, cl 5(d).
[93] Ibid cl 9.
[94] *Report of the Whistleblowing Commission on the effectiveness of existing arrangements for workplace whistleblowing in the UK* (2013), para 8.
[95] Interview with Cathy James, Chief Executive of PCaW, on 7 March 2014.

thought that about 10–11 per cent of the 3,000 calls to her organisation's telephone advice line each year were made anonymously; they could sometimes be properly investigated, although it was much harder to keep in touch with an anonymous complainant.[96] It is difficult, if not impossible, to get clarification of the details of an anonymous statement of concern and to provide the feedback which reassures the employee that the employer has taken his concerns seriously. For these reasons an informal Code of Practice for whistle-blowing drafted by PCaW in 2008 considers that employer whistle-blowing policies should not encourage concerns to be raised anonymously.[97] Open whistle-blowing is the ideal, as it enables the organisation to investigate the concern fully and 'to minimize the risk of a sense of mistrust or paranoia developing'.[98] But a whistle-blowing policy should provide for employees to approach someone with their concerns confidentially, though the organisation should make it clear that other employees may try to discover the identity of a whistle-blower.[99] In contrast to this approach, US law requires private corporation employers to provide facilities for fully anonymous allegations under the Sarbanes-Oxley Act which was enacted in 2002 in response to the Enron and other corporate scandals; anonymous speech, as we have seen,[100] is fully protected in the United States under the First Amendment, though the constitutional right does not bind private employers,[101] so this legislation extends the scope of the right to speak anonymously.[102]

The approach to anonymous whistle-blowing taken by Public Concern at Work, and in the context of litigation by the EAT, is coherent and can be supported. While open whistle-blowing represents much the best means of raising a concern at work, arrangements should be made for confidential reports in order to protect employees from reprisals from their colleagues as well as from management. There is a great deal of evidence to show that workers fail to speak up when they might otherwise raise their concerns, because they fear reprisals and ostracism by fellow employees.[103] A sensitive and responsible human resources officer, as in the *Ramsey* case discussed above, may act as an intermediary to verify the credibility of the employee

---

[96] Information provided in email from Cathy James, 1 June 2015.

[97] *Whistleblowing Arrangements*, Code of Practice drafted by PCaW in collaboration with British Standards Institution (BSI) (London, BSI, 2008) paras 3.5.4 and 4.6.

[98] Ibid para 3.5.2.

[99] Ibid para 3.5.3.

[100] See chapter 3, section II.

[101] Under the 'state action' doctrine, constitutional rights are only directly protected against infringement by federal or State laws or other government action: see E Barendt, 'State Action, Constitutional Rights and Private Actors' in D Oliver and J Fedtke (eds), *Human Rights and the Private Sphere* (Abingdon and New York, Routledge-Cavendish, 2007) ch 13.

[102] See TM Dworkin, 'SOX and Whistleblowing' (2007) 105 *Michigan Law Review* 1757 for a critical analysis of the Sarbanes-Oxley Act.

[103] *Report of the Whistleblowing Commission* (n 94) paras 27–28.

raising the concern, and more importantly to check whether his allegations are substantially accurate—even perhaps to warrant the dismissal of the employees against whom they are made. It is much more difficult to make comparable checks when concerns are raised in complete anonymity. While it would be wrong totally to disregard anonymous whistle-blowing, employer policies should not encourage it. As we will see in the next chapter, the distinction between the making of confidential and fully anonymous allegations can also be drawn when sources, whether or not they are whistle-blowers, give the press and other media stories—when it is journalists and editors, rather than human resources managers, who have to assume the role of responsible intermediaries.

5

The Protection of Anonymous Sources

I. INTRODUCTION

THE PRECEDING CHAPTER has shown that there is no strong right to speak or write anonymously in English law (see chapter 4, section III), in contrast to the position in the United States where a constitutional right to anonymous speech is guaranteed by the First Amendment (see chapter 3, section II). The bare freedom to write anonymously or to use a pseudonym is not explicitly recognised by any legislation in the United Kingdom, let alone by any provision in a constitution. But legislation does uphold a qualified right to anonymous speech through the media; section 10 of the Contempt of Court Act (CCA) 1981 provides that a court may not require a person responsible for a publication to disclose the source of information contained in it, unless it is established that disclosure is necessary for one of four specified purposes. So in this indirect way English law does appear to recognise the value of anonymous speech.[1]

This privilege not to reveal sources is not confined by the CCA 1981 to professional journalists, for it can be claimed by anyone responsible for a publication (for example, the editor of a parish newsletter) but in practice it is almost always used by the institutional media, and so it is invariably referred to, rather misleadingly, as 'the journalists' privilege not to disclose their sources'. The principle has been recognised by the Codes of Practice of the National Union of Journalists and of the Press Complaints Commission;[2] it is now incorporated into the Code of the new Independent Press Standards Organization, set up by most of the national newspaper industry in its response to recommendations in the Leveson Report.[3] Newspapers frequently rely on anonymous sources, variously identified, for instance, only as 'Whitehall sources', 'a government spokesman', 'some analysts' or

---

[1] The CCA 1981 applies throughout the United Kingdom, so this chapter draws contrasts between the legal position in the United Kingdom and that in the United States and in Canada.
[2] NUJ Code, art 7; Press Complaints Commission Code, art 14.
[3] HC 780, 2012.

'a close friend'.[4] To give a concrete example, in August 2014 (the time of writing this chapter) the *Guardian* reported that:

> sources have told [it] that ... publication [of an official report into the causes of a horsemeat scandal] has been blocked amid government concerns that the public would be frightened by the idea that criminals were still able to interfere with their food.[5]

In a very small handful of cases information may be provided by a wholly anonymous source,[6] but normally the journalist knows the identity of the source, with whom he may be extremely familiar; but the source's anonymity is preserved when the story is reported.

The principal question discussed in this chapter is why UK law recognises, and is right to recognise, a privilege—in practice claimed by professional journalists—not to disclose sources of information, and yet has, at least hitherto, not recognised a freedom of anonymous speech comparable to that upheld in the United States. One explanation is, of course, that the media constitutes a powerful lobby, which is able to make a persuasive case for recognition of journalists' privilege in the public interest; it is contended that, without an assurance that their identity will not be disclosed, sources will be reluctant to provide the media with stories, and as a result information of real public interest will not be published. There is no equivalent lobby for a strong freedom to write anonymously. But the media argument assumes that sources do, at least generally, provide important and accurate information which should be published in the public interest; this argument is much weaker, indeed virtually collapses, if it is clear that sources (perhaps government spokesmen) often manipulate journalists to publish stories which are misleading or distorted. Malicious sources might even be indirectly responsible for the publication in a newspaper of commercial fraud or of defamatory allegations.

It is these dangers which make unpersuasive the argument for a strong right to anonymous speech (see chapter 3, sections III and IV). The argument for source anonymity is therefore attractive only if journalists and editors act as responsible intermediaries who vouch for the credibility of the sources on which they rely and for the accuracy of the information given them—in the same way that a human resources manager may investigate and check a whistle-blower's allegations (and motives) and can then properly assure him that his identity will not be disclosed (see chapter 4, section IV). In these circumstances the dangers of anonymous speech would largely be averted, so readers and viewers can be confident that they are looking at accurate information from reliable sources.

---

[4] See the article by Roy Greenslade, *Guardian*, 23 February 2004.
[5] 'Row as horsemeat file shelved', *Guardian*, 17 August 2014.
[6] Two cases in a few years for a major newspaper group. (Interview with a newspaper lawyer conducted in August 2014.)

Section II of this chapter looks first at the UK law on the privilege of journalists not to disclose their sources of information. The object is not to provide an exhaustive statement of the law, which is well set out in other books,[7] but to bring out its main principles, especially important points made by English courts when they have assessed how the privilege should be balanced against various interests in disclosing the source's identity: the safeguarding of national security, the prevention of crime or an employer's interest in dismissing a rogue employee. The section also briefly examines US and Canadian law in this area, discussing in particular a famous case involving Judith Miller, a reporter for the *New York Times*, which nicely illustrates some of the difficulties in accepting without reservation the argument for a strong journalists' privilege.[8]

The arguments of principle concerning the privilege are fully considered in section III of the chapter. It will give examples of almost certainly inaccurate, or irresponsible, stories emanating from anonymous sources, for instance, the reports in US and UK newspapers before the invasion of Iraq in 2003 that Saddam Hussain had weapons of mass destruction. Section III will also examine the development of ethical codes in the US media to ensure that anonymous sources are used responsibly, and of comparable principles in the United Kingdom. Without such checks on the use of anonymous sources, it may be difficult to accept the case even for the qualified legal privilege not to disclose the identity of media sources recognised by the UK CCA 1981, let alone the absolute claim made by journalists in their professional codes. Finally, section IV considers how far the privilege should be extended, as it is under the CCA 1981, beyond professional journalists, so it can be claimed by bloggers, website operators and others who disseminate stories given them by anonymous sources.

II. LAW ON JOURNALISTS' PRIVILEGE

A. UK Law

A qualified statutory privilege is provided by CCA 1981, section 10:

> No court may require a person to disclose, nor is any person guilty of contempt of court for refusing to disclose, the source of information in a publication for which he is responsible, unless it be established to the satisfaction of the court that disclosure is necessary in the interests of justice or national security or for the prevention of disorder or crime.

---

[7] In particular, see D Eady and ATH Smith, *Arlidge, Eady and Smith on Contempt*, 4th edn (London, Sweet and Maxwell, 2011) ch 9; G Robertson and A Nicol, *Media Law* (London, Penguin Books, 2008) ch 5, paras 5-052–5-071.

[8] *In re Grand Jury Subpoena (Judith Miller)*, 397 F3d 964 (DC Cir 2005).

At common law the courts had recognised only a limited discretion not to order the media to disclose its sources;[9] normally, it would be liable, like any other persons involved, albeit innocently, in wrongful conduct to assist a wronged party by disclosing the names of the wrongdoer, for example, by identifying a source who had leaked information in breach of its duty of confidence to its employer.[10] The CCA 1981 introduced a privilege not to identify a source of information, which could be overcome only if the applicant showed that disclosure is necessary for one of the four specified purposes: to prevent disorder; to prevent crime; to safeguard national security; or 'in the interests of justice'.

Before considering how the courts balance these purposes against the public interest in the protection of sources, a few points should be made. The first is that the courts give the provision a broad interpretation, so that it applies not only to direct orders to identify the source of information but also to orders to hand over documents from which the identity of the source, perhaps the person supplying the documents to the media, might be revealed. This was determined by the House of Lords in *Secretary of State for Defence v Guardian Newspaper*,[11] where an unknown source sent the newspaper confidential documents discussing how the government proposed to handle the controversy which, it anticipated, was likely to follow the arrival of Cruise missiles in Britain. (The documents had marks on them from which the identity of the persons who had handled them could be determined, and the leaker might be traced.)[12] The same principle was followed in *Interbrew SA v Financial Times Ltd*,[13] where the Court of Appeal ordered the newspaper to deliver up documents, sent to it by an unidentified source, purporting to contain details of the applicant's proposals to take over a rival company; there was no doubt that CCA 1981, section 10 applied, but delivery of the documents was ordered, largely because it was presumed the source had the maleficent purpose of damaging the applicant company and the investing public.[14] It should be noted that in both these cases fully anonymous speech was indirectly protected through the privilege created by the CCA 1981; at the relevant time the journalists concerned did not know the identity of the leaker, whose story they proceeded to publish.

---

[9] *British Steel Corp v Granada Television Ltd* [1981] AC 1096.

[10] This is known as the *Norwich Pharmacal* principle, after the case in which it was upheld by the House of Lords: *Norwich Pharmacal Co v Customs and Excise Commissioners* [1974] AC 133.

[11] [1985] AC 339, 349–50.

[12] The leaker was subsequently identified as Sarah Tisdall, a clerk in the Foreign Office, after the decision of the courts to compel the newspaper to return the documents on the ground that it was necessary in the interests of national security to prevent further leaks of confidential information.

[13] [2002] EMLR 24.

[14] Ibid para 55. Subsequently, the European Court of Human Rights held that the Court of Appeal ruling infringed the right to freedom of expression guaranteed by ECHR, Art 10: *Financial Times v United Kingdom* [2010] EMLR 21.

A second point, which would merit much fuller treatment in a comprehensive discussion of this area of law, is that English courts must now interpret and apply the privilege in the light of the European Convention on Human Rights (ECHR), Article 10 guarantee of freedom of expression, incorporated into UK law by the Human Rights Act 1998. In its landmark ruling in *Goodwin*, the European Court of Human Rights emphasised the importance of protection of journalistic sources for freedom of the press; orders requiring the disclosure of a source's identity 'cannot be compatible with Article 10 of the Convention unless it is justified by an overriding requirement in the public interest'.[15] The Court has consistently upheld applications challenging national decisions requiring the media to disclose the identity of its sources, notably in two UK cases.[16] (Indeed, this is one of the few areas of freedom of expression law where European jurisprudence is more generous than that of the United States with regard to exercise of the freedom; as section II(B) shows, courts in the United States have often declined to recognise a constitutional right to keep sources confidential.) The House of Lords has accepted that section 10 of the CCA 1981 shares the same purpose as the freedom of expression guarantee of the ECHR 'in seeking to enhance the freedom of the press by protecting journalistic sources', and that the approach of the European Court of Human Rights in *Goodwin* should be adopted in applying the UK statute.[17]

The last point is that it is for the party seeking disclosure of the source's identity to show that this is *necessary* for one of the four specified purposes, and 'necessary' has a meaning lying 'somewhere between "indispensable" on the one hand, and "useful" or "expedient" on the other'.[18] So disclosure will not be ordered if the applicant could obtain it by other means, for example, by making inquiries at the place where the leaked document went missing.[19] The presumption is that it is in the public interest to protect the anonymity of the source of the story, and it is for the applicant to overcome that presumption by showing an overriding public interest in disclosure of the source's identity.[20]

The courts consider a number of factors in balancing or weighing the two competing public interests: that in freedom of the press and anonymity of sources, on the one hand, and that in one of the four purposes specified in CCA 1981, section 10, on the other. Much the most important, and

[15] *Goodwin v United Kingdom* (1996) 21 EHRR 123, 143.

[16] Ibid and *Financial Times v United Kingdom* (n 14).

[17] *Ashworth Hospital Authority v MGN Ltd* [2002] 1 WLR 2033, HL, para 38.

[18] *Re an Inquiry under the Company Securities (Insider Dealing) Act 1985* [1988] AC 660, 704, per Lord Griffiths.

[19] *John v Express Newspapers* [2000] 3 All ER 257, CA.

[20] See the statement of principle by Laws LJ in *Ashworth Hospital Authority v MGN Ltd* [2001] 1 WLR 515, CA, para 101, approved on this point by Sedley LJ in *Interbrew SA* (n 13) para 32.

problematic, of the latter is 'in the interests of justice'. In the leading case, *X Ltd v Morgan Grampian Ltd*,[21] this phrase was interpreted to include circumstances in which the applicant was attempting to assert his legal rights and to protect himself against serious wrongs, by, for example, taking steps to dismiss a disloyal employee who had given the press confidential information about his work. Lord Bridge listed the types of factors to be considered in determining whether the applicant's interests trumped the public interest in preserving source anonymity. Among them are the importance of the information and the public interest in its publication and whether the source obtained the information legally or illegally. If, for example, the story was given to the media in breach of an employee's duty of confidence, disclosure of the source's identity would probably be ordered, unless there was a clear public interest in its publication, because it revealed corruption or other serious wrong-doing.[22]

The weight of the factors listed by Lord Bridge has been considered in subsequent cases. One view is that the nature of the information leaked to the media and published by it is irrelevant. 'The public interest in the non-disclosure of press sources is constant, whatever the merits of the particular publication, and the particular source.'[23] It is also immaterial whether the source was disloyal or leaked the story for money. Sedley LJ in the *Interbrew* case disagreed with this view. Although the source's motive (personal spite or conscience) might be irrelevant, it was pertinent to decide whether the purpose of the leak was to draw the public's attention to wrong-doing or 'to wreck legitimate commercial activity'.[24] A distinction should be drawn between information of real public interest and prurient information, say, about a celebrity's sex life given the media by a 'close friend'. A similar approach appears to have been taken in the *Ackroyd* case, when the Court of Appeal upheld the decision of Tugendhat J refusing to order a reputable investigative journalist, Robin Ackroyd, to disclose his source for the medical records of the Moors murderer, Ian Brady, which he had passed on to the *Daily Mirror*; the courts took into account Ackroyd's record as a journalist, and the apparent absence of a financial motive for the supply of the records by the source.[25]

This approach is surely preferable to the alternative view under which the character of the information and the source's purposes are wholly irrelevant. That view is as hard to support as the positions that all anonymous speech has the same value and that there is a strong right to speak (and write)

---

[21] [1991] 1 AC 1.
[22] Ibid 43–45.
[23] Laws LJ in *Ashworth Hospital Authority v MGN Ltd* (n 20) para 101.
[24] *Interbrew SA* (n 13) para 42.
[25] *Mersey Care NHS Trust v Ackroyd (No 2)* [2008] EMLR 1, CA, upholding the decision of Tugenhat J [2006] EMLR 12.

anonymously (considered in chapter 3). On these perspectives, the rights of anonymous speakers and of the press are likely to be overvalued to the cost of other interests; for example, the interest of readers in credible stories of public importance or the public's rights not to be deceived or defamed. The probable truth or falsity of the information provided by the source is surely also relevant to the balancing exercise. In the *Interbrew* case, Sedley LJ said that if the falsity of the leaked documents (or part of them) had been established, that would have been a strong, additional factor in favour of overriding the protection given to the source under the CCA 1981. There is no public interest in the spread of false information.[26] Of course, it will sometimes be unclear to the media at the time of publication, or even subsequently, whether the source has provided false information. When the European Court of Human Rights upheld the application by the *Financial Times* that the UK courts' order to deliver up the documents to Interbrew had infringed ECHR, Article 10, it said that judges should be slow to assume, in the absence of compelling evidence, that a source had acted for improper purposes or had intentionally provided false information.[27] The coherence of the journalists' privilege depends on the assumption that sources generally provide accurate stories of public importance; there is little justification for upholding the privilege when it is clear that the media has been provided with false information.

B. Law in the United States and Canada

In *Branzburg v Hayes*,[28] the Supreme Court in a 5–4 decision rejected the claim of three journalists that they had a right under the First Amendment to protect the confidentiality of their sources, and so could refuse to appear before a grand jury and answer questions which would identify their sources of information concerning drugs and other offences. In his opinion for the Court, White J doubted whether a refusal to uphold a constitutional privilege would imperil freedom of the press; history showed that the press could flourish and report stories of public importance without protection for the confidentiality of its sources. He was also anxious not to create a new reporters' testimonial privilege, which would not be shared by other citizens. For one familiar question, discussed in section IV below, is whether a privilege to keep sources confidential should be confined to reporters from the institutional media, or should also be enjoyed by bloggers, citizen-journalists and website operators when they provide information given them by unnamed sources.

---

[26] *Interbrew SA* (n 13) para 57.
[27] *Financial Times Ltd v United Kingdom* (n 14) para 63.
[28] 408 US 665 (1972).

As David Anderson, a prominent commentator on press freedom in the United States, has argued,[29] it would be wrong to conclude that in *Branzburg* the Supreme Court wholly foreclosed the possibility of any constitutional protection for a reporter's privilege. White J explicitly stated that newsgathering was covered by the First Amendment; moreover, he envisaged that Congress might introduce legislation for such a privilege and that State legislatures could frame appropriate levels of protection in this area. (By 2006, over 30 States and the District of Columbia had enacted 'shield laws', many of which provide journalists with a more or less absolute privilege not to disclose their sources;[30] now 40 States have enacted these laws.) The Court in *Branzburg* was rejecting a claim for a constitutional privilege which would in that case have entitled the journalists to refuse to answer questions in a criminal investigation. It was not a strong context in which to raise the constitutional claim. Sources often provide stories of real public importance, just as much anonymous speech is valuable and should not be restricted. But equally, sources 'can be used to circulate trivial gossip, baseless rumors or malicious assaults'.[31] A constitutional privilege would allow journalists to refuse to identify their sources in those contexts, as well as in others where such a claim would be much more appropriate; if it is properly understood, the decision in *Branzburg* can be supported.

The Supreme Court decision to reject the claim to a constitutional privilege has been followed in some later federal cases,[32] notably by the District of Columbia Circuit Court of Appeals in the well-known *Judith Miller* case, which merits discussion at some length.[33] In July 2003, a retired diplomat, former ambassador Joseph Wilson, wrote a feature article in the *New York Times* stating that the Central Intelligence Agency (CIA) had asked him in 2002 to investigate claims that Iraq had attempted to buy uranium in West Africa to develop nuclear weapons, but he had been unable to find any evidence to support them. The article in effect contradicted part of the Bush administration's argument that Saddam Hussein had been developing weapons of mass destruction (WMD). A week later Robert Novak,

---

[29] DA Anderson, 'Confidential Sources Reconsidered' (2009) 61 *Florida Law Review* 883.

[30] See J Brabyn, 'Protection against Judicially Compelled Disclosure of the Identity of News Gatherers' Confidential Sources in Common Law Jurisdictions' (2006) 69 *Modern Law Rev* 895, 911–12, and WE Lee, 'The Priestly Class: Reflections on a Journalist's Privilege' (2006) 23 *Cardozo Arts and Entertainment Law Review* 635, 664–85.

[31] Anderson, 'Confidential Sources Reconsidered' (n 29) 900.

[32] See, eg, *In re Grand Jury Proceedings*, 810 F2d 580 (6th Cir 1987) and *McKevitt v Pallasch*, 339 F3d 530 (7th Cir 2003). But other federal courts have upheld claims to the privilege in the circumstances of the case: see, eg, *Zerilli v Smith*, 656 F2d 705 (DC Cir 1981); *United States v Caporale*, 806 F2d 1487 (11th Cir 1986).

[33] *In re Grand Jury Subpoena, Judith Miller*, 438 F3d 1138 (DC Cir 2006), cert denied by the Supreme Court: 125 S Ct 2977 (2005). (The decision is also reported at 397 F3d 964 (DC Cir 2005), but the later report, to which subsequent references are made, contains some passages redacted from the earlier one.)

a conservative columnist for the *Chicago Sun-Times*, in an attempt to discredit Wilson's statement, reported that the former ambassador had been assigned the mission because his wife, Valerie Plame, was a CIA official working on Saddam's WMD programme. Novak later disclosed that his sources were 'two senior administration officials'.[34]

The Bush administration appointed an independent special prosecutor, Patrick Fitzgerald, to investigate the leaks of information; he subpoenaed several journalists to answer questions before a grand jury. All of them agreed to give evidence, except Matt Cooper who had written an article for *Time* magazine about the Plame affair referring to his conversations with unnamed administration sources, and Judith Miller, a leading international reporter for the *New York Times*, who had in fact not written about Plame. The DC Circuit Court of Appeals upheld the decision of the District Court requiring Cooper and Miller to disclose their sources. Both were held to be in contempt for refusing to do so, and Miller served 85 days in prison.[35] She was released after negotiations between her lawyers and Fitzgerald, when her source, Vice-Presidential Chief of Staff, Lewis 'Scooter' Libby, made clear that he voluntary waived anonymity and encouraged her to testify to the grand jury.[36]

The Circuit Court in this case accepted that *Branzburg* precluded recognition of a constitutional privilege to refuse to disclose confidential sources in a grand jury investigation, though Judge Tatel in his full concurring judgment was unsure whether the Supreme Court had ruled out a constitutional privilege in all circumstances. Moreover, in contrast to the other two judges, he held that a federal common law privilege should be recognised, but it would be inappropriate to uphold it here. In leak cases such as this, the courts should balance the public interest in disclosure and the public interest in news-gathering, weighing the harm caused by the leak (the damage to Valerie Palme's employment and to her CIA colleagues' covert work) against the news value of the report, which in his view was very slight.[37] This approach is apparently unusual in US cases; generally when applying State shield laws, or common law rules providing for the privilege, courts treat the journalists' interest in news-gathering as fixed. The strength of that interest does not vary according to the importance of the information provided by the source.[38]

[34] For accounts of the affair, see M Carlson, *On the Condition of Anonymity* (Urbana, IL, University of Illinois Press, 2011) 38–39 and 117–19, and E Wasserman, 'A Critique of Source Confidentiality' (2005) 19 *Notre Dame Journal of Law, Ethics and Public Policy* 553, 556–60.

[35] Cooper's employer, *Time* magazine, much to his disgust, surrendered his notes to the grand jury, shortly after the Supreme Court declined to hear the journalists' appeal from the DC Circuit Court decision.

[36] See Lee, 'The Priestly Class' (n 30) 638–39.

[37] *In re Grand Jury Subpoena, Judith Miller* (n 33) 1175, 1179.

[38] D Abramowicz, 'Calculating the Public Interest in Protecting Journalists' Confidential Sources' (2008) 108 *Columbia Law Review* 1949, 1961–65.

Two other points in Judge Tatel's judgment are worth noting. In his view, it was irrelevant that the sources might have waived their confidentiality, because the privilege belongs to the reporter, who has the responsibility of determining whether confidentiality serves the public interest in the dissemination of information valuable to his readers.[39] This is an important point, for it suggests that the source him- or herself has no strong free speech interest in these circumstances; a reporter could decide to waive the privilege, perhaps on the ground that disclosure of the source's identity would add substantially to the credibility of the story.[40] That freedom for reporters would surely be incompatible with ascribing a strong anonymity right to speakers (see chapter 3, section III); the point is discussed further in section III below. Judge Tatel also rejected the journalists' argument that an absolute privilege was required, as otherwise sources would be without a secure guarantee that their identity would never be disclosed. Sources themselves should consider the harm occasioned by the story they have provided, as well as its news value; it was important that there was a disincentive against the manipulation of journalists by government officials seeking publication of damaging stories for partisan motives.[41] (On occasion English judges have used a similar argument in interpreting the qualified privilege provided by the CCA 1981. In *Camelot Group v Centaur Ltd*, a case involving a leak of draft accounts, the Court of Appeal emphasised that sources should reflect on the consequences of leaking confidential information and on how the courts might balance the arguments for and against a disclosure order, even though that might bring about a 'chilling effect' on the preparedness of other sources to talk to the media.)[42]

The Supreme Court of Canada has rejected the argument for recognition of a constitutional media privilege not to disclose its sources as an aspect of the right to freedom of expression guaranteed by section 2(b) of the 1982 Charter of Rights and Freedoms. In one case it doubted whether a requirement to testify and disclose their sources at a hearing before the Alberta Labour Relations Board would inhibit journalists' ability to gather information; it was not clear that sources would 'dry up', as the press had argued.[43] But the Court in that case did not decide whether journalists' privilege was covered by section 2(b) of the Charter. In *R v National Post*, however, it did clearly hold that it was not so covered.[44] The issue was whether police could

---

[39] *In re Grand Jury Subpoena, Judith Miller* (n 33) 1177.

[40] But the reporter would have no First Amendment immunity in these circumstances from an action by the source for breach of contract or promissory estoppel: *Cohen v Cowles Media*, 501 US 663 (1991).

[41] *In re Grand Jury Subpoena, Judith Miler* (n 33) 1178.

[42] [1998] 1 All ER 251, 261–62.

[43] *Moysa v Alberta (Labour Relations Board)* (1989) 60 DLR (4th) 1, 7–8 per Sopinka J.

[44] [2010] 1 SCR 477. (See D Carney, 'Truth and the Unnamed Source' (2012) 4 *Journal of Media Law* 117, 126–34 for a full discussion of the facts and an analysis of the decision.)

require the editor of the *National Post* to allow it to search its premises to look for a document given in confidence to one of its journalists; the document appeared to suggest that the then Prime Minister of Canada was improperly involved in a bank loan to a hotel in debt to the Prime Minister's family investment company. Forensic tests on the document, believed to be a forgery, might identify the source who had supplied it to the newspaper. Binnie J for the Court held that the newspaper had made a convincing case that unless it could offer anonymity where sources would otherwise refuse to talk to it,[45] freedom of expression would suffer, but he rejected its argument for a constitutional immunity from orders to disclose their identity. A constitutional immunity could not be confined to the traditional mass media, but could be claimed by anyone—a blogger or tweeter—for any sources it considered worthy of protection; further, its recognition would damage law enforcement and other constitutional values.[46] The Court also rejected the newspaper's argument for a class privilege, similar to that covering lawyer-client communications. There was no accredited class of journalists who could assert the immunity, nor was it clear whether the immunity belonged to the source or to the journalist. In the case of lawyer-client communications, it belongs to the client and cannot be waived by his lawyer. In contrast, it is uncertain whether a journalist is free to identify his source, if he becomes convinced that the latter has mislead him and the information provided is false.[47]

The Supreme Court therefore upheld only a qualified privilege or immunity, which would be granted on a case by case basis. The burden is on the media to show that a number of criteria are satisfied, including crucially that the public interest in protection of its source outweighs the public interest in disclosure of his identity, say, for the purpose of a criminal investigation.[48] Binnie J added that the case for the confidentiality of a source weakens if the journalist becomes sure that he has been misled, if, for example, in this case he had concluded that the bank documents sent to him had been forged.[49] Further, it would be wrong for a journalist to provide a source with a total guarantee of confidentiality. There is a risk that after all the circumstances have been taken into account a disclosure order will be made and the source identified. That means that 'a source who uses anonymity to put information into the public domain maliciously may not in the end avoid a measure of accountability', as evidenced by the fate of Lewis 'Scooter' Libby, Judith Miller's source, who was subsequently convicted on charges of perjury and obstruction of justice.[50]

---

[45] Ibid para 33.
[46] Ibid para 40.
[47] Ibid paras 43–49.
[48] Ibid para 60.
[49] Ibid para 63.
[50] Ibid para 69. For a short account of the proceedings against Libby, see Carlson, *On the Condition of Anonymity* (n 34) 129–35.

C. Conclusions

In neither the United States nor Canada has the case been accepted for a constitutional immunity for journalists from requirements to answer questions about their sources' identity. The UK Contempt of Court Act 1981 does provide journalists (and others responsible for a publication) with a qualified privilege. In applying this statute, English courts now take into account the jurisprudence of the European Court of Human Rights which provides a firmer guarantee of source anonymity than that afforded by the highest courts on the other side of the Atlantic. One reason for the reluctance of courts generally to provide stronger protection for source anonymity seems to be that they appreciate that on occasion sources mislead and manipulate journalists and may provide false information or documents; this apprehension surely underlies the reasoning of the Court of Appeal in *Interbrew*, of Judge Tatel in the *Judith Miller* case, and of the Canadian Supreme Court in *National Post*. Insofar as these fears are warranted, the case for any protection, let alone an absolute guarantee, of confidentiality is much weaker, or indeed it collapses altogether.

This account of the law on journalists' privilege provides the background for a full discussion in section III of the arguments for recognition of the privilege and for the reservations which can be made about such recognition. These arguments, as we have seen, are sometimes touched on by the courts, but are rarely developed at length. That is largely because the question for them is usually how the journalists' privilege should be balanced against the competing interests, whether public or private, in disclosure of the source's identity, rather than on the question of principle to what extent source anonymity is valuable. Legal literature, at least in the United Kingdom, is also entirely concerned with how courts conduct the balancing exercise, and takes for granted the value of source anonymity. But it is legitimate, as the next section shows, to question this value and to examine how journalists (and others) can act as responsible intermediaries to ensure that only accurate, and not false or misleading, anonymous reports and information are disseminated.

III. ARGUMENTS OF PRINCIPLE CONCERNING SOURCE ANONYMITY

A. In Favour of Source Anonymity

The classic argument for source anonymity is that without it many people would be unwilling to provide information to the media, and so stories of public importance and value would never be published. As the authors of a leading media law textbook in the United Kingdom have written, '[W]ere it not for "unofficial sources" obligingly talking off the record to journalists, there would simply be much less news in newspapers'.[51] Emphasis can be placed on the interests and concerns of the press and other media, on the public interest, or on the interests of the sources themselves; but however the emphasis is placed, the argument for keeping sources confidential is an extremely strong one. The European Court of Human Rights in *Goodwin* perhaps put most stress on the contribution the protection of source confidentiality makes to the role of the press. 'Without such protection, sources may be deterred from assisting the press in informing the public on matters of public interest.' The vital role of the press as public watchdog would be undermined and its ability 'to provide accurate and reliable information may be adversely affected'.[52] When it accepted the important part played by the use of confidential sources in the news-gathering function of the media, the Supreme Court of Canada brought out the public interest dimension of the argument: without source anonymity, '[i]mportant stories will be left untold, and the transparency and accountability of our public institutions will be lessened to the public detriment'.[53] It can be added, of course, that insofar as journalists' privilege is an aspect of freedom of speech, the interests of the public (the readers of the press and listeners and viewers) may be regarded as paramount.[54]

But the argument also takes account of sources' interests and concerns. Courts sometimes refer to the 'chilling effect' of an order to disclose a source's identity, meaning that it will deter other potential sources from coming forward to talk to the press, because they fear that eventually orders will be made to identify them.[55] The European Court of Human Rights also considers that disclosure orders may have a detrimental impact on the interests of 'future potential sources' as well as on those of the members of the public who have an interest in receiving information supplied by unnamed sources.[56] These are legitimate concerns which are proper to take into account as part of the overall argument for source anonymity. But another argument placing the source at the centre of the case for journalists' privilege is much less convincing. Geoffrey Stone has suggested that the logic of the privilege for sources is similar to that of the privileges claimed by the clients of lawyers and by the patients of doctors or therapists.[57] In all these situations society, and the law, want to encourage communication. But there are important distinctions between these privileges. The privilege

---

[51] Robertson and Nicol, *Media Law* (n 7) para 5-053.
[52] *Goodwin v United Kingdom* (n 15) 143.
[53] *R v National Post* (n 44) para 33.
[54] See the discussion of free speech principles in chapter 3, section III.
[55] See, eg, the judgment of Laws LJ in *Ashworth Hospital Authority* (n 20) para 101.
[56] *Financial Times Ltd v United Kingdom* (n 14) para 63.
[57] GR Stone, 'Why We Need a Federal Reporter's Privilege' (2005) 34 *Hofstra Law Review* 39, 41. Geoffrey Stone is a distinguished commentator on the First Amendment, and has argued vigorously for a statutory federal privilege for journalists not to disclose their sources.

claimed by the client of a lawyer or by the patient of a doctor or therapist is that the communications between them, whatever their character, are kept confidential, although the lawyer, doctor or therapist is usually free to reveal the names of their clients or patients. The purpose of the journalist-source privilege, in contrast, is to enable the media to disseminate information to the general public, while keeping the identity of the source secret, even if revealing his name would add credibility to the story. Journalists often claim a privilege not to hand over their notes, documents and other information, whether or not it is confidential. Moreover, the journalists' privilege, unlike the privileges claimed by clients and patients, is not dependent on any formal agreement between the parties. There may be an understanding between source and reporter, but it is usually regarded by journalists as a fundamental ethical principle necessary to conduct their work, which is binding on them whether or not the source has asked for a promise of confidentiality.[58]

Stone's argument has more than theoretical importance. On his view, the privilege essentially 'belongs' to the source, just as the other privileges are those of the client or patient. When the journalist invokes the privilege, he is acting as an agent of the source.[59] It would follow that only the source is free to waive it; a reporter is no more entitled to do this than a lawyer or doctor is the privilege which 'belongs' to the client or patient. That, however, is not the position in the United States, where courts have held that the privilege belongs to the reporter, as the press is in a better position to take responsibility for the public dissemination of information, which it is the purpose of the privilege to protect.[60] On Stone's approach, the source privilege would appear to be an extension of the freedom of anonymous speech, a matter of constitutional entitlement in the United States; anonymous speakers and writers are using the media to communicate their messages.[61] The argument that there is a strong *right* to anonymous speech was criticised in chapter 3, and this version of the argument—that sources have a strong right to anonymity—is no more persuasive. For there may indeed be some circumstances in which it is legitimate for the media to identify their source, even when they have not been compelled to do this by a court order: see section III(C) below.

The value of source anonymity can be illustrated by referring to some important stories which have been broken as a result of information provided

---

[58] The Press Complaints Commission Code, drawn up by a Committee of Editors, states that 'journalists have a *moral* obligation to protect confidential sources of information' (emphasis added).

[59] Stone, 'Why We Need a Federal Reporter's Privilege' (n 57) 50.

[60] See *United States v Cuthbertson*, 630 F2d 139 (3rd Cir 1980), and *In re Grand Jury, Subpoena, Judith Miller* (n 33) 1177 per Tatel J.

[61] This is the position in Sweden, where there is a right to anonymous speech (Freedom of the Press Act 1949, ch 3, s 1, and Fundamental Law on Freedom of Expression 1991, ch 2, s 1) and journalists may not disclose a source's identity without his consent (Freedom of the Press Act, ch 3, s 3, and Fundamental Law on Freedom of Expression, ch 2, s 3).

in this way. The stories about MPs' expenses, about 'Cash for Questions' and about 'Lords for Sale', all emanated ultimately from information and documents supplied by unidentified sources. The report in the *Sunday Times* that Israel was developing nuclear weapons came from a whistle-blower who had been working for a number of years at secret installations in the south of the country.[62] The BBC broadcast a story that the Blair government before the invasion of Iraq had 'sexed up' a dossier prepared by the intelligence services on the development of nuclear and chemical weapons by Saddam Hussain; it relied on a single source, later identified as David Kelly, a weapons specialist at the Ministry of Defence.[63] Nick Davies, an investigative journalist working for the *Guardian*, owed much to a source called Mr Apollo, and a number of other anonymous sources (including 'Mango', a press whistle-blower, and 'Jingle' and 'Karl', two police sources) for his exposure of phone hacking at the *News of the World*.[64] A very high proportion of political stories in the UK national press (perhaps over 90 per cent) are initially provided by sources off the record, though they might provide a tip which is then looked into and confirmed as a result of the reporter's own investigations. Confidential sources are also frequently crucial for stories about crime and national security.[65] Most famously in the United States, the exposure of the Watergate scandal by Bob Woodward and Carl Bernstein in the *Washington Post* owed much to their link with 'Deep Throat', a source only identified over 30 years later as Mark Felt, a former associate director of the FBI.[66] Whatever reservations (discussed in the following subsection) can be legitimately held about the case for source confidentiality, the argument in favour of it is an extremely powerful one, and it is strongly supported by the historical record.

B. Reservations Concerning Source Anonymity

Despite these examples of the valuable stories provided by unnamed sources and the powerful arguments of principle for source confidentiality, there are grounds for scepticism. Lillian BeVier, a leading sceptic, has argued that the empirical case for source confidentiality is unconvincing, as we can never be

---

[62] The whistle-blower, Mordechai Vanunu, was kidnapped in Rome by the Israeli secret service and has spent a number of years in prison in Israel: for a critical account of the affair, see N Davies, *Flat Earth News* (London, Random House, 2008) 296–301.

[63] Ibid 199–200. The BBC was heavily criticised in the report of Lord Hutton into the death of David Kelly for broadcasting an inaccurate story: *Report* (HC 247, 2004) paras 280–82. From para 278 it is clear that its reporter, Andrew Gilligan, did take some steps to corroborate the source's information.

[64] N Davies, *Hack Attack. How the Truth Caught up with Rupert Murdoch* (London, Vintage, 2015) 5, 16, 19, 112–13, 201, 306–7.

[65] Interview with a newspaper lawyer conducted in August 2014.

[66] Carlson, *On the Condition of Anonymity* (n 34) ch 4.

sure that sources would impart information only if they have been given a promise of confidentiality which will be honoured even in litigation when a court is asked to order disclosure.[67] Her point is that sources are primarily concerned that their identity will not be *published* by the media, not that it will never be revealed by a court order.[68] That point may be correct, but it lacks weight. Some sources, particularly if they have taken legal advice, will be aware of the risk that their identity could be disclosed in the course of litigation by court order, and might as a result refrain from talking to the media. Further, the fact that many sources are not worried about the possibility of such an order does not count much against the normative argument that their anonymity *should* be protected in order to encourage other whistle-blowers. While it may be true that there is a lack of compelling evidence to prove that sources would dry up in the absence of journalists' privilege to protect their anonymity, it would be wrong to rely on that ground of scepticism.

Lillian BeVier and other sceptics are, however, on much stronger ground with another argument: the public (readers, listeners and viewers) are completely dependent on the media's assessment of the reliability and integrity of their sources. It would be wrong for the public to assume that every source provides accurate stories out of a genuine concern for its welfare. Sources act from a variety of motives and may provide inaccurate information or misleading accounts of events.[69] A number of examples can be given. Both in the United States and in the United Kingdom, it now seems clear that the press published inaccurate stories about the development by Saddam Hussain of WMD in the run up to the invasion of Iraq; they relied on misinformation provided them by Iraqi exiles or by administration officials eager to promote the case for the invasion.[70] In reliance on official sources, the London *Sunday Times* carried inaccurate accounts in 1988 of the shooting by Special Armed Service (SAS) officers of suspected IRA terrorists in Gibraltar, wrongly stating that the terrorists had been armed and had a bomb on them.[71] In 2011, the *Guardian* reported the blog of

---

[67] L BeVier, 'The Journalists' Privilege: A Skeptic's View' (2006) 32 *Ohio Northern University Law Rev* 467, 475–6.

[68] Ibid 476. (See also A Lewis, 'A Preferred Position for Journalism?' (1979) 7 *Hofstra Law Review* 595, 616–17, where it is argued that investigative journalism in Britain was not impaired by the absence of journalists' privilege before the Contempt of Court Act 1981.)

[69] BeVier, 'The Journalists' Privilege' (n 67) 478; Abramowicz, 'Calculating the Public Interest in Protecting Journalists' Confidential Sources' (n 38) 1966–68; Wasserman, 'A Critique of Source Confidentiality' (n 34) 561–68, and Carlson, *On the Condition of Anonymity* (n 34) passim.

[70] Davies, *Flat Earth News* (n 62) 205–17; Carlson, *On the Condition of Anonymity* (n 34) 42–50.

[71] Davies, *Flat Earth News* (n 62) 303–11. See his account of the misinformation provided by 'Astroturf', the name PR groups gave to an organisation set up to defend the interests of the tobacco industry, and industries opposing climate change reforms: 168–69, 176, 188.

an 'anonymous Syrian lesbian blogger', until the blogger revealed himself as a middle-aged American living with his wife in Scotland.[72] *Newsweek* magazine published an article in 2005, claiming that a forthcoming US government report would confirm that guards at Guantanamo Bay had flushed a copy of the Koran down a toilet. Riots in Afghanistan followed. Within a week the anonymous source for the story withdrew the allegation; *Newsweek* apologised and retracted the story.[73] The newspaper story that Valerie Plame, a CIA agent, was responsible for the appointment of her husband, a retired diplomat, to investigate suspected attempts by Saddam Hussain to purchase uranium in West Africa was true; but it emanated from Bush administration sources anxious to discredit the diplomat's article in the *New York Times* in which he had stated that intelligence claims in the year before the invasion had exaggerated the threat from Iraq.[74] The sources had a discreditable motive for a story of little news value.

There are several reasons why reliance on unnamed sources may be dangerous. Sources may cultivate journalists, who are persuaded that they are getting a truthful inside story, and manipulate them into publishing inaccurate, misleading or harmful allegations. Anonymous sources remain unaccountable, as it is impossible for the public to confront them and ask them about the basis for the allegations which they have used the media to spread. Anonymity also precludes verifiability, or any checking of the story by the public. As Edward Wasserman has argued, 'confidentiality [of sources] poses ethical conflicts, chiefly because it may clash with two professional norms: accountability and verifiability. The result may impede truth-telling'.[75] The practice of allowing source anonymity may also damage the relationship of trust between the journalist and the reading (or viewing) public which is sacrificed so that the former can develop an (unhealthy) close relationship with his sources.[76]

The case for source anonymity assumes that generally sources are honest whistle-blowers, primarily concerned to provide the public with important information, which government or industry wants to deny it. That assumption may be warranted, but it seems misguided to ignore the fact that government officials, lobby groups, public relations officers and other sources have a variety of reasons for providing the media with stories, and may give it inaccurate, incomplete or misleading information. As Sedley LJ pointed out in the *Interbrew* case, it is the government which has been the principal beneficiary of the rule protecting source anonymity, for it is the source of

---

[72] See www.theguardian.com/world/2011/jun13/syrian-lesbian-blogger-tom-macmaster.
[73] Carlson, *On the Condition of Anonymity* (n 34) 74–76.
[74] Ibid 117–19, and see text at nn 33–34 above.
[75] Wasserman, 'A Critique of Source Confidentiality' (n 34) 563.
[76] Ibid 566–67, and see Carlson, *On the Condition of Anonymity* (n 34) 145–47.

most unattributed leaks to the media.[77] It would also surely be naive to view all whistle-blowers as necessarily honest and reliable.

These arguments echo the reasons given in earlier chapters of this book for doubting the case for a strong (constitutional) right to anonymous speech. The proscription or tight regulation of anonymous speech and writing would certainly deter some people from contributing to public discourse, but it would also ensure accountability for deceitful and defamatory speech and enable readers more easily to assess the credibility of authors, who would be compelled to communicate under their real name. As suggested in the introduction to this chapter, the case for source anonymity is only stronger than that for anonymous speech insofar as the press and other media act as responsible intermediaries—by vouching for the credibility of their sources and the accuracy of the information they provide. How far the media takes steps to do this is considered in the next subsection.

C. The Media as Responsible Intermediaries

Anxiety in the last few years about manipulation of the press by anonymous sources, particularly in the United States, has persuaded some newspapers and other media to tighten the rules governing their use.[78] Journalism professors had long argued for greater care in this context. In a much cited article, David Boeyink advocated the drafting of guidelines to ensure, so far as possible, the appropriate use of anonymous sources.[79] As a matter of principle, reporting should be truthful and fair to anyone charged in an article or broadcast with culpable behaviour; this entails responsibility in the use of anonymous sources. Among the particular guidelines suggested by Boeyink are those that anonymous sources should be used only when a story is important, and as a last resort when journalists find it difficult to report a story without reliance on them. Their use should be authorised by an editor, and the information provided by the source should generally be verified by a second source, independent of the first. Sources should be identified so far as possible, with an explanation provided for their anonymity. This last guideline is generally referred to as a requirement of *transparency*; it gives readers some information about the source of a story to help them assess its probable truth, though it is doubtful whether in practice it provides them with enough assistance for this purpose.

---

[77] *Interbrew* (n 13) para 7.

[78] See Carlson, *On the Condition of Anonymity* (n 34) ch 1, discussing the changes in editorial policy concerning the use of anonymous sources at the *New York Times* and the *Washington Post* following their reporting of administration claims about Iraq's development of WMD in the run up to the invasion in 2003. Also see Abramowicz, 'Calculating the Public Interest in Protecting Journalists' Confidential Sources' (n 38) 1971–74.

[79] 'Anonymous Sources in News Stories: Justifying Exceptions and Limiting Abuses' (1990) 5 *Journal of Mass Media Ethics* 233.

American newspapers and magazines have adopted many of these guidelines. In February 2004, the *New York Times* issued a memorandum emphasising that anonymous source should be used rarely, and only after careful deliberation between the journalist and the responsible editor; multiple unnamed sources should be independent of one another. Transparency requires that readers should be told as much as possible about the source and his motives.[80] *Time* magazine has also adopted detailed Editorial Guidelines for the use of anonymous sources: they require information to be validated from other sources, and every unnamed source to be made known to an editor, or in sensitive cases to the editor-in-chief. Reliance on clearly named sources is preferred. 'The more the reader knows about the source of the reporter's information, the better the reader can evaluate the accuracy and fairness of the information offered.'[81] The Associated Press (AP) News Values and Principles contain a number of rules, among them a requirement for approval of the use of an anonymous source from the news manager. Anonymity should be granted only when a source insists on it; it is not automatically granted as a straightforward matter of professional practice. AP 'routinely' requires more than a single source, and stories should not be published until attempts have been made to contact additional sources for confirmation.[82] Only rarely will a single source be sufficient. The story must say enough about the source to establish his credibility.[83]

The UK media have not imposed detailed requirements of this kind. The Editorial Code of the *Guardian* provides that, '[W]e should be honest about our sources, even if we can't name them', an oblique method of encouraging transparency.[84] It also warns against the use of anonymous quotations, citing the policy of the *New York Times*: direct quotations give the anonymous speaker an unfair advantage, for readers cannot assess his credibility. In practice both at the *Guardian* and at Times Newspapers (*The Times* and *Sunday Times*) journalists are expected to discuss the use of an anonymous source with the head of news or an editor, though in contrast to the policy at some American newspapers, they should not disclose the name of the source to the editor. There is no firm rule at these papers against reliance on a single source, though there is some caution after the criticism of the BBC in the

---

[80] Carlson, *On the Condition of Anonymity* (n 34) 41–42, and Abramowicz, 'Calculating the Public Interest in Protecting Journalists' Confidential Sources' (n 38) 1971–74, commenting on New York Times Confidential News Source Policy, available at www.abc.net.au/mediawatch/transcripts/0726_nyt.pdf.

[81] Time Inc., Editorial Guidelines (May 2012), available at www.timeinc.com/wp-content/.../04/editorial_guidelines_2012.pdf.

[82] *Newsweek* was heavily criticised for its use of a single source when publishing the story that the Koran had been flushed down the toilet at Guantanamo Bay: Carlson, *On the Condition of Anonymity* (n 34) 81.

[83] AP News Values and Principles, available at www.timeinc.com/wp-content/.../04/editorial_guidelines_2012.pdf.

[84] See www.theguardian.com/info/guardian-editorial-code.

Hutton Inquiry Report.[85] Strenuous attempts are generally made to verify information provided by a single source. However, *Financial Times* journalists are required as a general rule to have two independent sources for their stories.[86] At Times Newspapers there is a policy of disclosing as much information as possible about the source; a story about unrest in the Conservative party, for example, would be supported by information supplied by 'a senior Tory back-bencher' rather than just attributed to 'a source'.

The BBC Editorial Guidelines are a little fuller. Under Section 3, 'Accuracy', there are requirements to check and verify information to achieve due accuracy. 'We should be reluctant to rely on a single source. If we do rely on a single source, a named on-the-record source is always preferable.' The evidence of first hand sources should be corroborated.[87] Care is required with regard to user generated content, which should not be assumed to be accurate and for which verification is required; special care is advised for material which may have been supplied by members of a lobby group or anyone with a vested interest in the story.[88] The requirements for the use of sources and material supplied by third parties are seen in the context of the BBC's fundamental duty to provide accurate and truthful reporting. This is important, for there can be a conflict between that duty and an unrestricted reliance on anonymous sources, which, as we have seen, may enable the dissemination of inaccurate stories by the media.[89]

A similar emphasis can be found in the recent report of Lord Justice Leveson on the press.[90] Leveson refers to the anonymity of confidential sources in the context of his treatment of inaccuracy. He found that 'the use of anonymous sources can lead to an inability to assess whether the source is reliable, or even exists'.[91] Journalists can abuse the privilege in order to provide a camouflage for a non-existent source 'or one who is known or suspected to be unreliable, or one in respect of whom inadequate enquiry is made by the journalist'.[92] He accepted evidence that some newspapers adopted a 'cavalier approach to checking facts provided by a source' where there was little risk of litigation in which a disclosure order might be made.[93] The Report recommended that the new regulatory body should encourage the press to be as transparent as possible in relation to its use of sources, and to provide

---

[85] Information provided by newspaper lawyers. For the BBC's reliance on a single source and the Hutton Report, see text at n 63 above.

[86] Financial Times Editoriall Code of Practice, available at http://aboutus.ft.com/files/2013/11/131114-FT-Code-FINAL.pdf.

[87] Editorial Guidelines, ss 3.4.1 and 3.4.2, available at www.bbc.co.uk/editorialguidelines/page/guidelines-accuracy-gathering-material/.

[88] Ibid s 3.4.3.

[89] See Carney, 'Truth and the Unnamed Source' (n 44) 118–26.

[90] *An Inquiry into the Culture, Practices and Ethics of the Press* (HC 780, 2012).

[91] Ibid Part F, ch 6, para 9.12.

[92] Ibid para 9.14.

[93] Ibid para 9.17.

any information that would enable readers to assess the reliability of stories it provided.[94]

How then should journalists act as responsible intermediaries who vouch for the credibility of the sources on which they rely? The principal requirements are to verify, so far as possible, the source's story through independent research or by corroboration from a second source, entirely separate from the first. Transparency is also crucial, for by helping readers (or viewers) assess the reliability of stories provided by an anonymous source, it cements the relationship of trust between them and the newspaper (or other media). Sources should be used with caution and not relied on without discussion in the newspaper office: that requirement now appears generally to be observed both in the United Kingdom and in the United States. A further requirement may be suggested; journalists should make it clear to their source that confidentiality is conditional. They should explain that not only might they be required by court order to disclose a source's identity, but that they themselves might reveal it if they become convinced that the source has provided false information or has acted from clearly improper motives.[95]

This suggestion will be controversial. English newspapers would never countenance this step, though it has occasionally been discussed in some newspaper offices. Journalists consider it would be unethical for them to waive the privilege, which in their view belongs to the source.[96] In contrast, some American commentators would not rule out this course of action; it might be right for journalists to reveal a source in breach of a confidentiality agreement, if it becomes clear that they are being manipulated to reproduce mendacious or malicious stories. The possibility that this could occur 'would reduce the ability of sources to take advantage of their anonymity in purely self-serving ways'.[97] This course of action would be compatible with the legal position that the privilege 'belongs to' the reporter, not to the source.[98] The press is free to waive it and reveal the source's identity. This course of action would, of course, be a little less controversial, if it had been made plain to the source at the outset that his anonymity was conditional: his identity might be disclosed if it became clear that he had provided a seriously inaccurate story or had acted maliciously.

---

[94] Executive Summary of the Report, HC 779, para 63 and Recommendation 45. The key proposal of the Leveson Report was that the press should set up a regulatory body underpinned by statute to replace the Press Complaints Commission.

[95] See Carlson, *On the Condition of Anonymity* (n 34) 154–58, and A Quinn, 'Respecting Sources' Confidentiality: Critical but Not Absolute' in C Meyers (ed), *Journalism Ethics: A Philosophical Approach* (New York, Oxford University Press, 2010) 271, 277–80.

[96] Interviews with newspaper lawyers conducted in August 2014.

[97] Carlson, *On the Condition of Anonymity* (n 34) 155.

[98] See text at n 60 above.

Consider this hypothetical case, a variant of the facts of a leading Supreme Court decision in this area.[99] A senior Conservative Party back-bencher provides a newspaper with a story to the effect that a Conservative government minister is engaged in corrupt behaviour. The newspaper publishes the story, but it subsequently becomes clear to its journalists that it is largely false and that the source acted out of spite—perhaps because the minister had been promoted to a position which the back-bencher thought he had been promised. In these circumstances the newspaper would surely be right to identify its source, who had manipulated it to publish an inaccurate and defamatory allegation. His identity is crucial to a full account of the story. He should be accountable for his dishonesty. Of course, journalists and their editors should balance the public interest in the disclosure of the identity of a malicious source against the damage that this would do to the general principle of journalists' confidentiality and the risk that honest whistle-blowers might be deterred from coming forward to talk to the media. A decision to reveal should not be taken lightly. But it might sometimes be consistent with the role of journalists as responsible intermediaries. The public can be more confident that they are discharging this role conscientiously, if on the (hopefully) rare occasions when they know that they have been manipulated into publishing false and damaging stories, they ensure that their dishonest source is accountable. And honest sources would not be deterred from talking to the media, for they would still know that their identity would never be disclosed.

IV. WHO CAN CLAIM THE PRIVILEGE?

As noted in section I above, in the United Kingdom the privilege conferred by the CCA 1981 is not confined to professional journalists, but can be claimed by any person responsible for a publication, so, it is suggested, it might be invoked by a producer of a leaflet, an editor of a local magazine or a blogger. But it does not cover the operator of a website containing a number of discussion boards over which he exercises no editorial control. That was decided by Owen J in *Totalise plc v The Motley Fool Ltd*, where the claimant applied for disclosure of the identity of a contributor who had used the pseudonym 'Z Dust' when posting allegedly defamatory comments about it, its directors and officers. In the judge's view the defendant merely

---

[99] In *Cohen v Cowles Media Co*, 501 US 663 (1991), the Supreme Court held, 5–4, that a newspaper did not have a First Amendment right to break a promise to its source (a worker for the Republican candidate for the governorship of Minnesota) to keep his name confidential, even though disclosure of his name added to the story concerning criminal charges facing the Democrat candidate. Souter J, joined by three other Justices, dissented on the ground that disclosure of the identity of the leaker added to the information provided to the electorate. I agree with the dissenting judgment.

'provided a facility by means of which the public at large is able publicly to communicate its views'.[100] It took no responsibility for what was posted on its discussion boards.[101]

State shield laws in the United States vary in their definitions of the beneficiaries of the privilege. Some of them confine it to 'professional journalists' regularly employed or engaged in work for the traditional media (newspapers, magazines, news agencies and broadcasting stations), so excluding book authors and publishers, and academic researchers. But a few take a broader approach. The Minnesota law, for example, covers anyone engaged in the gathering, editing and publishing of information for the purpose of disseminating it to the public—which seems in effect similar to the UK provision.[102] In at least two federal cases, courts have held that the qualified privilege they were prepared to recognise extended to anyone acting with this purpose, 'regardless of the medium used to report the news to the public'.[103]

The question who might be the beneficiaries of any privilege to keep sources anonymous worried the Supreme Court when it declined in *Branzburg* to recognise a constitutional privilege.[104] The Court considered it wrong in principle to allow reporters working for the traditional media immunity from answering questions, which other people such as independent researchers similarly engaged in gathering information for the purpose of publication would not enjoy. This discrimination would be even harder to support now, when bloggers, citizen-journalists and tweeters regularly provide information to the public. Why should they not be entitled to rely on the privilege to keep their sources confidential, which historically has been claimed by reporters working for the mass media?[105]

This question may be answered by reflection on how far the various types of news provider act as responsible intermediaries when they disseminate information from anonymous sources. As has been seen in the previous section (section III(C)) professional journalists are often required by editorial codes to verify anonymously provided information, and to take other steps to ensure, so far as possible, that their readers can assess the reliability of the stories supplied by their sources. Alternatively, as is more usual in the United Kingdom, they may take steps of this kind as a matter of professional practice. Other news providers, for example, bloggers and website

---

[100] [2001] EMLR 29, para 26.

[101] The position of website operators and other Internet intermediaries disseminating anonymous defamatory messages is considered in the next chapter (see chapter 6, section III(D)).

[102] See Lee, 'The Priestly Class' (n 30) 670–78.

[103] Judge William A Norris in *Shoen v Shoen*, 5 F3d 1289, 1293 (9th Cir 1993), finding the earlier ruling in *Bulow v Bulow*, 811 F2d 136 (2d Cir 1987) to this effect persuasive. In *Shoen* the author of a book was held entitled to claim the privilege.

[104] *Branzburg v Hayes* (n 28). Also see the judgment of Judge Sentelle in the *Judith Miller* case, 397 F3d 964, 979–81 (2005).

[105] The question is posed by Anderson, 'Confidential Sources Reconsidered' (n 29) 903–4.

operators, should enjoy the same privilege as professional journalists to keep their sources confidential, insofar as they take real responsibility for their publications; this requires them to take at least some minimal steps to ensure that they do not disseminate false information from malicious sources. On the other hand, if there is no evidence that they can, or do, take these steps, it would be wrong to allow them to claim the privilege. The crucial question is whether the person claiming the privilege is engaged in a process intended to disseminate *truthful* information; one element in this test is how far there are procedures in place to verify the truth of the story reported, and another is whether readers or viewers of, say, the blog or website have enough information to enable them to judge its credibility.[106]

---

[106] See the article by LL Berger, 'Shielding the Unmedia: Using the Process of Journalism to Protect the Journalist's Privilege in an Infinite Universe of Publication' (2003) 39 *Houston Law Rev* 1371, 1411–16.

6

Anonymity on the Internet

I. CULTURE OF ANONYMITY

A. Introduction

IT IS VERY common for communications on the Internet to be sent anonymously or with the use of a pseudonym. Indeed the Internet now provides the context for the most vigorous debate on the pros and cons of anonymous speech, a matter which has largely been resolved, at least in the United Kingdom, in the older contexts of newspaper journalism and literary reviews (see chapter 2). The anonymity of blogs and of communications on social media such as Facebook (despite that site's real name policy discussed in section II below) has been crucial for the development of freer political speech under the authoritarian regimes in Tunisia and Egypt during the Arab spring of 2011, and for what free speech exists today in Iran and China.[1] Moreover, in any society many people, for example, whistle-blowers, can speak much more freely on the Net if they can do this without revealing their identity. Anonymity also enables the victims of sexual abuse and of domestic violence to use the Net to protest against their treatment.

On the other hand, anonymity seems to encourage the dissemination of extremist political speech, in particular neo-Nazi hate speech directed at minority ethnic groups;[2] Anders Breivik, who murdered 77 people in Norway in July 2011, wrote his 1,516 page online manifesto under a pseudonym, Andrew Berwick.[3] It may be used to encourage people to provide active support for terrorist groups, even to fight for them in Iraq and Syria. Anonymity also enables material to be uploaded with relative safety on child pornography websites.[4] Young people may feel more secure in sharing anonymously their darker thoughts on 'self-harm' sites discussing anorexia, bulimia and depression; these sites may provide vulnerable teenagers

---

[1] See R MacKinnon, *Consent of the Networked* (New York, Basic Books, 2012) esp 145–53.
[2] J Bartlett, *The Dark Net* (London, Windmill Books, 2014) ch 2.
[3] Ibid 50–51.
[4] Ibid 127.

with valuable advice and support, but equally, of course, the sites might encourage them to persist with dangerous habits or even to commit suicide.[5] So there is an enormous range of anonymous (and pseudonymous) speech on the Internet of widely varying quality.

Of particular concern recently has been the phenomenon of 'trolling' on the Net: abusive and insulting communications directed, often on social media (see section II below), at particular individuals. In some cases the abuse amounts to threats of violence, or even of rape or murder. On one view this phenomenon is encouraged by anonymity. In *The Offensive Internet*,[6] distinguished American academic commentators drew attention to the number of vicious attacks, particularly on women students, which are posted on websites anonymously. Anonymous cyber mobs and hate groups target vulnerable people: young women, gays, lesbians and bisexuals.[7] Jamie Bartlett in a recent book, *The Dark Net*, concluded that the easiest way to deal with trolling would be to outlaw anonymity and to insist that all communication on the Internet is conducted by people with the use of their real name,[8] though he added that there are good reasons why it would not be right to take this step. The arguments for and against controlling the use of anonymity and pseudonyms will be considered shortly.[9]

At this point it is worth noting that concern about the effects of anonymity (and the use of pseudonyms) in trolling has perhaps led to something of a backlash against anonymity, particularly in the social media.[10] At the very least, what was taken a few years ago as a distinctive advantage of communication on the Net—the freedom conferred by anonymity, enabled by the absence of the editorial checks familiar in the traditional press and broadcasting media—is now perceived to carry a major disadvantage: the absence of accountability to those damaged by anonymous trolling. In authoritarian societies, and even some which would be regarded as relatively liberal, bloggers and users of online services have been required to register under

---

[5] Ibid ch 7, and see S Turkle, *Alone Together* (New York, Basic Books, 2011) 229–31 for the use of the Internet by young people for 'confessional' statements.

[6] S Levmore and MC Nussbaum (eds), *The Offensive Internet* (Cambridge, MA, Harvard University Press, 2012).

[7] DK Citron, *Hate Crimes in Cyberspace* (Cambridge, MA, Harvard University Press, 2014) 57–69. In her book Danielle Citron explores the disproportionate impact of cyber-hate on women and LBGT (lesbian, bisexual, gay, transgendered) people; ibid 13–17.

[8] Bartlett, *The Dark Net* (n 2) 42. Chapter 2 of his book discusses the origins and varieties of trolling.

[9] In section I(B) below.

[10] B Hogan, 'Pseudonyms and the Rise of the Real-Name Web' in J Hartley, J Burgess and A Bruns (eds), *A Companion to New Media Dynamics* (Chichester, Blackwell Publishing, 2012) 290; M Kaminski, 'Real Masks and Real Name Policies: Applying Anti-Mask Case Law to Anonymous Online Speech' (2013) 23 *Fordham Intellectual Property Media and Entertainment Law Journal* 815, 824.

their real names in order to counteract the spread of what are regarded as subversive or antisocial messages.[11]

Anonymity on the Internet may be distinguished from the *privacy* of the *content* of Internet communications and searches, a topic which has been much discussed recently, particularly after Edward Snowden's revelations about the scope of the surveillance conducted by security agencies in the United States and the United Kingdom. Internet users are often understandably concerned about the monitoring of their communications by the police and security services, and also by the communication of their preferences by social media platforms to advertising agencies or for other commercial purposes; or a user may not want authorities to know that he frequently visits pornographic sites. The primary concern in these circumstances is with the privacy of the information communicated or looked at, rather than with the identity of the user, who may generally be willing to be identified. In these circumstances anonymity on the Net supports the right to personal privacy, for anonymity (or the use of a pseudonym) prevents, or at least makes more difficult, the linking of Internet users to identifiable individuals living at a particular address. In *R v Spencer*, the Supreme Court of Canada regarded anonymity on the Net as the foundation of a privacy interest which could be protected under the Canadian Charter of Rights; in *Spencer*, it provided a subscriber protection against the disclosure by an Internet Service Provider (ISP) of his name and address when the police investigating child pornography offences obtained this information from the ISP without a warrant.[12] Equally, as was explained in section 5 of chapter 1, personal privacy provides a strong argument for anonymity on the Net, though it must meet the objection that blogging and other varieties of Internet communication are, like most types of speech, essentially not self-regarding, private activities, but public.[13] Privacy and anonymity may therefore reinforce, or support, each other.

But these privacy arguments are not the subject of this book, which is concerned with anonymous *speech*, in particular the question how far a right to anonymous communication can be justified as an aspect of freedom of speech (see the arguments canvassed in chapter 3). So this chapter is not concerned with, for example, the justifications which may be given for Internet hacking by groups such as Anonymous, which rest primarily

---

[11] *Report of the UN Special Rapporteur on the Promotion and Protection of the Right to Freedom of Opinion and Expression*, (2015) A/HRC/29/32, paras 49–50 refer to requirements of this kind in Iran, Russia, China and South Africa. For the law in South Korea imposing an obligation on websites to require visitors to supply real names and addresses, with national ID card numbers, see MacKinnon, *Consent of the Networked* (n 1) 90–92. The law was held unconstitutional in August 2012 for infringing freedom of expression.

[12] [2014] 2 SCR 212.

[13] See the decision of Eady J in *Author of a Blog v Times Newspapers* [2009] EMLR 22, discussed in chapter 4, section III.

on (almost certainly specious) privacy arguments, rather than on freedom of speech.[14] Nor is it relevant to the themes of this chapter that courts may allow parties to bring legal proceedings anonymously, so that their identity may not be disclosed by the media, including the Internet. Such permission protects the privacy of the victims of cyber-harassment or hate, and allows them more comfortably to bring proceedings against perpetrators.[15]

Another preliminary point is whether anonymity can be effectively secured for Internet communications.[16] Every Internet connection has a unique Internet Protocol (IP) address, which identifies the user; websites record the IP address each time they are visited, saving it indefinitely, so the user can always be traced. But various devices and techniques can be adopted to conceal an IP address and its user, so enabling anonymous and pseudonymous communications and searches.[17] The encryption of emails and other communications, or the use of a temporary email address, may make identification more difficult,[18] though encryption safeguards the *content* of the message, rather than masking the identity of the sender. The use of web proxies, such as anonymous.org, or anonymizer.com, providing an intermediary between the user and the visited sites, hide the user's IP address from everyone except the proxy. But authorities may compel the proxy to reveal the user's IP address.[19] Virtual Private Networks (VPNs) provide encrypted connections between a specific IP address and the VPN server; in principle they should be secure, but in practice it appears that security services and other authorities can break them and identity an IP address.

Probably the most effective device for protecting anonymity is use of Tor software, providing a network of 'onion routers' which conceals the origin and destination of communications on the Internet and which repeatedly encrypts their content.[20] Tor has often been used in Iran and the Middle East by dissidents to protect their anonymity.[21] Determined security authorities may be able to break into the network to identify users; anonymity can never be absolutely guaranteed, though it may be protected effectively enough in many circumstances. But individual victims of an anonymous

---

[14] This group is the subject of P Olson, *We are Anonymous* (New York, Little, Brown and Co, 2012) and G Coleman, *Hacker, Hoaxer, Whistle-blower, Spy* (New York, Verso, 2014).

[15] Citron, *Hate Crimes in Cyberspace* (n 7) 162–64.

[16] For a general discussion of encryption and other techniques for protecting privacy and anonymity on the Internet, see R Cohen-Almagor, *Confronting the Internet's Dark Side* (Cambridge, CUP, 2015) 43–47.

[17] See *Report of the UN Special Rapporteur* (n 11) para 9.

[18] Bartlett, *The Dark Net* (n 2) 79–80.

[19] For a discussion of web proxies and their limitations, see EJ Stieglitz, 'Anonymity on the Internet: How Does It Work, Who Needs It, and What are Its Policy Implications?' (2007) 24 *Cardozo Arts and Entertainment Law Journal* 1395, 1401–2.

[20] Ibid 1402–3, and see Bartlett, *The Dark Net* (n 2) 2, and 141 for the use of Tor Hidden Services for drug sales.

[21] MacKinnon, *Consent of the Networked* (n 1) 58, 229–30.

attack, whether it takes the form of cyber-harassment, hate speech or defamation, may find it too difficult or costly to find out the identity of its perpetrator for the purpose of bringing civil proceedings against him. Whether or not anonymity is effectively secure, it is generally felt to be sufficiently secure for its use to be keenly defended by bloggers and others communicating on the Net.

The final point to make in this introduction is that communication on the Internet is clearly covered by the right to freedom of speech, or the right to freedom of expression, the term used in the European Convention on Human Rights (ECHR) and in many national constitutions. The United States Supreme Court held in its landmark decision in *Reno v American Civil Liberties Union* that there was no basis for qualifying the protection afforded by the First Amendment guarantee of freedom of speech in the context of the Internet;[22] the Court rejected the argument that the Net could be subject to special content regulation of the kind which has traditionally constrained broadcasting. Of more relevance to the subject of this chapter, the *McIntyre* ruling upholding a right to anonymous speech has been followed in the context of the Internet.[23] A federal District Court held invalid as infringing the First Amendment a Georgia statute which had made it an offence to transmit messages over the Internet under a false name.[24] But the right to communicate anonymously on the Net is not absolute. It is an offence under a federal statute to use a telecommunications device, without the user disclosing his identity, with intent to abuse, threaten or harass any specific individual.[25] The law would almost certainly survive constitutional challenge, as true threats instilling a real fear of violence are not protected by the First Amendment.[26] German courts have also upheld a freedom to communicate anonymously on the Net: see the discussion of the *Spickmich* case in section IV below.

The treatment of anonymous online speech by the European Human Rights Court has been rather more equivocal. In *KU v Finland*, it ruled that any guarantee of privacy and freedom of expression rights for a person placing an anonymous advertisement is not absolute and must give way to other rights and interests, such as the prevention of crime and the protection of the rights of others.[27] Finland had therefore infringed the right of the applicant, a young boy aged 12, to respect for his privacy, when under its law at the relevant time it could not compel an Internet Service Provider to reveal

---

[22] 521 US 844 (1997).
[23] See chapter 3, section II, discussing *McIntyre v Ohio Elections Commission*, 514 US 334 (1995).
[24] *ACLU v Zell Miller*, 977 F Supp 1228 (ND, Ga 1997).
[25] 47 USC s 223(a)(1)(c), discussed in Citron, *Hate Crimes in Cyberspace* (n 7) 124–25.
[26] *Planned Parenthood of the Columbia/Williamette Inc v American Coalition of Life Activists*, 290 F3d 1058 (9th Cir, 2002).
[27] *KU v Finland*, Application no 2872/02 (2009) 48 EHRR 52.

the identity of a user who had placed an advertisement on a dating site in the applicant's name; the advert claimed he was looking for an intimate relationship with an experienced boy of his age or older. But in the later *Delfi* case[28] (to be discussed below in section III(D)) the Court attached more importance to the freedom of anonymous communication on the Net, when it declined to hold in infringement of freedom of expression the imposition of responsibility on a news portal for publishing anonymous comments; in its view, to require a claimant to take proceedings against the authors of these comments, rather than the news portal, would chill freedom of anonymous expression.

It should be noted that under English law there is, as with the traditional mass media, a freedom to communicate anonymously on the Internet, though it is not a matter of constitutional right (see chapter 4 for a general discussion of English law on anonymous communication). Internet communication is of course subject to the same general legal restrictions as publication in the press or on the broadcasting media, for example, those imposed by public order laws, the laws prohibiting hate speech, obscenity laws, and the Protection from Harassment Act 1997.[29] One important provision should be mentioned: section 127 of the Communications Act 2003 makes it an offence to send through a public electronic communications network a message which is 'grossly offensive or of an indecent, obscene, or menacing character'. It applies to any type of communication sent on the Net, whether from a computer or a mobile phone, and its scope has been examined in a number of cases. The most notable of these is *Chambers v DPP*,[30] where the court upheld the appeal of a man who had been convicted of the offence for sending by Twitter a jokey message threatening to blow up an airport after his flight had been cancelled; the message properly understood should not have been understood as 'menacing'.

B. Justifications for Anonymity

At least two general questions should be carefully distinguished from each other. The first asks why there has been such a prevalent culture of anonymity on the Internet, so much so that for many users anonymity, or more generally the use of a pseudonym, appears natural or instinctive, and any suggestion that the practice might be curbed attracts the most vociferous protest. The second question is whether the culture can be justified, leading

---

[28] *Delfi AS v Estonia*, Application no 64569/09 (2014) 58 EHRR 29 (First Section Chamber); [2015] EMLR 26 (Grand Chamber).
[29] See J Rowbottom, 'To Rant, Vent and Converse: Protecting Low Level Digital Speech' (2012) 71 *Cambridge Law Journal* 355, 357–65 examines the different types of legal restrictions on Internet communication.
[30] [2012] EWHC 2157 (QB).

perhaps to the conclusion that there is a right to communicate anonymously on the Internet. That right might not be absolute, but it should perhaps be limited only in the most pressing circumstances, where, for example, it is necessary to identify people who use the Net in preparing acts of terrorism or to threaten murder or other violence. But it would not be legitimate on this perspective always to unveil the identity of the sender of a defamatory message, the topic of section III below. Another issue is relevant to the legitimacy of anonymity bans: does anonymity, or the use of a pseudonym, on the Net encourage trolling, for example, cyber-bullying or threats against targeted individuals, or is it completely irrelevant to this sort of abuse of the Internet?

Online anonymity may have developed from the use of initials and other short forms of pseudonym in the early days of the Net, but by the early 2000s it had become a cultural expectation on the part of many Net users, so it became offensive to ask for information concerning their off-line identity.[31] Users preferred to construct a separate identity in the initially strange new world of the Internet. Almost certainly there was a mixture of personal and ideological reasons for their decisions. Psychologists have identified anonymity as one of the principal factors for an *online disinhibition effect*, under which many people are prepared to say things in cyberspace which they would not do in a face to face encounter in real life. They can easily hide their identity, believing they cannot be linked to the messages they send and so held responsible for their consequences.[32] For many adolescents this trend may be reinforced by the practice of creating separate identities (avatars) when playing games in online worlds.[33] Pseudonyms may be adopted simply because they are fun or to parody public figures.[34] Young people may also become more comfortable in disclosing their anxieties and attempting to make friends online under a pseudonym rather than with their own name.[35] For one or other of these reasons, online and offline identities become disassociated from each other.

It is more controversial how far the adoption of anonymity is itself responsible for unacceptable behaviour on the Internet, or whether that is primarily attributable to other factors, perhaps the mere fact that communication on the Net is not the same as face to face speech or that it is generally conducted among a large group of strangers. People encouraging others to join terrorist groups or sharing pornographic images might use a pseudonym only to avoid detection; anonymity, or use of a made-up name, might

---

[31] Malcolm Collins, 'The Ideology of Anonymity and Pseudonymity', (2 August 2013) www.huffingtonpost.com/malcolm-collins/online-anonymity_b_369585.

[32] J Suler, 'The Online Disinhibition Effect', (2004) 7 *CyberPsychology and Behaviour* 321, 322.

[33] Turkle, *Alone Together* (n 5) 179–86, 212–19; VS Ekstrand, 'The Many Masks of Anon: Anonymity as Cultural Practice and Reflections in Case Law' (2013) 18 *Journal of Technology Law and Policy* 1, 15–16.

[34] Ekstrand, ibid, 17, 23.

[35] Turkle, *Alone Together* (n 5) 189–98, 229–31.

not itself be responsible for this conduct.[36] The link between anonymity and undesirable speech cannot be proved, but it is surely plausible to believe that the adoption of a pseudonym does make some people less inhibited and cautious when they comment on a blog or use social media, and therefore significantly contributes to the phenomenon of trolling and other unacceptable communication on the Net. Moreover, it is inconsistent for proponents of anonymity on the Net to argue that it enables, as it certainly does, whistle-blowers, political dissidents and others safely to communicate valuable messages, but plays little part in encouraging the dissemination of less attractive types of communication.

The principal justification for a right to anonymous speech on the Net is, of course, that it enables more people to communicate their ideas and to provide important information of value to the public than would be the case if their speech were chilled by requirements to use their real name. In authoritarian countries almost everyone will be reluctant to speak freely online, as well as offline, if they fear the imposition of legal sanctions. That is the reason why David Kaye, the UN Special Rapporteur on the promotion of freedom of expression, has strongly supported a right to communicate anonymously on the Net.[37] Anonymity enables the circumvention of the myriad restrictions on the exercise of freedom of expression imposed by authoritarian governments. In liberal societies more tolerant of political dissent, anonymity is essential for whistle-blowers who would otherwise be vulnerable to dismissal or social ostracism from work colleagues, for the victims of family or sexual abuse, and for asylum-seekers and immigrants.[38] The arguments which were considered at length in chapter 3 apply at least as strongly to the Internet as they do to the traditional mass media.

There is one argument in support of anonymity which focuses on the particular character of the Internet. As the District Court Judge said in a leading US case on regulation of the Internet, 'it is the most participatory form of mass speech yet developed'.[39] Individuals are free to communicate their views on any topic they like by blogging, commenting on others' blogs, through websites and social media platforms, by email and in discussion groups. There are only minimal entry costs for access to the Web. As Jack Balkin, a leading American commentator on the implications of digital communication for freedom of speech, has written, 'technological changes have

---

[36] KS Williams, 'On-Line Anonymity, De-individuation and Freedom of Expression and Privacy' (2006) 110 *Penn State Law Review* 687, 693–97 reviews the arguments, and concludes that anonymity is not a significant causative factor. See also D Rowland, 'Griping, Bitching and Speaking Your Mind: Defamation and Free Expression on the Internet' (2006) 110 *Penn State Law Review* 519, 531–35.

[37] *Report of the UN Special Rapporteur* (n 11) paras 23 and 31.

[38] E Stein, 'Queers Anonymous: Lesbians, Gay Men, Free Speech and Cyberspace' (2003) 38 *Harvard Civil Rights—Civil Liberties Law Review* 159, 199, argues for the importance of online anonymity to enable gay people to contribute freely to public discourse.

[39] *Reno v American Civil Liberties Union*, 929 F Supp 824, 833 (ED Pa, 1996) per Dalzell District J.

made it possible for large numbers of people to broadcast and publish to audiences around the world, to be speakers as well as audiences'.[40]

In the Internet context *speakers* therefore have a particularly strong claim to the right to freedom of speech (or expression), because the Net provides them with a facility they have not enjoyed in the context of the mass media where their access is controlled by various 'gatekeepers': newspaper editors, radio and television producers, and book and magazine publishers. In the traditional mass media contexts more emphasis is usually placed on the interests of readers, viewers and other *recipients* of speech who are generally concerned to know the identity of the journalist or broadcaster in order to assess his reliability (see chapter 3, section III). On the Internet in contrast, users may be more tolerant of anonymity,[41] either because it is generally accepted or because they have lower expectations of the reliability of the information provided on many sites or of the expertise of bloggers and commentators. Too much should not be made, however, of the latter point. Some users may rely, for example, on the anonymous reviews of hotels and restaurants on travel advice sites, such as Trip Advisor, while online commentators using a pseudonym may build up a reputation for expertise or straight dealing and win the trust of Net users.[42] The anonymity of Wikipedia surely contributes to its authority, just as unsigned articles in newspapers were considered to carry more weight than they would have done had they carried the journalist's by-line (see chapter 2, section IV(A)).[43]

On the other hand, some features of the Internet may make online communication potentially more damaging than comparable remarks offline.[44] Online communication tends to permanence, certainly more so than broadcasts or newsprint.[45] Search engines like Google provide users with links to harmful communications, so they remain easily accessible long after they were first made.[46] So these communications are more likely to be seen by the public, including potential employers of a victim of cyber-hate or harassment, and for a longer time, than similar communications in the traditional media. The absence of entry costs enables anyone to blog, comment on

[40] JM Balkin, 'The Future of Free Expression in a Digital Age' (2009) 34 *Pepperdine Law Review* 427, 440. See also JM Balkin, 'Digital Speech and Democratic Culture: A Theory of Freedom of Expression for the Information Society' (2004) 79 *New York University Law Review* 1.

[41] Ekstrand, 'The Many Masks of Anon' (n 33) 18.

[42] Bartlett, *The Dark Net* (n 2) 150–52.

[43] Wikipedia material is entitled to authority only insofar as its accuracy is carefully checked and open to correction: see the text at n 120 below.

[44] Citron, *Hate Crimes in Cyberspace* (n 7) 4–12.

[45] This is the subject of V Mayer-Schönberger, *Delete: The Virtue of Forgetting in the Digital Age* (Princeton, NJ, Princeton University Press, 2009).

[46] See B Leiter, 'Cleaning Cyber-Cesspools: Google and Free Speech' in S Levmore and MG Nussbaum (eds), *The Offensive Internet* (Cambridge, MA, Harvard University Press, 2012) 155. In C-131/12 *Google Spain; Mario Costeja Gonzalez* [2014] EMLR 27, the European Court of Justice upheld a right to be forgotten, requiring Google to remove links in search engine results to stale information in a newspaper about attachment proceedings in connection with Costeja's social security debts in 1998.

blogs, and communicate in other ways online, without any control from editors and media lawyers who can, and should, remove potentially defamatory or other harmful content in the absence of justification for its publication, for example, a defence to a libel action or a public interest argument. So it is unlikely there will be any preliminary check to ensure that the Net is not used for the dissemination of hate speech, cyber-bulling or harassment, or defamation.

Two aspects of *anonymous* online communication are particularly important, and provide the strongest argument for the imposition of restrictions on anonymity in this context. The first is the absence of responsible intermediaries, compared with the position for publication in the traditional media.[47] In the case of book publishing, newspapers, journals and broadcasting, the publisher and editors (or other comparable figures) can usually vouch for the integrity and reliability of the anonymous author (or the source for a newspaper or broadcast story). They can check the story before publication, and their lawyers should remove material which carries unwarranted legal risks. It is in contrast unusual for any intermediary to assume this responsibility in the online world. It is relatively difficult for website operators or social media platforms such as Facebook actively to monitor the thousands of communications which are daily sent to their sites, and absolutely impossible for ISPs (generally acting merely as conduits for the transmission of messages) to do this. If the victim of an anonymous defamatory allegation is to have any chance of receiving compensation for reputational damage, the legal choice is either to impose liability on the website operator or ISP, which may deter Internet intermediaries from providing their service, or to persuade or compel them to assist in the identification of the anonymous (or pseudonymous) author. This topic is considered at length in section III below.

The problem occurs in fields other than defamation law: the control of pornography, particularly child pornography, of communications encouraging or soliciting acts of terrorism, and of hate speech, cyber-harassment and bullying. If authors cannot be identified, and easily prosecuted, there are frequently calls for ISPs and other intermediaries to exercise greater control over the content of the messages they carry. For example, under the Terrorism Act 2006, they may face criminal prosecution if they fail to take down unlawful 'terrorism-related' material after receiving appropriate notice;[48] this possibility provides some remedy for one type of anonymous communication on the Net, though it also applies where the author is identifiable.

The other aspect of Internet communication which may be especially disturbing when anonymous is this: the victim of hate speech or a threat of violence has no idea where it comes from. A woman facing anonymous online threats of rape (see the example discussed in the next section) does

---

[47] S Levmore, 'The Internet's Anonymity Problem' in S Levmore and MG Nussbaum (eds), *The Offensive Internet* (Cambridge, MA, Harvard University Press, 2012) 50, 54–55.
[48] Terrorism Act 2006, s 3.

not know whether they were made by neighbours who are able to follow her movements near her home or were made by people living miles away. She can therefore never be certain if she will face an imminent physical attack. This uncertainty makes even more terrifying the impact of cyber mobs who attempt to silence women and members of minority group by forcing them offline.[49]

For these two reasons the anonymity of damaging Internet communications creates real difficulties; it may make the harm more acute and it is much harder for its incidence to be reduced through effective monitoring by responsible intermediaries as in the case of the traditional mass media. It is hard to disagree with the conclusion of Saul Levmore, a leading American commentator on Internet regulation, that anonymity, coupled with the lack of effective regulation on the Internet, has made it 'the preferred medium for juvenile communications'.[50] But it does not follow that anonymity should simply be banned, as has happened in China and other authoritarian countries, where users have been required to register under their real names. Anonymity—in practice the use of pseudonyms—does enable more people to communicate freely and openly on the Net, and the advantages of this medium would be lost if the law significantly restricted its use, let alone banned it altogether. The optimum solution is to allow the practice, while at the same time to enable the authorities and the victims of defamatory allegations to identity the authors of harmful communications for the purpose of legal proceedings when it is right to hold them accountable.

II. ANONYMITY IN THE SOCIAL MEDIA

Anonymity in the social media (sometimes described as social networking sites) has been particularly controversial, for two reasons. First, its frequent use for trolling, in particular the cyber-bullying of adolescents, has been held largely responsible for a number of tragic episodes, among them the suicides of its victims. Secondly, the adoption by some social media of real name registration policies has been heavily criticised by those commentators who regard them as contrary to the ethos and culture of the Internet. These policies have certainly had an adverse impact on free political speech under authoritarian regimes and attracted fierce protest in Iran and Tunisia.[51] The arguments for and against regulating anonymity and pseudonyms in the social media are identical to those made in the context of

---

[49] See the essay by DK Citron, 'Civil Rights in our Information Age' in S Levmore and MG Nussbaum (eds), *The Offensive Internet* (Cambridge, MA, Harvard University Press, 2012) 31, and her book, *Hate Crimes in Cyberspace* (n 7) 8–9, 195–97, and T McGonagle, *Paper for Council of Europe on Online Hate Speech*, MCM (2013)005 (2013) 31–32.

[50] Levmore, 'The Internet's Anonymity Problem' (n 47) 50, 56–57.

[51] MacKinnon, *Consent of the Networked* (n 1) 159–64.

other communications on the Net, considered earlier in this chapter. But they have particular resonance in this context, given the widespread use of social media by political dissidents and young people.

Many of the most widely used social networking sites have adopted policies, under which users are required to register under their real names and provide an email address. Facebook does not allow registration under pseudonym, though it may permit registration under a well-established stage name if the star's identity has been verified.[52] In its view people are more responsible in debate and social commentary when they use the site under their real name.[53] It is strict in enforcing these requirements, though it relies on reports from users that someone is using a false name on their account. Facebook even insisted that Salman Rushdie registered under his rarely used actual first name, Ahmed. Subsequently, it relented and allowed the author to register under his usual name. For Facebook's founder, Marc Zuckerberg, openness and transparency are crucial: 'Having two identities for yourself is an example of a lack of integrity.' (Google+ was even stricter in enforcing a real name policy: see below for further discussion.) Some social media sites require users to provide their name, but make little or no attempt to check that it is real and not made up. On others, notably Twitter, where an account may be created under the user's own name or under a pseudonym, checks are made to verify only the accounts of celebrities such as Stephen Fry, so followers can be sure that they are reading his tweets.

Facebook's real name policy has been challenged in Germany which does allow anonymity and the use of pseudonyms on social media. Section 13, VI of the Telemedia Act of 2007 provides that service providers must allow the anonymous or pseudonymous use of their services insofar as this is technically possible and reasonable, while the federal Data Protection Act of 2003 (as amended in 2009) requires the aliasing or rendering anonymous of personal data so far as this is possible.[54] The Data Protection Authority in Schleswig-Holstein ruled that Facebook's real name policy infringed German data protection law, but this ruling was successfully challenged in the state Administrative Court on the ground that the law only applied when the data controller was established in Germany or in a non-EU state. The Court accepted Facebook's argument that it was established in Ireland, which did not prescribe any freedom to communicate anonymously.[55]

---

[52] Ibid 150; Citron, *Hate Crimes in Cyberspace* (n 7) 238.

[53] Facebook Guidelines of March 2015 for the removal of hate content.

[54] Data Protection Law, s 3a. The terms 'aliasing' and 'rendering anonymous' are defined in s 3, VI of the Law. The real name policy could not be challenged on constitutional grounds in the United States, since the First Amendment freedom of speech is guaranteed only against state, not private, interference.

[55] For discussion of this controversy, see S Schmitz, 'Facebook's Real Name Policy' (2013) 4 *Journal of Intellectual Property, Information Technology and Electronic Commerce Law* (online journal) 190.

In complete contrast to Facebook, some social networking sites have explicitly adopted anonymity policies under which users are free to communicate under a pseudonym or without any identifying name. Among them are Social Number (users are identified by number, not name); Gaia Online, a gaming site; Ask-fm; Evsum; and Anonyming. One of the best known is the controversial site 4chan, launched in 2003 by Christopher Poole under the pseudonym 'moot'; its /b/image board is widely used for trolling and the dissemination of pornographic images.[56] Registration is not required, or even possible except for members of staff. The site has excited considerable controversy over its use for Internet attacks and for the posting of threats of violence.[57] In the last two years mobile versions of these sites have been developed with the evolution of mobile apps. The only obstacle to the expansion of these sites and apps is the difficulty in attracting advertising revenue, because they cannot identify particular users to advertisers.

When Google+ (or Google Plus) was launched in June 2011, it required users to register under their 'common name', the name by which they were known to family, friends and work colleagues. It adopted an algorithm which identified likely pseudonyms, and automatically suspended the accounts of their holders, even though those users were generally known by a pseudonym or a nickname. Users and commentators rounded on Google+. The Electronic Frontier Foundation in the United States argued that Google's 'common name' policy chilled the online speech of women, minorities and activists in authoritarian regimes. The clash between Google and Google+ users has been referred to as 'the Nymwars', a fight over the right claimed by online users to adopt a pseudonym or communicate anonymously if they preferred.[58] Google defended its policy as necessary to promote the safe use of the Net and to prevent the dissemination of anonymous spam, but commentators argued that its real object (and that of other sites with a real names requirement) was to sell the names of subscribers to advertisers.[59] The Nymwars could, therefore, be presented as a clash between free speech rights and the commercial interests of social media platforms and the advertisers financing them. Taken aback by the volume of criticism, Google announced in October 2011 its intent to allow the use of pseudonyms, and the common name policy for Google+ was finally abandoned in July 2014.[60]

---

[56] Bartlett, *The Dark Net* (n 2) 35–37, 170.
[57] See https://en.wikipedia.org/wik/4chan; and see Citron, *Hate Crimes in Cyberspace* (n 7) 52–55.
[58] See www.eff.org/deeplinks/2011/12/2011-review-nymwars; and see Hogan, 'Pseudonyms and the Rise of the Real-Name Web' (n 10).
[59] See Laurel Papworth, *Social Network Identity: Anonymity, Pseudonymity, and Accountability*, Media 140, (10 November 2011) available at http://laurelpapworth.com/social-network-identity-anonymity-pseudonymity-and-accountability-media140/.
[60] See https://en.wikipedia.org/wiki/Nymwars.

The use of anonymity on the social media continues to be vigorously debated. Some organisations have strongly defended it. The British Medical Association backs the right of doctors to use social networks in a personal capacity anonymously, though the General Medical Council recommends that they should identify themselves if they mention their work. Unsurprisingly, Alcoholics Anonymous suggests that members do not reveal that they are AA members on the social media, as they could be inadvertently identifying another member. That is however not the same as support for anonymity or the use of a made-up name. Anonymity is supported by free speech organisations such as the Electronic Frontier Foundation in the United States, and Article 19. On the other hand, its use has been criticised; the prominent freedom of information campaigner, Heather Brooke, regards anonymity as the tool of bullying cowards, and Julie Zhuo has argued in the *New York Times* that disclosure of an author's identity is vital for improving the quality of online debate—though it should be noted that she worked for Facebook.[61]

It is easy to give examples of the clear abuse of anonymity on social media. There have been several episodes of anonymous cyber-bullying on the Latvian-based question and answer site Ask-fm.[62] Bullying on this site led to the suicide of a 14-year-old girl, Hannah Smith.[63] Using a false name, a Facebook user in South Shields, Tyneside, posted a message on Facebook threatening to kill at least 200 US high school students.[64] Perhaps the best known case is the conviction of two Tweeters for sending anonymously vicious threats of violence, including rape, to Caroline Criado-Perez for campaigning for a woman to appear on Bank of England notes, and to Stella Creasy, MP, for supporting her campaign. The judge said that the anonymous character of the tweets 'heightened the fear', as the victims could not tell how dangerous the tweeters were and how to recognise and avoid them.[65] Like the Facebook user in South Shields, the tweeters were convicted of the offence of sending 'grossly offensive' and 'menacing' messages contrary to section 127 of the Communications Act 2003.

In the United States, social networking sites have enabled college students to spread gossip about each other anonymously. The site JuicyCampus, now defunct, boasted that it would not itself be liable for helping in the dissemination of defamatory or other illegal messages, because of the immunity conferred by section 230 of the Communications Decency Act of 1996,[66]

---

[61] See www.nytimes.com/2010/11/30/opinion/30zhuo.html?_r=4&.
[62] *Guardian*, 10 August 2013.
[63] Ask f-m has been linked to at least five teenage suicides, and the comparable US site Formspring to three: A Binns, 'Facebook's Ugly Sisters: Anonymity and Abuse on Formspring and Ask.fm' (2013) 4 *Media Education Research Journal* 27.
[64] *Guardian*, 27 April 2013.
[65] See www.theguardian.com/uk-news/2014/jan/24/two-jailed-twitter-abuse-feminist-c....
[66] See the discussion in section III(D) below.

and that it did not ask its users for their name, email address or other identifying features.[67] In one particularly egregious case, the AutoAdmit social networking site carried several pseudonymous posts sexually abusing and threatening named women law students at Yale.[68] The women brought legal proceedings, successfully requesting that the site identify those who had posted the threatening and harassing messages: see section III below for discussion of the proceedings. Martha Nussbaum has questioned whether the posters should have been allowed anonymity in the first place; university sites should in her view compel users to identify themselves as a condition for posting messages.[69]

To some extent users of social media can protect themselves by, for example, declining to accept anonymous messages on sites such as Ask f-m or by refusing to reply, so preventing dissemination of the exchange with their tormenter.[70] But it is clearly wrong to expect a victim to leave a site altogether, as Caroline Criado-Perez did for a time after receiving abuse from over 80 Twitter accounts for her bank note campaign. The abuser then silences his victim as well as creating anxiety and fear. The victim may also find it more difficult to obtain employment if they abandon use of social media platforms such as Facebook and LinkedIn.[71]

The real challenge is for the social media platforms themselves: whether they should do more to limit threats of violence and abuse stemming from anonymous users without going so far as to enforce a real name registration policy. It is clearly impossible for the most popular sites to monitor or vet the millions of messages carried each week in the same way, for example, that the voluntary contributors to Wikipedia ensure the accuracy of its entries.[72] But they should react immediately when they receive notice from a victim of cyber-harassment or of cyber-bullying, by suspending the accounts of the perpetrator and identifying him to the police and other relevant authorities. Insofar as they have previously allowed anonymity or the use of a pseudonym, they should require that in future the authors of hate speech or abuse uses a real name on the social media platform; as Danielle

---

[67] DJ Solove, 'Speech, Privacy, and Reputation on the Internet' in S Levmore and MG Nussbaum (eds), *The Offensive Internet* (Cambridge, MA, Harvard University Press, 2012) 15, 24, and Levmore, 'The Internet's Anonymity Problem' (n 47) 50, 58. (See also Cohen-Almagor, *Confronting the Internet's Dark Side* (n 16) 86–88.)

[68] For details of the threats and slurs, see Citron, 'Civil Rights in Our Information Age' (n 49) 31, 34–35, and MC Nussbaum, 'Objectification and Internet Misogyny' in S Levmore and MG Nussbaum (eds), *The Offensive Internet* (Cambridge, MA, Harvard University Press, 2012) 68, 73–75.

[69] Ibid 85.

[70] Binns, 'Facebook's Ugly Sisters' (n 63) 27, 33–34.

[71] Citron, *Hate Crimes in Cyberspace* (n 7) 8–9.

[72] See Levmore, 'The Internet's Anonymity Problem' (n 47) 59.

Citron puts it in her study of online hate speech, 'anonymity would be a privilege that can be lost'.[73]

In the context of libel law, as will be discussed in the next section, a frequently suggested remedy is the adoption of a notice and take-down procedure, under which a platform removes a message immediately it is put on notice by the victim of a defamatory allegation. But if an Internet intermediary is induced to take down defamatory (and other illegal) messages because it may itself otherwise be exposed to legal liability, there is an obvious danger that it will act as a free speech censor by immediately removing material which might turn out to have lawful content. That objection may not be a strong one in the context, for example, of incitements to violence or cyber-bullying where the illegal character of the message is usually very clear. It has rather more weight in the context of defamation, where it is much harder for a website operator or other intermediary to determine whether there is legal liability. Apart from that context, it is surely right to expect social media platforms to do as much as they can to assist the victims of abuse and cyber-bullying, even if that means sacrificing their users' interest in communicating anonymously.

III. DEFAMATION LAW AND ANONYMITY ON THE INTERNET

A. General

The law of defamation balances the interest of the claimant in vindicating his reputation by securing damages from a defendant who has libelled him against the interest of the defendant (usually a branch of the traditional mass media) in freedom of expression. Historically, greater weight has been attached by English common law to the former, the claimant's right to protect his reputation, than to the defendant's free speech rights. For example, in English law it is for the defendant to prove the truth of the allegations which are presumed to be false, and until recently there was no defence if the press or other branch of the media published inaccurate defamatory statements, even though they were believed on good grounds to be true.[74] By contrast in the United States, after the landmark decision of the Supreme Court in *New York Times v Sullivan*,[75] a public official could only win libel

---

[73] Citron, *Hate Crimes in Cyberspace* (n 7) 239. But she opposes Facebook's real names policy as contrary to freedom of speech.

[74] In *Reynolds v Times Newspapers Ltd* [2001] 2 AC 127, the House of Lords upheld a public interest privilege for untrue defamatory communications, provided that the information was in the public interest and that the defendant observed the requirements of 'responsible journalism'; the defence has now been replaced by Defamation Act 2013, s 4.

[75] (1964) 376 US 254.

damages if he proved that the defendant had published the allegations with 'actual malice', defined as knowledge that they were false or reckless indifference to their truth or falsity. This principle was later extended to cover actions by public figures, with the consequence that it is virtually impossible in practice for a celebrity to win a libel action.[76]

The application of the principles of defamation law to communications on the Internet raises a number of issues: should, for example, defamatory blogs or other communications on the Net be treated as libel or slander, and to what extent should a website, which itself is without defamatory content, be liable if it links to another site which does contain a defamatory allegation?[77] Further, there are complex questions of jurisdiction and choice of law where a defamatory allegation is uploaded in one state—such as a US State which under the principle in *New York Times v Sullivan* provides generous free speech defences—but is read in another state where the libel laws, like those in England, are considered more friendly to claimants.[78] These questions arise whether the author of the defamatory allegations is identified or is anonymous and are not considered here; the discussion is concerned with the problems of applying defamation law to anonymous communications.

Obviously a claimant faces the difficulty of identifying the author of an anonymous message so that he can take legal proceedings against him: to what extent can an ISP be compelled to help the claimant identify him, and how far might the ISP, or other intermediary, itself be liable in defamation for publishing the allegation? The questions are considered later (see sections III(C) and (D) below). This section also examines (section III(B)) whether the fact that an online allegation was made *anonymously* or by someone writing with a *pseudonym* should be relevant to its interpretation: on one view an anonymous message is less likely than one by a named author to be taken seriously, and should not therefore be understood as making an allegation of fact likely to cause the claimant serious harm.

Under the most radical approach to the application of defamation law in this context there would be no liability at all for blogs and comments on the Internet, particularly if they have been made anonymously.[79] Blogs, and *a fortiori* other communications on the Net, are, it is said, not relied on in the same way as comparable material in newspapers and on the broadcasting

---

[76] For a summary of this line of authority, see Barendt, 206–10.

[77] In *Crookes v Newton* [2011] SCR 269 the Supreme Court of Canada held that the hyperlinker should not be liable for defamatory content in the linked material.

[78] For the relevant UK statutes, see Defamation Act 2013, s 9 and Private International Law (Miscellaneous Provisions) Act 1995, ss 11 and 13.

[79] An even more radical line, now rarely taken, is that it is wrong for national law to attempt to regulate any aspect of the Internet, which should be governed by its own cyber-laws; see DR Johnson and D Post, 'Law and Borders: The Rise of Law in Cyberspace' (1996) 48 *Stanford Law Review* 1367.

media; further, victims can easily reply to defamatory online allegations, perhaps through their own blogs.[80] To apply the usual principles of defamation law, developed for communication on the mass media, would be to stifle spontaneous anonymous, communication on the Net, and this risk requires the application of special, more lenient legal principles. But online newspapers would remain subject to standard libel law.[81]

One objection to this proposal is that it ignores the impact that defamatory Internet content may have in the real world—on the social standing and self-esteem of ordinary people, or on the commercial standing of corporations.[82] The instantaneous, global character of Internet communications means that a reputation can be destroyed throughout the world in a few seconds, and it seems silly to argue that it can be restored by a blog or email in reply. The anonymity of much Internet communication is at most only a factor to take into account when considering the modification of the usual principles of defamation law, rather than a ground for departing from them altogether. Moreover, the adoption of more lenient principles of defamation law for the Internet would be to discriminate in favour of that medium and against the traditional mass media. The law, as Kirby J pointed out in *Dow Jones and Company, Inc v Gutnick*, should be 'technology-neutral',[83] and it should not confer on the Internet privileges which are not enjoyed by other media in competition with it. So it is better to consider how the principles of defamation law should be applied with sensitivity for the special characteristics of Internet communication, in particular the frequent resort to anonymity, rather than to depart from them altogether. This was the approach taken by a Joint Committee of the House of Lords and House of Commons when it considered the government's draft Defamation Bill (now the Defamation Act 2013) in 2012: in its view defamation law should in principle apply to publications on the Net as it does to the more traditional mass media.[84] That is surely correct.

B. Anonymity and Interpretation

The meaning of language alleged to be defamatory of a claimant is often critical. Indeed, a committee reviewing the reform of English libel law

---

[80] See GH Reynolds, 'Libel in the Blogosphere: Some Preliminary Thoughts' (2006) 84 *Washington University Law Review* 1157, 1166–67.

[81] Y Karniel, 'Defamation on the Internet: A New Approach to Libel in Cyberspace' (2009) 2 *Journal of International Media and Entertainment Law* 215.

[82] See M Hadley, 'The *Gertz* Doctrine and Internet Defamation' (1998) 84 *Virginia Law Review* 477, 491–98, and SE Malloy, 'Anonymous Bloggers and Defamation: Balancing Interests on the Internet' (2006) 84 *Washington University Law Review* 1187, 1191.

[83] (2002) 210 CLR 575, para 125.

[84] HL Paper 203, HC Paper 930-1 (2011–12), para 93.

in 1975 identified it as the single most important issue in defamation litigation.[85] It is crucial in determining whether the words complained of are defamatory or merely abusive, whether they amount to an allegation of fact or are the expression of an opinion, and whether the defendant has proved the truth of any factual allegations as interpreted by the court ('the imputation conveyed by the statement complained of').[86] In defamation law the judge ascribes a single meaning to the language of which complaint is made, an approach not adopted in other legal proceedings such as an action for malicious falsehood; although controversial, the single meaning rule can be defended as striking a necessary balance between the different interpretations which may be placed on the language by different groups of readers and which may be contended for by the claimant and the defendant.

One question to be considered here is whether the courts should take a different approach to understanding the words used in Internet communication from that they adopt when interpreting press and broadcast reports. Secondly, is it relevant in interpreting their language that the allegations were made anonymously or by someone using a pseudonym? In determining meaning courts take into account the context in which the words were used, for example, the terms of the whole of an article in which the allegedly defamatory allegation is embedded, and the mode of publication. So they do take into consideration the informal character of much Internet communication and the exaggerated, hyperbolic language in which it is often couched. In a leading US case, the California Court of Appeal thought the concealment of speakers' identities was responsible for this characteristic of speech on the Net: 'the relative anonymity afforded by the Internet forum promotes a looser, more relaxed communication style'.[87] So anonymous posts calling the female claimant and other officers of a Florida company 'boobs, losers and crooks', and purporting to outline the sexual fantasies of the company's legal officer about the claimant, were 'rude and childish' and characterised as an expression of opinion rather than as an allegation of fact.[88] On the other hand, a court in New York rejected the argument of an anonymous blogger that references to a fashion model as 'whoring' and 'skanky' in the captions to photographs of her in sexually provocative postures did not contain assertions of objective fact; the court upheld the petitioner model's application for an order directing Google, the provider of Blogger.com, to identify the blogger.[89] But the anonymity of Internet communications is

---

[85] *Report of the Faulks Committee on Defamation*, Cmnd 5909 (1975) para 92.
[86] Defamation Act 2013, s 2(1).
[87] *Krinsky v Doe 6*, 72 Cal Reporter 3d 231 (Cal App 6 Dist 2008).
[88] Ibid 250. For commentary on this case, see LB Lidsky, 'Anonymity in Cyberspace: What Can We Learn from John Doe?' (2009) 50 *Boston College Law Review* 1373, 1381–84.
[89] *Liskula Cohen v Google, Inc*, 887 NYS2d 424 (Supreme Ct NY County, 2009). 'Skank' means someone disgustingly foul or filthy, or considered sexually promiscuous.

often regarded in American case law as one reason for not treating them as making credible allegations of fact. On that ground, the claimant may fail to make out a prima facie libel case sufficient to persuade a court to compel the ISP, or other intermediary, to help him identify the author of an anonymous or pseudonymous message (see further section III(C) below).

English courts have adopted a similar approach to the interpretation of defamatory communications on the Internet. In *Smith v ADVFN plc*, Eady J halted 37 libel proceedings brought by the claimant in respect of comments on bulletin boards which were highly critical, indeed abusive, with regard to his behaviour in attempting to co-ordinate a shareholders' action group. In the judge's view, bulletin board communications are 'rather like contributions to a casual conversation ... are often uninhibited, casual and ill thought out; those who participate know this, and expect a certain amount of repartee, or "give and take"'.[90] The participants mostly used pseudonyms in their exchanges, and did not take the remarks seriously. They should be treated as more like slander, or as mere abuse.[91] The claims were dismissed as without merit.

In another case, the character of postings on a football club supporters' website was taken into account in deciding whether to compel the website operator to disclose the identity of the posters.[92] They had invariably adopted a pseudonym (for example, 'half-pint', 'xdanielx' and 'Auckland Owl') as their user name. A disclosure order was made only in respect of serious allegations of the greed, untrustworthiness and dishonesty of the claimants, directors of Sheffield Wednesday FC, where their rights trumped 'the right of the authors to maintain their anonymity and their right to express themselves freely'.[93] It would in contrast have been a disproportionate interference with freedom of speech to make a disclosure order in respect of merely trivial or abusive postings.

This approach of taking into account the informal character of Internet publications was approved by the Joint Committee of the House of Lords and House of Commons considering the draft Defamation Bill in 2012:

> many derogatory and mocking statements on blogs and social networking sites may be read casually, remain fleeting in their impact and be given limited credence by readers when compared, for example, to material published by reputable media organisations.[94]

This consideration should, in the Committee's view, be given appropriate weight by courts when they determine whether the publication is likely to

---

[90] [2008] EWHC 1797 (QB), para 14.
[91] Ibid paras 15–17.
[92] *Sheffield Wednesday Football Club and others v Hargreaves* [2007] EWHC 2375 (QB).
[93] Ibid para 18 per Richard Parkes QC, sitting as a Deputy Judge. Also see the decision of Sharp J in *Clift v Clarke* [2011] EWHC 1164 (QB).
[94] HL Paper 203, HC Paper 930-1 (n 84) para 95. See Rowbottom, 'To Rant, Vent and Converse' (n 29) 370–79 for support for lenient treatment of low level speech on the Internet.

cause serious harm to the claimant's reputation—a requirement now for a successful libel action under section 1 of the Defamation Act 2013.[95] The anonymity of the publication would almost certainly have some relevance in determining the seriousness of that harm.

However, there is a good argument against attaching decisive (or perhaps even much) weight to the use of anonymity or a pseudonym when interpreting language alleged to be defamatory. Too ready an interpretation of anonymous aspersions as mere abuse or as the expression of an opinion, rather than as defamatory allegations of fact, would encourage the use of anonymity (and pseudonyms) by speakers who know that they are on that account less likely to be held liable in libel proceedings. This would place a further obstacle for libel claimants, in addition to the difficulty they may have in identifying an author against whom proceedings may be taken. This argument would, of course, not be accepted by proponents of strong free speech anonymity rights, but it should be taken seriously by those who want to discourage the use of anonymity, except in those circumstances where it is supported by strong arguments (see chapter 3, section V).

C. Identification of Anonymous Internet Authors

Is a court entitled to compel an Internet intermediary (a website operator or an ISP) to identify, so far as it can, the user from whose computer an allegedly defamatory message was sent? In the view of the European Court of Human Rights this course may be required in certain circumstance; the public interest and the well-being of the victim required the identification of the person who had placed an advertisement on an Internet dating site in the applicant's name, purporting to look for an intimate sexual relationship.[96] The question has arisen in a few English cases,[97] and in many in the United States where the strong protection afforded the right to anonymous speech has led to some complex law.[98] A leading English decision is that of Owen J in *Totalise plc v The Motley Fool Ltd*, where he granted the claimant (itself an ISP) an order to compel the defendants, operators of websites

---

[95] Reynolds, 'Libel in the Blogosphere' (n 80) 1166–67 recommends that the level of harm should be 'fairly high' for claimants in the United States to recover damages in Internet cases.

[96] *KU v Finland* (n 27). The Court rejected the argument that the possibility of obtaining damages against the ISP was a sufficient remedy in this case: ibid para 47.

[97] It also arose in a recent Scottish case; the Court of Session rejected an application to compel TripAdvisor to disclose the names of authors of two allegedly defamatory reviews of a guesthouse, on the ground that the contract provided for the exclusive jurisdiction of courts in Massachusetts:seewww.scotsman.com/lifestyle/travel/guest-house-couple-fail-to-unmask-online-critics-1-3297405 (I am grateful to Gillian Morris for referring me to this case).

[98] For a survey of legal problems in this area, see M Collins, *The Law of Defamation and the Internet*, 3rd edn (New York, OUP, 2010) paras 5.63–5.74 (UK and Commonwealth authorities) and 30.23–30.31 (US authorities).

with discussion boards, to disclose the identity of 'Z Dust' who had posted seriously defamatory allegations against it on their boards.[99] It was granted under the principles established in *Norwich Pharmacal Co v Customs and Excise Commissioners*,[100] under which a person who has facilitated wrong-doing may be required by an order for discovery to provide information to enable a claimant to identify the wrong-doer. The judge rejected the defendants' argument that it could claim the journalists' privilege not to disclose its sources conferred by section 10 of the Contempt of Court Act 1981 (see chapter 5, section II). The defendants did not take any responsibility for the comments which appeared on their discussion boards, but simply provided a facility by which members of the public could communicate their views.[101] Owen J exercised his discretion to grant the disclosure order, largely because the allegations were very serious and the user was 'hiding behind the anonymity afforded by access to the defendants' discussion boards'. Further, there was no other way by which his identity could be discovered.[102]

On appeal in this case (brought solely on costs), the Court of Appeal did say that it would sometimes be legitimate to protect an anonymous speaker's identity, and also that it may be appropriate for the website operator to inform the author and give him an opportunity to produce reasons to the claimant and to the court for preserving his anonymity.[103] As noted earlier, anonymity may be protected where the court considers the allegations too trivial to cause serious harm.[104] Now, however, under section 5 of the Defamation Act 2013, discussed in the next subsection, a website operator's own defence to defamation proceedings is conditional on its assistance of a libel claimant to identify an anonymous author; anonymity is in this way discouraged. The impact of this new statutory provision on the earlier case law is not yet clear.

Applause Store Productions and Firsht v Raphael is an instructive case,[105] bringing out many issues in this area of law. A false Facebook profile was created in the name of the second claimant, Matthew Firsht, and shortly afterwards a Facebook group was set up, linked to this profile, which contained seriously defamatory matter concerning Firsht and his company, Applause Store. Both the profile and the group were established by one of the two computers using an IP address accepted to have been the defendant's; the question for the court was whether the defendant, Grant Raphael, was the author of the defamatory messages, or whether, as he contended,

---

[99] [2001] EMLR 29.
[100] [1974] AC 133, HL.
[101] *Totalise plc* (n 99) paras 25–26.
[102] Ibid para 27.
[103] [2002] 1 WLR 1233, CA, paras 25–26.
[104] *Sheffield Wednesday Football Club v Hargreaves* (n 92).
[105] [2008] EWHC 1781 (QB).

the profile and group had been set up by one of the three or four acquaintances who had stayed at his flat during the relevant time. Facebook had complied with a *Norwich Pharmacal* order to identify the IP address of the computer which had set up the false material.[106] The judge determined on the basis of his assessment of the evidence concerning the Facebook activity log and the movements of people at the flat that it was implausible that anyone other than the defendant was responsible for the defamatory material.[107] (The judgment also resolved a straightforward issue concerning the meaning of the allegation on the group page.)[108]

In English law, therefore, an intermediary can usually be compelled to disclose the IP address of the computer from which the defamatory material was sent, but it may be harder to identify the individual responsible for it, as in *Applause Store* or where the messages are sent from a computer in an Internet café.[109] The position in the United States is quite different, because of its strong protection of anonymous speech. In the courts' view, the easy identification of anyone sending defamatory messages online would chill freedom of speech on the Internet and therefore be incompatible with the First Amendment. They therefore require a claimant to satisfy a threshold test before they are willing to compel an ISP or other intermediary to disclose the IP address of a subscriber from whose computer a defamatory message has been sent. First, the anonymous author must be given notice of the libel action and an opportunity to have it dismissed to protect his anonymity; notice can be given by posting it on the site where the allegedly defamatory allegation had been placed. Secondly, the usual test is that the claimant must establish a prima facie case of defamation, and he must then show under a balancing standard that his interest in discovering the author's identity in order to take proceedings to vindicate his reputation outweighs the defendant's right to speak anonymously.[110]

On this balancing approach account is taken of the character of the speech, so an author of anonymous *political* speech (for example, criticism of a town council member) is less likely to be unmasked than an author of defamatory *commercial* allegations, to which less weight is attached under the First Amendment.[111] Nor is inane anonymous gossip protected as strongly as political speech. A federal District Court compelled an ISP

---

[106] Ibid para 10.
[107] Ibid para 62.
[108] Ibid para 8.
[109] See the evidence of Mark Gracey, Chair of the Internet Services Providers Association Content Liability Sub-Group to the Joint Committee, HL Paper 203, HC Paper 930-1 (n 84) vol II, 286 and n 124.
[110] *Dendrite International Inc v Doe*, 775 A2d 756 (NJ Superior Court, AD 2001). See Kaminski, 'Real Masks and Real Name Policies' (n 10) 882–83.
[111] Compare *Doe v Cahill*, 884 A2d 451 (Del 2005) (comments on political blog about mental state of a town councillor) with *In re Online Anonymous Speakers*, 611 F3d 653 (9th Cir 2010) (commercial smears directed at business practices of a distribution company).

to identify the subscribers to its service who had posted under pseudonym scandalous comments on the sexuality and sexual conduct of female Yale law students; it was rightly unimpressed by the argument for anonymity, where the subscribers' comments 'were seriously defamatory and had little or no free speech value.[112] The court also robustly rejected the argument that the subscribers had a reasonable expectation of privacy when the ISP privacy policy clearly indicated that it would comply with a court order to identify them to a third party. So although it is much more difficult in the United States than in England to compel an intermediary to help a claimant identify an anonymous author, it is far from impossible, particularly where the case does not concern highly protected political speech.

D. Responsibility of Internet Intermediaries

If an anonymous author of an online defamatory allegation cannot be identified, or the claimant is reluctant to go through the procedure for requiring an ISP to assist in the author's identification, may a claimant take proceedings against the intermediary itself? A website operator or ISP can be treated as a secondary publisher, or as a distributor, of libellous allegations which in the offline world is as liable in defamation as the original author or publisher of a book or newspaper. ISPs might be held liable just as printers, newsagents and libraries may be—though as with these other secondary publishers the law might afford them special defences unavailable to the original author and publisher.

US law provides a robust answer to the question posed in the preceding paragraph: Internet intermediaries are immune from defamation (and other tort) liability under section 230(c)(1) of the Communications Decency Act of 1996, which provides that '[N]o provider or user of an interactive computer shall be treated as the publisher or speaker of any information provided by another information content provider'. In the leading case on the interpretation of this provision, *Zeran v America Online, Inc*,[113] the Fourth Circuit Court of Appeals took a broad view of its scope. The provision conferred immunity on ISPs, even though they might be considered as distributors, rather than as publishers (the term used in the provision), and it applied even though, as in this case, AOL had been given notice of the defamatory character of the message it was carrying and failed to take it down within a reasonable time. The court explained that in enacting

---

[112] *Doe I and Doe II v Individuals* ('Auto-Admit case'), 561 F Supp 2d 249 (D Conn 2008): see Lidsky, 'Anonymity in Cyberspace' (n 88) 1386–89 for commentary on this case, and see Citron, *Hate Crimes in Cyberspace* (n 7) 39–45, and 133–34, who points out that only seven of the 39 posters could be identified.
[113] 129 F3d 327 (4th Cir 1997).

section 230, Congress intended to foster the development of Internet services free from the risks of tort liability and to encourage ISPs and other intermediaries to devise systems of self-regulation.[114]

The drastic implications of the ruling can be seen from looking at the facts of the case. Zeran was the victim of anonymous pranksters who posted messages on an AOL bulletin board advertising T shirts (and subsequently other items) with offensive slogans associated with the Oklahoma City bombing a week earlier. People interested in buying the shirts were invited to phone 'Ken' at Zeran's home in Seattle. As a result he received a huge volume of angry calls, including threats of death; five days after the original posting he received an abusive phone call every two minutes.[115] His business which he conducted at home was in effect destroyed. He made several attempts to get AOL to close the accounts from which the messages had been sent, but it was several days before it took this step, and AOL refused as a matter of policy to post retractions of the messages. In a footnote, the Circuit Court reports without comment Zeran's claim that AOL made it impossible to identify the author because of the inadequate records it kept of its users. In any event his life had been ruined without compensation from the intermediary, which had failed to act promptly on being notified that it was carrying seriously defamatory messages. Even if they had been eventually identified, it might have been difficult to get adequate compensation from the pranksters.

Several American commentators have called for the repeal, or at least the reform, of section 230, so some redress can be provided to the victims of defamatory or privacy infringing online communications; they might find it difficult, or too costly, to take proceedings against authors who have blogged anonymously or under a pseudonym.[116] As will be explained shortly, in English law intermediaries have been held liable if they fail promptly to take down material once they have been notified that it is defamatory; it would be possible to reform section 230 to provide for liability on this 'notice and take down' basis. Moreover, that procedure applies to infringements of intellectual property rights in the United States, which do not enjoy the immunity granted by section 230.[117] But the existing section has its defenders. The imposition of liability would, it is argued, deter some intermediaries from providing their services and stifle the creativity (what is now often

---

[114] Ibid 330–31.

[115] Ibid 329.

[116] See the essays in *The Offensive Internet* (n 6) by Solove, 'Speech, Privacy, and Reputation on the Internet' (n 67); Citron, 'Civil Rights in Our Information Age' (n 49); Levmore, 'The Internet's Anonymity Problem' (n 47); and Leiter, 'Cleaning Cyber-Cesspools' (n 46), at 23–27, 48–49, 66 and 155–57, respectively.

[117] For the notice and take down procedure applicable to intellectual property rights, see Digital Millennium Copyright Act of 1998, s 512.

termed the 'generativity') of the Internet.[118] If liability were based on a failure to act promptly on notification of any defamatory (or other unlawful) content, ISPs would feel compelled to act as censors, irrespective whether or not the message was defamatory, and without any appeal from the persons whose messages were summarily removed from the Net. Liability on notice would have a chilling effect on freedom of speech.[119]

Another argument develops that made by the Fourth Circuit Court in *Zeran*: Congress intended intermediaries to establish and enforce their own systems of self-regulation, which can be more effective than reliance on legal control through tort actions. Particular Web communities such as Wikipedia and social networking sites can develop their own rules and practices to ensure that defamatory (and other false or damaging) messages are removed expeditiously from the Internet. Wikipedia's practices where entries are checked by volunteers, overseen by levels of administrators, provide a good model.[120] Some social media platforms also try to ensure that their services are not used for threatening or abusive messages, though their record is not always very impressive (see section II above). But this argument is unconvincing. ISPs and website operators providing platforms for bloggers are unlikely to develop practices like those of Wikipedia. They usually carry far too much traffic to monitor its content, although they can, and should, take some steps (the issue of detailed codes of conduct for their users, and warnings that users must comply with them on pain of losing service) to reduce the incidence of inappropriate content.[121]

Section 230 (and its expansive interpretation by the courts) should be seen in terms of the American preference for free speech over other competing rights and interests, in particular the right to reputation (and privacy rights) though not, it may be noted, over intellectual property rights. *Zeran* attached enormous weight to freedom of speech and the development of the (then) young Internet, and none at all to the claimant's reputation rights (and it might be added to his personal safety). The effect in that case was to allow unchecked the dissemination of abusive anonymous speech, where it was almost certainly impossible to secure redress from the speaker.

English law has provided a different answer to the question considered in this subsection: libel proceedings may be brought against intermediaries such as ISPs and website operators, at least if they fail to take down a

---

[118] Balkin, 'The Future of Free Expression in a Digital Age' (n 40) 433–36, and BH Choi, 'The Anonymous Internet' (2013) 52 *Maryland Law Review* 501, 530–38. The term 'generativity' is associated with the writing of Jonathan Zittrain: see especially *The Future of the Internet and How to Stop It* (London, Allen Lane, 2008) ch 4.

[119] This argument was made by the Circuit Court in *Zeran* (n 113) 333.

[120] See Zittrain, *The Future of the Internet and How to Stop It* (n 118) ch 6, and HB Holland, 'In Defense of Online Intermediary Immunity: Facilitating Communities of Modified Exceptionalism' (2008) 56 *Kansas Law Rev* 101, 132–35.

[121] Cohen-Almagor, *Confronting the Internet's Dark Side* (n 16) chs 6 and 7.

defamatory message once they have been notified of its content. Thus, in a recent leading case, *Tamiz v Google Inc*,[122] it was held by the Court of Appeal that a defendant providing a platform for blogs, such as Google in this case, might be liable if it failed within a reasonable time to take down postings which the claimant had told it were defamatory of him.[123] The postings had been made anonymously on a blog bearing the pseudonym 'London Muslim', so it is hardly surprising that the claimant chose to take proceedings against Google.

Intermediaries have had special defences under English libel law in addition to the general defences enjoyed by authors and other primary publishers (for example, newspaper editors, book and magazine publishers, broadcasting channels) such as truth, fair comment (now 'honest opinion' after the Defamation Act 2013), and privilege. Broadly, the Electronic Commerce (EC Directive) Regulations 2002, introduced to give effect to the EU Electronic Commerce Directive conferred complete immunity from civil (and criminal) liability on 'mere conduits', that is ISPs which simply transmit information on a communications network,[124] while under Regulation 19 of these Regulations 'host provider' intermediaries which only store information in respect of which complaint is made,[125] such as website operators and hosts of newsgroups, are immune, until they have actual knowledge that they are hosting unlawful information and fail to act expeditiously on obtaining this knowledge to remove it. These provisions provide more generous defences for Internet intermediaries than those provided for them (and other secondary publishers) by the Defamation Act 1996.[126] But both that Act and the Regulations in effect provide for a 'notice and take down' procedure.

This procedure has long been open to criticism for much the same reasons that persuaded the Circuit Court in *Zeran* that the generous immunity provided by Congress was necessary to protect freedom of speech. In 2002 the Law Commission feared that ISPs might remove material on notification of its possibly defamatory content, even though its publication might be in the public interest. Further, the material might be true.[127] Unlike newspaper publishers, ISPs would not want to contest the defamatory character of the material in the courts, or be concerned with its truth. It was far simpler for

---

[122] [2013] EWCA (Civ) 68, [2013] EMLR 14.

[123] Google was not liable, as the blogger removed the comments five weeks after notification of their allegedly defamatory content, and it was held that it was highly improbable that many readers would have accessed them in this time. It would have been an abuse of process for the court to have entertained a libel action.

[124] Electronic Commerce (EC Directive) Regulations 2002, SI 2002/2013, reg 17.

[125] For interpretation of the scope of this regulation, see *Kaschke v Gray* [2010] EWHC 690 (QB), paras 47–76.

[126] Defamation Act 1996, s 1. For a comparison of the defences afforded by the 1996 Act and the 2002 Regulations, see Collins, *The Law of Defamation and the Internet* (n 98) paras 16.30–16.92, esp 16.44–47 and 16.75–79.

[127] Law Commission, *Defamation and the Internet*, Scoping Study no 2 (2012) para 2.41.

them to remove it. Much the same points were made by the Internet Service Providers Association (ISPA) when it gave evidence to the Joint Committee considering the government's draft Defamation Bill in 2011–12.[128] ISPs naturally tended to err on the side of caution. Index on Censorship, a free speech campaigning organisation, argued that a claimant should be required to obtain a court order before an obligation was imposed on an ISP to remove allegedly defamatory material.[129]

The Joint Committee accepted these suggestions, coupling their recommendations with a promotion of 'a cultural shift towards a general recognition that unidentified [that is anonymous] postings are not to be treated as true, reliable or trustworthy'.[130] It had found that posts and blogs are often anonymous, and that, while encouraging free speech, anonymity 'also discourages responsibility, as people feel free to make abusive or untrue comments without fear of any comeback'.[131] The Committee therefore proposed that defamation law should distinguish between the treatment of Internet material sent by an identified author and that sent anonymously. In the case of the former, a claimant would have to apply to a court for a take-down order. On the other hand, an intermediary would be required to take down material written by an unidentified person, unless authors promptly replied to a request to identify themselves. But an intermediary could apply to the court for an exemption from the take-down procedure and secure a 'leave up' order if it thought that there were good public interest reasons for publishing the anonymous material, perhaps because the author was a whistle-blower. Intermediaries complying with these requirements would not be liable for the publication of anonymous material. The Committee hoped that in the long term people would pay less attention to material on the Net which is anonymous.[132]

The government approved the Committee's objective of discouraging anonymity on the Internet, but did not consider workable its recommendation for a two-track system for dealing with defamatory material. Instead, it opted for a procedure under which, as a condition for having a defence, a website operator must act as a liaison point between a libel claimant and the person who had posted defamatory material where the claimant was unable to identify the latter. The procedure has been enacted in section 5 of the Defamation Act 2013 and the complex regulations made under it. A website operator has a defence if it shows that it did not post the allegedly defamatory statement,[133] although that may be defeated if the claimant

---

[128] Evidence of ISPA to the Joint Committee, HL Paper 203, HC Paper 930-1 (n 84) vol II (Ev 56), 267.

[129] Evidence of Index on Censorship to the Joint Committee, ibid vol II (Ev 48), 83.

[130] Ibid para 103.

[131] Ibid, para 102.

[132] Ibid para 105.

[133] Defamation Act 2013, s 5(2).

shows that the operator acted with malice in relation to its posting.[134] More importantly, the defence is defeated if the claimant shows that it was not possible for him to identify the person who had posted the statement; that he gave the operator a notice of complaint (satisfying the terms of section 5(6) and the Regulations); and that the operator failed to comply with requirements specified in the Regulations. It is not possible, it should be noted, for claimants to 'identify' a poster unless they have sufficient information to take proceedings against him, that is, they know his physical address.[135]

Regulations set out what the operator must do to take advantage of the defence.[136] Within 48 hours of receiving a notice of complaint, he must send the poster a copy of it and notification that the statements complained of may be removed from the website unless the operator receives a response from the poster within the deadline (five days of notification of the complaint to the poster), which indicates whether the poster wishes to have the statement removed or provides the operator with its full name and address, and indicates if it consents to the passing on of these details to the complainant.[137] If the poster fails to respond by the deadline specified by the operator, the latter must remove the statement within the next 48 hours,[138] and he must also do this if the poster indicates that he wishes that to be done.[139] If, however, the poster indicates that it does not wish that course to be taken, the operator should within 48 hours inform the complainant of this decision and provide the latter with the poster's full name and address or notify him that the poster does not want these details to be passed on.[140] The expectation is that generally the defamatory allegations will be removed within a few days of notification by the claimant or that he will have received from the operator details of an unidentified author's name and address so that he can take proceedings against the latter. But posters can insist on anonymity and decline to have their defamatory statements removed from a website—a privilege which may be claimed by people trolling as well as by whistleblowers who might be acting with noble intentions.

It is as yet unclear whether the new defence will encourage website operators to reduce the incidence of anonymous blogging and comments, as the Joint Committee had hoped its recommendations would do. It might have that effect, as they have a complete defence when a libel victim is aware of the name and address of the defamer. In other cases, rather than relying on section 5 and the complex regulations made under it, platform providers

---

[134] Ibid s 5(11).
[135] J Price and F McMahon (eds), *Blackstone Guide to the Defamation Act 2013* (Oxford, OUP, 2014) para 6.36.
[136] Defamation (Operators of Websites) Regulations 2013, SI 2013/3028, Sch.
[137] Ibid Sch para 2.
[138] Ibid Sch para 5.
[139] Ibid Sch para 7.
[140] Ibid Sch para 8.

which do not moderate the content of their websites may prefer to use the 2002 Regulations, for it provides them with complete immunity until they receive notice that they are hosting unlawful defamatory allegations, that is, those which cannot be defended as true or covered by some other defence to libel proceedings.[141]

Other intermediaries such as ISPs cannot rely on the section 5 defence, which is confined to website operators. Instead, they can invoke section 10 of the Defamation Act 2013, primarily introduced to strengthen the protection given offline secondary publishers such as booksellers: a court does not have jurisdiction to hear a defamation action against a person who was not the author, editor or publisher of the material, unless it is not reasonably practicable for an action to be brought against one of those primary publishers. It would probably be reasonably practicable to take proceedings against an anonymous online author, if an ISP can be compelled to identify him under the *Norwich Pharmacal* procedure.[142]

The ECHR may afford less generous protection, at least to some website operators, than that now provided by English law. In *Delfi AS v Estonia*, the Grand Chamber of the European Court rejected the application of a large news portal, publishing up to 330 news articles and receiving 10,000 comments (mostly pseudonymous) daily, that its freedom of expression had been infringed when it was held liable for publishing defamatory comments, many of them hateful and threatening, posted against the director of a public ferry company.[143] (The First Section Chamber had previously come to the same decision.)[144] The applicant had criticised the conduct of the ferry company on its portal and invited comments on this article. The Court emphasised that the Delfi news portal exercised substantial control by prohibiting threatening, insulting or obscene comments and by automatically deleting identified vulgar words. The portal could not therefore be regarded as a merely passive, technical service provider.[145] In these circumstances, the Court was unpersuaded that it was enough for the applicant to have taken down the hateful, threatening and defamatory comments on receipt of notice from their victim; Delfi should have acted promptly to remove clearly unlawful comments without such notice.[146]

Of most relevance to the theme of this chapter, the Court took account of the importance to Internet users of their freedom to communicate anonymously, a principle recognised in a Council of Europe Declaration.[147] In its

---

[141] See n 125 above, and *Blackstone Guide* (n 135) paras 6.53–55.
[142] See the text at n 100 above.
[143] [2015] EMLR 26.
[144] [2014] 58 EHRR 29.
[145] *Delfi AS v Estonia* (n 143) paras 144–46.
[146] Ibid 159.
[147] Ibid paras 147–49. (Principle 7 of a Declaration of the Council of Ministers on freedom of communication on the Internet, adopted in May 2003, recognises the importance of anonymity.)

decision, the First Section Chamber had said it would be wrong to require a claimant to have identified the authors of defamatory comments for the purpose of taking civil proceedings against them; Delfi could have required commenters to register with it, so its decision not to take that course entailed an assumption of responsibility for their remarks.[148] The Grand Chamber referred to the difficulty in identifying the authors of anonymous comments and the lack of steps taken by the applicant company to help claimants bring legal proceedings against them. These points justified the imposition of liability on Delfi itself.[149] Under English law, a company in its position would now be able to take advantage of the defence afforded by section 5 of the Defamation Act 2013, provided it complied with the requirements set out in the Regulations to assist a libel victim identify the author. The decision in *Delfi* should not be taken to approve the imposition of liability on any website operator, let alone any service provider; it does not apply to social media or other platforms where the provider itself does not offer any content.[150] It holds only that those which play an active part in encouraging and moderating comments may be held liable in defamation, compatibly with freedom of expression. It would be wrong to treat all Internet intermediaries in the same way; some of them should be held responsible for hosting defamatory comments, at least when as in *Delfi* they also threaten violence and amount to hate speech, but others, particularly ISPs which merely carry messages of this kind, should not.

IV. THE *SPICKMICH* CASE IN GERMANY

The final section of this chapter discusses an interesting German decision concerning anonymity on the Internet. The complainant in the *Spickmich* case was a school teacher who wanted her name and the details of her school to be removed from a community schools portal, www.Spickmich.de. In particular, she objected to its publication of anonymous assessments of her teaching by a number of pupils on the scale 1–6.[151] (Her average assessment was 4.3.) After 12 months the assessments were removed from the site. Access to the portal was through registration by providing the user's name and email address, and details of the relevant school. The complainant argued that the storage and publication of the information infringed her right to informational self-determination, an aspect of her privacy rights which is strongly protected in German law. The case, therefore, involved a

---

[148] (2014) 58 EHRR 29, para 91.
[149] *Delfi AS v Estonia* (n 143) para 151.
[150] Ibid para 116.
[151] Decision of 23 June 2009, Neue Juristische Wochenschrift (NJW) 2009, 2888. The Federal Constitutional Court declined to consider the case: 1 BvR 1750/09.

conflict between two rights: the school-teacher's privacy right to determine whether information about her teaching qualities should be accessible to registered users of the portal, and the freedom of expression of the students assessing these qualities anonymously. The Bundesgerichtshof (Federal Supreme Court) upheld the lower court rulings and dismissed the complaint.

The Court was unconcerned that the student assessments were made anonymously and might consequently be considered of little value by registered users of the site. In its view anonymity is inherent in use of the Internet, as had been recognised in an earlier decision of the Court which had held that contributors to a discussion forum must accept the risk of personal attack from pseudonymous participants.[152] Further, anonymity is protected in Germany by the Telemedia Law provision requiring services providers to enable the anonymous and pseudonymous use of their services so far as this is technically possible and reasonable.[153] To these considerations, the Court added an argument of principle: an obligation to identify an individual with the expression of a particular view, would generally, as well as in the school context, lead to self-censorship from fear of the negative consequences of identification.[154] The imposition of such an obligation would be incompatible with the freedom of expression guaranteed by article 5, I of the German Basic Law. The Court added that the schools portal also met the interests of school students, parents and teachers in receiving relevant information.[155] (Freedom to receive information is also guaranteed by article 5, I.)[156] To make the storage and publication dependent on the teacher's consent, as she argued, would be in effect to render impossible any communication of valuable information to which she objected.[157] Moreover, it was far from clear that she would suffer any significant injury from disclosure of the assessments, which were not published to the world at large and were removed after a year.

The reasoning underlying this decision reveals the strong attachment of German law to the freedom to use the Internet anonymously. The Court did not pause to consider whether other systems might have been used which did not permit anonymous assessments to be downloaded by every registered user; arguably, it was unnecessary for all of them, as well as for other teachers, to be aware of the students' views about the teaching ability of the complainant.[158] As already discussed in this chapter, the provisions of

---

[152] Decision of 27 March 2007, NJW 2007, 2558.
[153] See section II above.
[154] Decision of 23 June 2009 (n 151) para 38.
[155] Ibid para 40.
[156] Barendt, 60, 111–12.
[157] Decision of 23 June 2009 (n 151) para 43.
[158] See A-B Kaiser, 'Bewertungs-portale im Internet—Die spickmich-Entscheidung des BGH' (2009) *Neue Zeitschrift für Verwaltungsrecht* 1474, 1476.

the Telemedia Law and the Data Protection Act requiring services to allow anonymous and pseudonymous communications on the Internet entail the illegality, according to the German authorities, of Facebook's real name policy (see section II above). The Bundesgerichtshof took this principle further: the freedom of anonymous Internet speech trumps an important competing right: the right to informational self-determination as an aspect of personal privacy.

7

Anonymous Speech, the Secret Ballot and Campaign Contributions

I. INTRODUCTION

W HILE THE FOUNDATIONS of a right to speak anonymously are vigorously contested, both generally and in the context of the Internet (see chapters 3 and 6), there is one important context in which anonymity is regarded as a basic right, indeed as one of the foundations of a political democracy: the secret ballot at public elections. The right of electors to cast their vote secretly, so that they cannot be identified with voting for a particular candidate or party, may intuitively seem very different from an entitlement to write anonymously, so authors are not identified as responsible for the contents of, say, a political pamphlet. But the arguments for and against anonymity in both these contexts are strikingly similar. Indeed, discussion in the nineteenth century of the case for and against anonymous writing, particularly in literary reviews, sometimes drew attention to the contemporary campaign for the introduction of the ballot. While some writers, notably Anthony Trollope, favoured openness rather than anonymity in both contexts,[1] others drew a distinction between writing and voting. The generally, perhaps universally, held view today is that while the case for signed reviewing and other journalism is overwhelming, so is the argument for the secret ballot.

But is that view clearly right? Nobody now make a serious case for open voting, but it was made by many commentators in the nineteenth century, notably by John Stuart Mill in his *Thoughts on Parliamentary Reform* (1859), much of which was later reproduced in chapter X of *Considerations on Representative Government*.[2] His arguments are considered in section II below, which explores the differences between speech and voting. It also discusses some fascinating court rulings in the United States on questions such

---

[1] See his *Autobiography* (N Shrimpton (ed), Oxford, OUP, 2014) 121 (in favour of signed articles in literary reviews) and 187 (opposition to the secret ballot).
[2] In *On Liberty and Other Essays* (J Gray (ed), Oxford, OUP, 1991) 353–69.

as whether election candidates may be required by State law, compatibly with the First Amendment guarantee of free speech, to disclose their authorship of mass mailings to the electorate, and whether a requirement to reveal the identity of those signing a petition for a referendum to repeal a State law contravenes the First Amendment. These constitutional questions are complex, because they have to be considered in the light of the landmark ruling in *McIntyre v Ohio Elections Commission*[3] (considered in chapter 3, section II), upholding a right to distribute election and referendum material anonymously; the statutory proscription of such distribution without disclosing the name of the person responsible for it infringed the First Amendment guarantee of freedom of speech. The fundamental issue in many US cases is, therefore, the scope of this anonymity right, and the extent to which it may be limited to safeguard the interests of voters in a fair electoral process.

Another set of questions concerns the identification of people and groups making donations to political parties or contributions to candidates' election expenditure: may the law in the interests of transparency require the disclosure of their identity, or is there a right to make donations and contributions anonymously? This topic is considered in section III below; the law in both the United Kingdom and in the United States requires disclosure. Statutory provisions requiring disclosure have been upheld as constitutional in the United States—a striking conclusion, given that under the First Amendment, restrictions on election expenditure are generally regarded as unconstitutional abridgements of freedom of speech. But in this particular context the Supreme Court has ruled that the interest of voters in knowing the identity of those financing electoral campaigns trumps any claim to a First Amendment right to make donations anonymously. The scope of *McIntyre* has not been extended to cover such a right.

II. SECRET BALLOT AND RELATED QUESTIONS

A. Secret Ballot

The secret ballot is now universally regarded as an essential aspect of the right to vote in free and fair elections. It is recognised, for example, by the Universal Declaration of Human Rights (1948)[4] and by Article 3 of the First Protocol to the European Convention on Human Rights (ECHR). Indeed, the ECHR provision imposes a duty on the contracting states 'to hold free elections at reasonable intervals by secret ballot', so there is now in Europe an absolute obligation to satisfy the right. But this was not always the position. The secret ballot was introduced in the United Kingdom only

---

[3] 514 US 334 (1995).
[4] Universal Declaration of Human Rights, Art 21(3).

in the late nineteenth century by the Parliamentary and Municipal Elections Act 1872, always known simply as the Ballot Act.[5] Previously, voting at elections had been open; votes were generally given orally (though in some towns they were given by a show of hands or the deposit in a box of beans or coloured balls).[6] The Conservative Party would have preferred to keep it that way. But Gladstone, the Liberal Prime Minister from 1868, wanted to bring John Bright, a keen proponent of secret voting, into the Cabinet and was also impressed by the stories of intimidation at the recent general election by manufacturers of the urban voters who had been enfranchised by the 1867 Reform Act. Gladstone's new enthusiasm for the ballot was decisive in ensuring the passage of the Ballot Act.[7]

The Select Committee which had been set up in 1869 by Gladstone's Liberal government to consider the introduction of the ballot (and other voting reforms) heard evidence about the experience in Australia of secret voting and the consequent decline there in intimidation and bribery during election campaigns.[8] The Australian experience was also influential in persuading American States to introduce the secret ballot from the 1880s. Previously voting at elections in the United States had been by voice or by a show of hands, while the first ballots were held on paper produced by the parties themselves rather than by neutral State officials.[9] In a decision in 1992 the Supreme Court recognised that States have a compelling interest to ensure that citizens enjoy the right to vote freely, so the secret ballot can be said to be an implicit constitutional right, although it is not guaranteed explicitly.[10] But it should be noted that recently Scalia J has said that the Court has never upheld a right to vote anonymously.[11]

One of the arguments deployed by the Conservatives (and a few Liberals) opposing the introduction of the ballot was that secret voting was contrary to the English cultural traditions of honesty and openness; it would lead to habits of falsehood and deception.[12] Voters would lie about the candidates

---

[5] For the history of proposals to introduce the ballot in the nineteenth century and the debates on the Ballot Bills in 1871–72, see B Kinzer, *The Ballot Question in Nineteenth-Century English Politics* (New York, Garland Publishing, 1982).

[6] See M Crook and T Crook, 'Reforming Voting Practices in a Global Age: The Making and Remaking of the Modern Secret Ballot in Britain, France and the United States, c.1600–c.1950' (2011) 212 *Past and Present* 199, 203–6, and J Mitchell, *The Organization of Opinion: Open Voting in England 1832–1868* (London, Palgrave Macmillan, 2008).

[7] Kinzer, *The Ballot Question in Nineteenth-Century English Politics* (n 5) 102–6. Before 1868, Gladstone had opposed the secret ballot, or at least had been very sceptical of its merits: see Roy Jenkins, *Gladstone* (London, Macmillan, 1995) 354–56.

[8] Kinzer, *The Ballot Question in Nineteenth-Century English Politics* (n 5) 121, 125. For the introduction of the secret ballot from the 1850s in the Australian States, see Crook and Crook, 'Reforming Voting Practices in a Global Age' (n 6) 217–25.

[9] *Burson v Freeman*, 504 US 191, 200–3 (1992).

[10] Ibid 208.

[11] *John Doe v Reed*, 177 L Ed 2d 493, 520 (2010): see section II(B) below for discussion of this case and Scalia J's judgment.

[12] Kinzer, *The Ballot Question in Nineteenth-Century English Politics* (n 5) 29–33.

or parties they voted for, just as some of them are now, it seems, not always straightforward when giving answers to opinion pollsters. This argument is similar to that increasingly made in the nineteenth century for signed literary reviewing: anonymity encourages inaccuracy and dishonesty, while signature would compel reviewers to be more careful and open (see chapter 2, section II(B)). *The Times* even seems to have equated open voting with the open expression of opinion: 'Nobody can wish to conceal his vote, unless he wishes also to conceal his opinions; but such a thing cannot be found in this country as a man with decided opinions but too prudent to avow them'.[13] That perspective had no time either for the secret ballot or for anonymous speech.

JS Mill's argument against secret voting was rather different. In the 1830s, like his father, the philosopher James Mill, he had supported the introduction of the ballot, but he changed his mind by the early 1850s.[14] For JS Mill, voting was a public trust, so electors should consider the public good; they were under some responsibility to those who did not yet enjoy the franchise. As a consequence of the voter's 'absolute moral obligation to consider the interest of the public, not his private advantage', the duty of voting 'should be performed under the eye and criticism of the public'.[15] These arguments would apply in Mill's view even after universal suffrage was introduced. Open voting would still be necessary to ensure that people did not vote on the basis of their personal or class interest. Mill conceded that there are exceptional cases when secret voting would be desirable to protect electors against intimidation, but he thought the force of coercion over them had declined, at least in the more advanced states of Europe. Gladstone would have disagreed with that view; he considered the ballot was needed to protect voters both in the English towns and in Ireland.

Mill also argued that insofar as electors were now able to cast their vote freely, they were in the much the same position as Members of Parliament; publicity was indispensable.[16] If all men were entitled to vote, whether they voted for a candidate supporting the interests of women was a matter of legitimate interest to their wife and daughters.[17] Mill might have added that legislators vote openly; it would be wrong for them to vote in secret, for that would run counter to their responsibility to the electorate. The making of legislation is an essentially public act. But if voters enjoy the same rights of freedom of speech as their representatives in Parliament and Congress— an argument accepted by the US Supreme Court in the famous *New York*

13 8 March 1850, quoted in ibid 70–71.
14 R Reeves, *John Stuart Mill* (London, Atlantic Books, 2007) 130, 239.
15 Mill, *On Liberty and Other Essays* (n 2) 355.
16 Ibid 358.
17 Ibid 359.

Times case[18]—and like them participate in a democracy by voting, perhaps they should speak and vote as openly as MPs and members of Congress.

Voters, however, are in a different position from Members of Parliament or Congressmen, first, because they are much more likely to be intimidated, harassed or bribed; recent election scandals in Birmingham and in Tower Hamlets show that this risk cannot be lightly dismissed.[19] The secret ballot is vital to protect the right of electors to cast their vote freely and to ensure that elections are conducted fairly without coercion. Moreover, voters are not responsible for how they vote, unlike legislators who are accountable to the electorate—an accountability which is promoted by transparency.

Voting is therefore not the same as legislative action. But how does it differ from speech? If the case for the secret ballot remains powerful despite Mill's contrary arguments, does it follow that we should accept anonymous speech for similar reasons? Of course, on another approach the secret ballot may be treated as exemplifying a long tradition of respect for anonymous speech; that was the view of Stevens J in his judgment for the Court in *McIntyre*.[20] But there are some obvious differences between speech and voting, even though both may be regarded as belonging to the realm of essentially public, rather than private, activity. For a start, voting produces legal consequences—the election of one of the candidates—whereas speech is part of a continuing dialogue or process without necessarily having any legal effects. (Paradoxically, this point was used in one nineteenth century review to justify anonymity in journalism, but the open ballot!)[21] Secondly, there are powerful free speech arguments for public knowledge of the identity of a speaker or writer: the audience usually wants to assess his reliability and credibility (see chapter 3, section III). There are no comparable arguments for a general awareness of how particular individuals vote, though that may certainly be of enormous interest to a few people: to members of their family or, more sinisterly, sometimes to others living in the same local or religious community or conceivably to an employer. But it is the intensity of these interests which justifies the secrecy of the ballot, for it creates the clear risk of coercion and intimidation.

The secret ballot can be justified as a general prophylactic rule adopted to counteract that risk. The risk of intimidation may be regarded now as very remote in most constituencies in developed liberal democracies, but

---

[18] *New York Times v Sullivan*, 376 US 254, 282–83 (1964). In this case the Court extended the free speech privileges enjoyed by Congressmen and public officials to cover anyone libelling a public official without malice.

[19] Election results in two Birmingham wards were held invalid in 2005 for fraud in relation to postal ballots by Election Commissioner, Richard Mawrey QC [2005] All ER (D) 15. He invalidated the Mayoral Election in Tower Hamlets for widespread fraud and undue influence over voters: [2015] EWHC 1215 (QB).

[20] *McIntyre* (n 3) 343.

[21] See the anonymous article in (1859) LXXXV *Blackwood's Edinburgh Magazine* 180, 189.

a general rule is surely preferable to reliance on, say, the detection and prosecution of individual acts of intimidation or bribery during election campaigns. Moreover, the secret ballot also removes the risk of family and social pressure on individual voters, falling short of intimidation—such pressure could not be met by the criminal law. It should be added that the secrecy is not absolute: marked ballot papers may be inspected where an order has been made to consider a disputed election petition or in a prosecution for an election offence, and the vote of a particular elector may be disclosed if a court has ruled it invalid.[22] In contrast, a general right to anonymous speech to safeguard the freedom of everyone to communicate their views is much harder to justify (see chapter 3, section III); that freedom can be secured by reliance on the media (see chapter 5) or by procedures to allow vulnerable individuals, in particular whistle-blowers, to communicate their concerns through trustworthy intermediaries (see chapter 4, section IV).

B. Anonymity in Other Election Contexts

Do the arguments for anonymous speech or for secret voting apply in other election contexts where citizens might oppose legal requirements to disclose their identity? This issue has arisen in a number of cases in the United States in which the courts have balanced the State's interests in the conduct of a fair election or referendum and the interests of an informed electorate against the right to speak anonymously formulated by the Supreme Court in *McIntyre*.[23] The *McIntyre* ruling was followed by a unanimous Court in *Buckley v American Constitutional Law Foundation*,[24] in which it invalidated a requirement in a Colorado law compelling circulators of petitions to wear name badges when they requested signatures for initiatives to be put on election ballots; the requirement would infringe the circulators' right to speak anonymously to the electorate when trying to persuade them to support the initiative. But the Court upheld other requirements in the Colorado law: that imposed on the sponsors of ballot initiatives to disclose their names and the amounts they spent on the collection of signatures, and that imposed on the circulators of the petition to disclose their names and addresses on affidavits to be submitted subsequently with each section of the petition. These *subsequent* reporting requirements were justified as necessary to regulate the electoral process and to identify individual circulators who had engaged in misconduct; unlike the badge requirement they did not

---

[22] Representation of the People Act 1983, Sch 1, rule 56(1)–(3). Parliament provided for scrutiny of disputed ballot papers in the 1872 Act, despite the reservations of the government: Kinzer, *The Ballot Question in Nineteenth-Century English Politics* (n 5) 234–35.

[23] See chapter 3, section II.

[24] 525 US 182 (1999).

have an impact on circulators' speech at the time it was made. As will be explained in section III below, the same distinction supports the requirements to disclose contributions to election expenditure; they operate after the money has been paid to the campaign funds.

In contrast, *McIntyre* played little part in the Supreme Court's treatment of the disclosure requirement in *John Doe v Reed*.[25] It upheld in general terms, with only Thomas J dissenting, a requirement to disclose the names and addresses of those citizens who had signed a petition to challenge a State law by referendum. The requirement arose under Washington State public records legislation, when a State law extending benefits to same-sex couples was challenged by conservative groups who feared that identification of their members might lead to their harassment; in this ruling the Court did not consider whether disclosure of the identity of these particular petitioners would infringe their First Amendment rights, but left it open for them in subsequent proceedings to produce convincing evidence that disclosure would lead to the taking of reprisals against them. In his opinion for the Court, Roberts CJ acknowledged that signing a petition was expressive and so was covered by the First Amendment, even though it produced a legal effect—the suspension of the law which was challenged. The State's interest in preserving the integrity of the electoral process (ensuring that only valid signatures supported the petition and that they had not been obtained by fraud) was strong enough to support disclosure, which also ensured transparency and accountability. Interestingly, the Court opinion did not even refer to the seminal *McIntyre* decision; in its view the signature of a petition is far removed from pure political speech, and has more in common with law-making, which is, as noted earlier, an essentially public activity to be discharged openly.

The separate concurring judgments of Sotomayor J, Stevens J and Scalia J did all refer to the protection of anonymous speech in *McIntyre*, but ruled that it did not govern the requirement to disclose the names of petition signers. *Doe v Reed* did not concern a restriction on either speech or voting. In a typically robust judgment, Scalia J, who had dissented from the Court's decision in *McIntyre*, even referred to the long tradition in the United States of legislating and voting in public, though, as already discussed, open voting ended with the introduction of the secret ballot by the States from the 1880s. In his view '[r]equiring people to stand up in public for their political acts fosters civic courage, without which democracy is doomed'.[26] Almost certainly JS Mill would have agreed.

The decision in *Doe v Reed* is surely right; the State does have a strong interest in protecting the integrity of referendum petitions and there was not really any significant impairment of freedom of speech in that case: citizens

---

[25] *John Doe v Reed* (n 11).
[26] Ibid 522.

remained free to campaign anonymously, on and offline, for or against the petition.[27] But the resulting position and the Court's reasoning are rather unsatisfactory. There is now a well-established practice of secret voting and the Court has upheld a right to circulate anonymously leaflets taking a stand on a referendum issue. But State law may require disclosure of the names of those signing a petition for a referendum. The Court should have explained more fully why that is not entitled to the secrecy which is enjoyed by both voting and speech.

Circuit Courts have usually upheld the constitutionality of requirements imposed either by federal or State law on candidates and their supporters to identify themselves as responsible for the circulation of campaign material,[28] or as paying for or authorising an advertising campaign which advocates the election or defeat of a particular candidate.[29] These requirements can be justified in the interests of an informed electorate; they tell voters whether a candidate, or an independent group, is communicating a particular message or whether, for example, negative campaign advertising was financed by an opposition candidate, to whom voters might have wrongly attributed the advertisements. Disclosure prevents deception and promotes a fairer election process. *McIntyre* was distinguished as concerning the anonymity of *referendum* literature rather than of material promoting an election candidate or calling for his defeat. In *Majors v Abell*, the Seventh Circuit Court of Appeals upheld an Indiana statute, which required political advertising explicitly advocating the election or defeat of an identified candidate to indicate who had paid for the advertisements, as compatible with the First Amendment. Posner J for the Circuit Court reasoned that a speaker's credibility often depends on his identity, so voters have a real interest in knowing who was responsible for financing campaign advertising.[30] But Easterbrook J dismissed that argument as paternalistic;[31] readers were in his view capable of assessing the credibility of anonymous election literature. And a different Circuit Court has invalidated a Nevada law imposing a requirement on persons responsible for financing election or referendum material to provide their names and addresses on the material as incompatible with First Amendment freedom of speech.[32] Following *McIntyre*, the court rejected the argument accepted by other Circuit Courts that the State was entitled to protect voters' interests in knowing the identity of those responsible for campaign material and advertising.

---

[27] For a defence of this decision, see C Boudin, 'Publius and the Petition: *Doe v Reed* and the History of Anonymous Speech' (2011) 120 *Yale LJ* 2140.

[28] *Griset v Fair Political Practices Commission*, 884 P 2d 116 (Cal 1994). (The case was decided before *McIntyre* was considered by the Supreme Court.)

[29] *Federal Election Commission v Public Citizen*, 268 F3d 1283 (11th Cir 2001); *Majors v Abell*, 361 F3d 349 (7th Cir 2004).

[30] Ibid 352–55.

[31] Ibid 357.

[32] *American Civil Liberties Union v Heller*, 378 F3d 979 (9th Cir 2004).

The Supreme Court decision in *McIntyre* upholding a constitutional right to anonymous speech was criticised in chapter 3, in particular for under-valuing the interest of readers and other audiences in knowing the identity of the speaker in order better to assess his credibility. Whether that interest should always trump the speaker's interest in anonymity is certainly debate-able. But it is surely clear that the electorate has a particularly strong interest in knowing the identity of the persons responsible for election litera-ture and advertising, so they can determine whether they are associated with one of the candidates or parties, or are genuinely independent. In the United Kingdom, the position for a long time has been that election material must be published with the name and address of the printer and of the promoter (the election agent) and of any person on behalf of whom the material is published (the candidate).[33] This requirement is justified in the interests of an informed electorate and a fair election process, interests which clearly outweigh any interest in anonymous election speech and advertising; it has never been challenged as incompatible with freedom of expression.

III. ANONYMITY AND DONATIONS TO POLITICAL PARTIES

Is there a right to give donations to political parties anonymously, or should parties be required to disclose the identity of their donors? The apparent simplicity of the question conceals an ambiguity: an anonymous or secret donation may mean one where the recipient political party is itself unaware of the donor's identity, or it may refer to a financial contribution where the party knows who the donor is, but the public does not. Disclosure require-ments imposed on the parties themselves obviously apply to the latter. In both the United Kingdom and the United States, as well as in other democ-racies, disclosure requirements have been imposed when donors provide more than the amount prescribed by legislation. Further, under UK law, a party must not accept a donation where it is unable to identify the donor, unless it is not more than £500.[34] So the short answer to the question posed at the beginning of this paragraph is that in the United Kingdom there is no right to donate more than a trivial sum of money to a political party anonymously, and the identity of donors, known to the recipient party, of more than a prescribed amount (at present £7,500) must be disclosed to the public.

Disclosure requirements are one aspect of the legal restrictions which may be imposed on the expenditure and financing of political parties and

---

[33] Representation of the People Act 1983, s 110, reproduced with amendments in the Political Parties, Elections and Referendums Act 2000, Sch 18, para 14.

[34] Political Parties, Elections and Referendums Act (PPERA) 2000, s 54(1)(b). Under s 52(2)(b) of the Act, a donation of not more than £500 is to be disregarded.

of election candidates, a topic of enormous controversy (and complexity) on both sides of the Atlantic. They form only a small part of this broad package of restrictions. Among the other restrictions are limits on spending by political parties, by individual candidates, and by third parties, particularly during election campaign periods, and limits on the amounts which individual donors (people or companies) may give to political parties. The appropriateness of these restrictions is outside the scope of this book, as are other aspects of the funding of political parties, for example, the issue of state support for their work.[35] The justifications for disclosure requirements may be similar to those given in support of other limits and restrictions, but the merits of these particular requirements can be considered separately from the broader restraints.

The disclosure requirements in the United Kingdom are imposed by the Political Parties, Elections and Referendums Act (PPERA) 2000, which was enacted to implement proposals made in the Fifth Report of the Committee on Standards in Public Life chaired by Lord Neill of Bladen.[36] The background to this Committee's Report was general concern over the increasing, but unregulated, expenditure by the two main political parties before the general elections in the 1990s and over the very large donations made to the Conservative Party by wealthy donors from abroad.[37] The Neill Committee discussed the arguments for and against the introduction of disclosure requirements in chapter 4 of its Report. It started from the premise that it was undesirable that political parties should be dependent on donations from a few wealthy individuals, who might, on a cynical perspective, provide funding to obtain access to government ministers, to buy influence over policy, or perhaps to be considered for an honour. (The Committee's worry seems to have been with the potentially corrupting impact of large donations, rather than with their size as such.) In November 1997, concerns arose over the revelation that Formula One head, Bernie Ecclestone, had given the Labour Party £1 million, shortly before the new Labour government proposed to exempt motor racing from a ban on tobacco advertising.[38] The argument in favour of transparency and the disclosure of the identity of persons making donations to political parties is, therefore, at root the fear of corruption (broadly understood as donations given in expectation of some political favour) or the public suspicion that money is given for improper 'corrupt' motives.[39]

---

[35] For discussion of these and other questions, see KD Ewing, *The Cost of Democracy: Party Funding in Modern British Politics* (Oxford, Hart, 2007), and J Rowbottom, *Democracy Distorted: Wealth, Influence and Democratic Politics* (Cambridge, CUP, 2011) ch 5.

[36] *The Funding of Political Parties in the United Kingdom*, Cm 4057-I (1998).

[37] Ewing, *The Cost of Democracy* (n 35) 3–7.

[38] Neil Committee, *The Funding of Political Parties* (n 36) paras 4.3–4.5, and para 4.11.

[39] See Ewing, *The Cost of Democracy* (n 35) 43–45 and 87–89, and J Rowbottom, 'Corruption, Transparency and Reputation: The Role of Publicity in Regulating Political Donations' (unpublished, 2015), both of which explore the different conceptions of 'corruption'.

The Neill Committee also considered the opposing arguments in favour of continuing with the practice of secrecy, under which donors had been free to fund political parties and candidates without public disclosure of their identity. Money might be given simply to express a donor's enthusiasm for a political party, a free speech argument which has been taken seriously in the United States.[40] Moreover, there are no requirements to disclose gifts made to charities, and privacy and the desire for anonymity should be respected. The secret ballot supported the argument from privacy; voters should also be entitled to donate to the party of their choice in secret.[41] (However, this last argument ignores the point that a donor's identity is almost always known to the recipient party, but the ballot is wholly secret.) Widespread disclosure of individuals' financial support for a particular party or candidate might discourage them from this form of political participation.[42] Despite these arguments the Committee concluded that there was a compelling case for mandating disclosure, where the public had a 'need to know when a donation is made to a political party which is significant enough to prompt questions or to raise suspicion about its purpose'.[43] Disclosure should be required where donations of more than £5,000 (now £7,500) were made annually to a national party, or more than £1,000 (now £1,500) to a local constituency party. The PPERA 2000 enacted these recommendations by imposing detailed requirements on political parties to report donations at three monthly intervals to the Election Commission and more regularly during election campaigns.[44]

One puzzling aspect of the Neill Committee's Report is its treatment of wholly anonymous donations—those where the party is unaware of the donor's identity. In a brief paragraph it concluded that a consequence of its recommendation for disclosure requirements was that political parties should refuse anonymous donations, excluding gifts of less than £50 (now £500). The Committee reasoned that, although some people preferred to give anonymously, 'in the political arena this aspect of privacy has to cede to the public interest in the shape of openness and transparency'.[45] But the principal argument for transparency in this context (the need to avoid corruption or suspicion about the motives for a gift) hardly applies to fully anonymous donations, where the party does not know the identity of its beneficiaries. In theory at any rate, an anonymous donor cannot be

[40] See text at notes 49–50 below.
[41] Neill Committee, *The Funding of Political Parties* (n 36) paras 4.16–4.26.
[42] These privacy arguments are supported (in the American context) by W McGeveran, 'Mrs McIntyre's Persona: Bringing Privacy Theory to Election Law' (2011) 19 *William and Mary Bill of Rights Journal* 859, 876–78. Also see Rowbottom, 'Corruption, Transparency and Reputation' (n 39).
[43] Neill Committee, *The Funding of Political Parties* (n 36) para 4.28.
[44] PPERA 2000, ss 62–63.
[45] Neill Committee, *The Funding of Political Parties* (n 36) para 4.49.

attempting to purchase influence or gain access to government ministers. The Committee also rejected the tentative suggestion of the Conservative Party that anonymous gifts might be made to a Political Donations Institute, which would pass them on to the political party indicated by the donor without revealing his identity. In the Committee's view the proposal would have enabled the making of large donations by wholly anonymous donors in an age of transparency,[46] but that risk could have been prevented by the introduction of caps or limits on the amount of permissible donations. But the Neill Committee declined to recommend that step; caps on the size of donations to political parties have still not been introduced in the United Kingdom.

A better argument for significantly limiting a freedom to make wholly anonymous donations is that this restriction makes it easier to enforce other constraints, for example, a ban on donations from foreign or other proscribed donors. It also prevents wealthy people from making extravagant gifts to political parties or candidates anonymously, though, as has just been pointed out, that risk can be easily averted by the introduction of contribution caps. And it is doubtful whether anonymity can really be kept in these circumstances; it is easy for donors or their friends to hint that they have funded a party, from which they can now expect favours. On the other hand, if an analogy can be drawn between the secret ballot and the freedom to donate to political parties as two similar modes of political participation,[47] there is a strong argument for permitting fully anonymous donations, provided this is accompanied by caps on their permissible amount to ensure that the democratic process is not distorted by gross differences in the level of funding provided to the political parties. Everyone, it might be argued, has an equal right to vote in secret and to make a small anonymous donation to the political party of their choice, but only a few can afford to make a financial contribution above, say, £200.

In the United States, it has been suggested that electoral campaign contributions should be made anonymously to the Federal Elections Commission (FEC) which would set up a blind trust for their receipt. The beneficiary of the contribution would be indicated on a separate form.[48] In the proponents' view, anonymity in giving should be as strongly protected as secrecy in voting. The idea is similar to that of the Conservative Party for making anonymous donations through an independent Institute, which was

---

[46] Ibid paras 4.27(b) and 4.37. The Committee was also hostile to the blind trusts which had been used to provide anonymous financial support for Tony Blair when he was Leader of the Opposition: paras 4.71–4.72.

[47] The analogy is drawn by Rowbottom, *Democracy Distorted* (n 35) 124–27, and McGeveran, 'Mrs McIntyre's Persona' (n 42) 867 and 872.

[48] B Ackerman and I Ayres, *Voting with Dollars: A New Paradigm for Campaign Finance* (Newhaven, CT, Yale UP, 2002).

briskly dismissed by the Neill Committee. It has not been taken further in the United States, where it is much more common to compare campaign donations with political speech than it is to draw an analogy between the former and voting.

The requirements in the United States to disclose campaign contributions were considered by the Supreme Court in its landmark decision in *Buckley v Valeo*.[49] In that case, the Court treated election expenditures and contributions to election campaigns as covered by the First Amendment guarantee of freedom of speech; however, it upheld the limits imposed by the Federal Elections Campaign Act of 1971 on contributions to election funds as necessary to prevent corruption or its appearance, while it invalidated as infringing the First Amendment its provisions on independent election expenditure by candidates and their supporters.[50] The Court recognised that the obligations on candidates and political committees to keep records of those donating more than US$10 and to file quarterly reports with the FEC disclosing the source of contributions of more than US$100 impinged on freedom of speech and of association. But these duties survived the strict scrutiny required under the First Amendment of any restrictions on the exercise of the freedoms. It was necessary to prevent corruption or its appearance (the same argument as that made in the Report of the Neill Committee) and it provided the electorate with information about the sources of a candidate's financial support. As noted earlier,[51] this information is of enormous interest to voters in evaluating rival candidates, and it surely outweighs the interest of contributors in keeping their identity secret—even though that interest is covered by the First Amendment freedoms. However, Burger CJ dissented from the Court's decision on the disclosure obligations, on the ground that it was fanciful to hold that a contribution of as little as US$10 or US$100 might create a risk of corruption, so the provisions in his view infringed the freedom to make anonymous contributions.

The Court in *Buckley* left open the possibility that the imposition of the disclosure requirement might impose an unduly heavy burden on the exercise of First Amendment rights, if there was evidence that disclosure would lead to reprisals against those contributing to election funds.[52] In that event the provision of financial support might well be deterred, just as it can be argued that the prohibition of anonymity might chill speech, particularly that of members of vulnerable groups likely to be harassed for expressing unpopular views (see the discussion in chapter 3, section II). In *Brown v Socialist Workers'74 Campaign Committee*, the Court did indeed hold that a minority party in Ohio could challenge the application to it of the

---

[49] 424 US 1 (1976).
[50] For a brief discussion of the decision, see Barendt, 89–90 and 480–82.
[51] See the Circuit Court decisions discussed in section II(B) above.
[52] *Buckley v Valeo* (n 49) 74.

requirements in the 1971 legislation to disclose contributions to election funds, because it was established that those providing this support faced threats and harassment.[53] The exception recognised in *Buckley v Valeo* and upheld in *Brown*, might, however, be much too narrow; many people might be put off making financial contributions to political parties or candidates from fear of social ostracism or unpopularity in the community as a result of the disclosure requirements. The Internet ensures that such disclosure reaches a wide audience.[54] In the United Kingdom, the Neill Committee also envisaged that there might be situations where it would be wrong to require disclosure because donors or their businesses might fear they would be victimised if their financial support for a party was revealed; but with the exception of the provision of support for the political parties in Northern Ireland, it did not think there was a strong case for exemptions from the general transparency rules.[55]

In two subsequent decisions, the Supreme Court has upheld disclosure requirements in the Bipartisan Campaign Reform Act (BCRA) of 2002, which made substantial amendments to the earlier legislation considered in *Buckley*. In *McConnell v Federal Elections Commission*, it dismissed a challenge to provisions requiring any person and organisation paying more than US$10,000 a year for election communications to file a statement with the FEC, and requiring him or it to identify in the statement anyone making a contribution of more than US$1,000.[56] The Court followed *Buckley* in holding that the State's interests in avoiding corruption or its appearance and in providing the electorate with information justified the disclosure requirements. It referred approvingly to a passage in the District Court judgment pointing to the danger that groups could finance election advertising 'hiding behind dubious and misleading names'.[57] That danger is met by the requirements in BCRA on these organisations to disclose their identity and that of persons contributing to their funds. Thomas J dissented from the ruling in *McConnell*, arguing that *McIntyre* overturned the ruling in *Buckley* insofar as the latter had held that disclosure was necessary to provide the electorate with more information. For him, the funder's free speech rights trumped the electorate's interest in information which might help its decision for whom to vote. But the Court in *McIntyre* itself had found it easy to distinguish *Buckley*:[58] there is a distinction between the mandatory identification of an author, as in *McIntyre*, and the disclosure of the source

---

[53] 459 US 87 (1982).
[54] McGeveran, 'Mrs McIntyre's Persona' (n 42) 863–64 and 866–67; LH Mayer, 'Disclosures About Disclosure' (2010) 44 *Indiana Law Journal* 255, 276–77.
[55] Neill Committee, *The Funding of Political Parties* (n 36) paras 4.67–4.70.
[56] 540 US 93 (2003). Donations of more than US$200 must now be disclosed: US Code, s 434(b)(3)(A), (c)(2)(C).
[57] 251 F Supp 2d 176, 237 (DC Cir 2003).
[58] *McIntyre* (n 3) 354–56.

of political campaign funding. The latter is much less intrusive on freedom of speech.

The second decision upholding the disclosure requirements in the BCRA is more striking, in that the Court in the *Citizens United* case invalidated some long-standing restrictions on corporate election expenditure, taking an exceptionally broad view of the freedom of corporate speech.[59] Nevertheless, the Court upheld the application of the disclaimer requirements in the BCRA that electoral communications clearly indicate that they are not authorised by any candidate and that they display the name and address of the person or group funding them; the requirements were applied in *Citizens United* to advertisements for a documentary critical of Hillary Clinton (then, as in 2016, a candidate for the Democratic Presidential nomination). In the Court's view, the requirements were justified in the interests of an informed electorate, so that it is not deceived into believing that a candidate was responsible for advertisements with which he was not associated. The electorate's informational interest was in itself sufficient to justify the application of this disclaimer and the general disclosure provisions in the BCRA to the Hillary Clinton advertisements. '[T]ransparency enables the electorate to make informed decisions and give proper weight to different speakers and messages.'[60]

The Court's consistent upholding of campaign funding disclosure requirements is significant, given both its general treatment of restrictions on election expenditure and contributions and its decision in *McIntyre* upholding a right to speak anonymously. At first glance the approval of the disclosure provisions appears to be at odds with its strong protection of anonymity in that case. On one view, as the Supreme Court itself said in *McIntyre*,[61] the explanation may lie in the distinction between the mandatory identification of authorship and the disclosure of expenditure, which seems to enjoy less protection than pure speech. Money is speech, but it does not have quite the same status under the First Amendment. But perhaps the disclosure cases also show the relatively weak force of the *McIntyre* ruling. It was argued in chapter 3 that the decision is hard to support on the basis of freedom of speech principles; in particular, it privileges the concerns of an author or speaker who wants to communicate anonymously over the strong interest which readers and audiences generally have in knowing his identity. When that interest is very strong, as it is in the case of the voters' interest in information about those financing election campaigns, the arguments for anonymity are correspondingly weak.

---

[59] *Citizens United v Federal Elections Commission*, 175 L Ed 2d 753 (2010). Thomas J dissented from this part of the judgment.

[60] Ibid 802 per Kennedy J for the Court.

[61] See text at n 58 above.

Index